John H. Tice

Over the Plains, on the Mountains

Or, Kansas, Colorado, and the Rocky Mountains: agriculturally, mineralogically and aesthetically described. Vol. 2

John H. Tice

Over the Plains, on the Mountains
Or, Kansas, Colorado, and the Rocky Mountains: agriculturally, mineralogically and aesthetically described. Vol. 2

ISBN/EAN: 9783337317119

Printed in Europe, USA, Canada, Australia, Japan

Cover: Foto ©Andreas Hilbeck / pixelio.de

More available books at **www.hansebooks.com**

ON THE

MOUNTAINS;

OR,

KANSAS, COLORADO,

AND THE

ROCKY MOUNTAINS;

Agriculturally, Mineralogically

—AND—

AESTHETICALLY DESCRIBED.

By JOHN H. TICE.

Copyright Secured.

St. Louis, Mo.:
PRINTED BY THE "INDUSTRIAL AGE" PRINTING CO.
1872.

Entered according to Act of Congress in the year 1872, by
JOHN H. TICE,
In the Office of the Librarian of Congress, at Washington.

PREFACE.

This volume contains the result of personal observations made in Kansas and Colorado in the Summer of 1871. By a resolution adopted by the Missouri State Board of Agriculture, it was determined in a body and in their official capacity, to take an excursion through Kansas, Colorado, Wyoming, and if found practicable, to Utah. The object was to gain information by personal observation, of the natural resources and agricultural capabilities of the great Plains and of the mountain territories, to ascertain the state of the branches of industry to which they were adapted, the character of the soil and climate, the mode of culture, and the probable extent to which they would be dependent upon other sections for supplies especially agricultural products. An invitation was extended to the Kansas State Agricultural Society, to join us in the excursion, which was cordially accepted. To the liberality of the North Missouri, the Kansas Pacific, the Colorado Central, the Denver Pacific and the Boulder Valley railroads we are indebted for free passes in going and returning over their roads; and for which they will please accept the most grateful and cordial thanks of the whole party.

During the excursion, I took full notes of everything that fell under my observation, and also of facts elicited from conversations with those familiar with the Mountains; not with the remotest intention however, of perpetrating the infliction of a book upon the patient public, but for my own gratification and satisfaction.

After my return home, I wrote out a few pages of the notes for the Sunday number of one of our leading dailies.

These were so favorably received, and excited so much interest, as to draw upon me scores of letters from all parts of the country where these sketches found their way. Some of these were from persons familiar with the scenes described, thanking me for the gratification the reading of my notes afforded them in reviving the recollections of the sublime and grand scenery of these matchless Mountains, and of enabling them mentally to renew the wild enjoyments, excitements and pleasures of a rude mining life. Other letters were from parties having various objects in view; some from those desirous of seeking new homes; some from those seeking investments, or solicitous of engaging in new enterprizes, and others from invalids, borne down by disease, anxious to know if a cure, or an amelioration of their infirmities would not be effected by a sojourn in the delightful and salubrious climate of the Mountains. All these wanted full and definite information on the points in which they felt interested.

The number of these letters, and the intense anxiety the writers expressed for accurate information, first suggested the idea of writing out the notes in full and publishing them in book form.

I have endeavored to meet the expectations and gratify the desires of all these questioners, as far as my observations extended. Moreover, I have endeavored to supply a want much needed by pleasure seekers, by making known the variety, extent, grandeur and sublimity of the matchless scenery of these gigantic Mountains. There is a large and increasing class who have the means and leisure to spend the hot summer months in fleeing to cooler localities for relaxation, recreation and recuperation. Many, but they are not the lovers and admirers of Nature, go to the seashore, or some fashionable watering place, where they pass through the same routine of inane amusements and frivolous excitements day after day and year after year; and return home without their minds enlarged by acquired knowledge, their sentiments refined, their taste for the grand and the beautiful quickened, or even their bodies invigorated. Yea, worse than that, positively damaged physically, socially and morally, by being irremediably inoculated with the virus of the frivolities, follies and vices of fashionable life; not only mind, heart and taste infected and perverted, but wasteful and expensive habits contracted. These "like Ephraim, are joined to their idols," and must be let alone. But there are those who are not yet drawn into the vortex of the maelstrom of fashion. To these it will be doing a good office and a grateful service, to direct their attention to the untrodden and as yet unfashionable routes of pleasure seekers in these wild, picturesque and indescribably grand and lofty Mountains, where in silence and solitude they can hold communion with Nature in her most awful, sublime, majestic and imposing forms; and whence they will return home with their thoughts enlarged, their affections ennobled, their sentiments elevated, their taste refined and their bodies invigorated, moreover, with lighter and kinder hearts and heavier purses. Aye, go upon the mountains as Moses did, and God will appear unto you and converse with you face to face. His laws and commandments there written on stones, will be transcribed and engraven on your hearts; and you, like the Hebrew Lawgiver, will also return to your friends with an overflowing heart and a shining face.

OVER THE PLAINS AND ON THE MOUNTAINS.

CHAPTER I.

On the evening of the fifth of June we set out on our journey on board of the evening Express train of the North Missouri Railroad. The day had been intensely sultry, and a lowering sky in the West indicated the approach of a storm. The air seemed stagnant; for not a breeze was stirring; and the heat was sweltering and oppressive. Glad were we, when the train commenced moving us through the air, relieving us from the smothering effects of heat, it having the same cooling effect as a wind would have of a velocity of twenty-five miles per hour. We were therefore soon quite comfortable, which together with the novelty of our situation, starting out to experience a new sensation, contributed to raise our animal spirits, and we became as cheerful and vivacious a crowd as ever had cast dull care aside; and had set out to test how much relish and enjoyment, new and strange scenes would add to pleasure. Clear of the mephitic city air, and through the bluffs, we were soon flying through the beautiful Florissant (pronounced Florissaw) Valley, the Arcadia of Missouri. At dusk we came to a halt at the end of the bridge opposite St. Charles, which spans the muddy and turbulent Missouri here. A moment and we are in motion again, but slowly and cautiously we move over the immense iron structure; already a new sensation for the completion of the structure had only been celebrated a few days previously. Then there was still lingering a vague feeling of insecurity induced by the croakings of ill-omened birds, who like Dickens'

> "Thompson with a P
> Think the world is going to the Devil
> If they are not hallooing *Gee.*"

This feeling of want of safety was intensified by some brainless would-be wag, having the morning of our leaving perpetrated the miserable pun, "that a whole train of the North Missouri Railroad had gone through the bridge;" which for a while had found credence in its literal sense.

The ebon shade of night soon fell upon the landscape and closed out all save our fiery steed and his luminous train. The sky was overcast, and from the west the dark storm cloud was rolling up with flash on flash of vivid lightning. Soon at intervals the hoarse rumbling of the thunder coming nearer and nearer notified us that we were approaching the storm.

I had gone to a forward car to chat with an acquaintance, and when I returned, my attention was arrested while on the platform by a most singular display made by myriads of fireflies, (*Photynus pyralis*). My first thought was that they were sparks from our engine, and with it came the thought of danger to the train from being set on fire and burned up, for no structure of wood could live in such a shower of sparks as that. But I soon saw that they were fireflies. Sometimes they emitted a continuous flash, and then after a little intermission, it broke out again like platoon firing. I also soon observed that they were almost exclusively confined to within a rod or so to the railroad on both sides. I therefore concluded that they had gathered from the woods on the young herbage along the sides of the railroad; and being alarmed by the train, had taken wing. Back into one of Pulman's sleeping cars, I was soon stowed away in one of its ample berths. But before I fell asleep the storm had set in. The rain was pouring down in torrents, and the wind was driving it splash, splash against windows and sides of the car, and then the lightning's glare, and the peals of thunder were terrific. I fell asleep and woke and fell asleep again, and still the storm raged on and beat against our frail shelter. Day had dawned ere we ran from under the rain cloud, yet the sky was still black and overcast. It was nine o'clock before the blue sky appeared. Day overtook us at Lexington Junction, where the branch railroad from Lexington to St. Joseph crosses. The country here generally is level prairie, and consequently water was standing everywhere, and the cornfields looked as if they were drowned out. The creeks were booming full to overflowing, and were floating down immense quantities of driftwood, which, lodging in the narrow passages between the abutments of the bridges, was threatening danger to the structures. From the same cause the culverts were choked up and the water was collecting in lakes on the north side of the road. Everywhere, the indications were of an immense rainfall; the broken limbs of trees indicated a severe wind storm also. The soil here is regarded as one of the most fertile and productive in the West, being intensely black, but extremely friable and mellow. The road passes up along the north bank of the river, having the muddy Missouri surging in its sandy bed on one side, and a most beautiful country of fine farms alternated with dense forests, on the other. In the forests I could not but admire the varied æsthetic forms of Nature, and observe how much of the science of the beautiful man has yet to learn from her teachings. Here was the *Tecoma radicans* smothering a half grown tree, or reclothing with verdure the trunk of a dead one, and adorning both with its cluster of large trumpet shape orange flowers. There the frost grape, *Vitis cordifolia*, had obtained the mastery over a well grown elm or hickory, and its long pendant vines were swaying to and fro, and often trailing on the ground. Yonder the American Ivy, the *Ampelopsis quinquefolia* has decked the trunk of some large elm, sycamore or oak, with unsurpassing beauty, making it a green column supporting an immense " coronal of green leaves."

We soon arrived opposite Kansas City and recrossed the Missouri to the south side on the railroad bridge. Here we were joined by two portions of our party, one who had preceded us, and the other who came up on the Missouri Pacific Railroad on the south side of the river. Kansas City claims 40,000 inhabitants and has them too, but appears only a small village, being mostly hid by the high and immense bluffs, on which and amongst which, it is built. It is a natural question to ask ones self: why a location should be selected for a city that will cost millions to prepare the site, when a mile or so above and a few miles below, a better site was already prepared by nature. I heard here an anecdote related, which perhaps contains the philosophy of the selection made here: A stranger either in quest of a new field for speculation, or of a new home for location, desired to know the price of a corner lot perched fifty feet above the grade. Two thousand dollars was the price asked. "Why that's enormous" said the stranger: "do you not see it will have to be graded down fifty feet before it can be used." "That's true" replied the owner, "but don't you see the fix the owner of the corner lot behind on the next street is in? He is just as much below the grade, and he will pay me twenty-five hundred dollars for my surplus dirt, and cart it off himself to fill up his." Not quite satisfied with this prospect for a speculation, he went in quest of the owner of the other corner to ascertain his price. Two thousand dollars was the reply. "What," said the stranger "two thousand dollars for that gully; don't you see that it is fifty feet below the grade, and will have to be filled up?" "That's so," replied the owner, "but don't you see the fix the owner of the other corner is in? He will not have any where to put his surplus earth, and he will pay me twenty-five hundred dollars for the privilege of filling up my lot."

The knights of Wall Street are credited with having invented many clever schemes in getting up corners of various kinds, but no genius has ever appeared there equal to the task of getting up such a brilliant scheme as the location of Kansas City, where the owner not only sells his corners for enormous prices, but the purchasers gets them for nothing and a large bonus besides.

After breakfast at the State Line, we got abroad of the train of the Missouri Pacific for Atchison in Kansas, forty seven miles distant. Crossing the Kaw or Kansas river, we passed through the western edge of Wyandotte, a flourishing and thrifty town, lying to our right on the west bank of the Missouri, which here has a general course nearly south though after receiving the Kaw it turns east. The bluffs soon make their appearance to our left, intermitting sometimes however to afford a passage for a creek, and leaving a level plain of extent enough for a number of fine farms. These bluffs are covered with the timber generally abounding in Illinois and Missouri, including the Coffee Nut, (*Gymnocladus Canadensis*,) and a dense thicket of hazle sumach, and other undergrowth. The soil consists of broken chert and limestone, covered by a black loam and vegetable *humus*. We soon passed the city of Leavenworth, which the railroad and expressmen spell "11worth" for short, and the Fort of same name, situated on a high bluff just north of the city, around whose base the railroad winds. Opposite the Fort, a railroad bridge is constructing over the Missouri River for the South-West Railroad. The piers, consisting of immense tubular colums of iron filled with grout, were up and ready to receive the superstructure. The railroad will land on the top of the bluff in the military grounds.

Several small pleasant villages lie on our route before we reach Atchison one of the tastiest, handsomest and most thriving towns in the West. It claims a population of 10,000, and is as busy, wide awake and enterprising a city as can be found anywhere; and which is making itself the railroad centre of northeast Kansas. It has railroad connections with the Hannibal and St. Joseph Railroad which connects it with Chicago and the East by the roads running through Central Illinois; with the North Missouri and Missouri Pacific Roads which connect it with St Louis and the South and East with the Central Branch of the Union Pacific, which will ultimately connect it with the West and the coast of the Pacific; with the Atchison and Nebraska Railroad now constructing and graded to the State line, connecting it with Omaha and the North; and with the South and Southwest by the following roads partly constructed or under contract and work commenced, namely: Atchison, Topeka and Sante Fe Railroad; Atchison Oskaloosa and Lawrence Railroad. It is not a mushroom town, but its growth has been gradual, steady and permanent. It has three large flourmills, four sawmills, two wagon manufactories, one large furniture manufactory, etc.

On our arrival we were received by Mayor Smith in behalf of the large concourse of citizens assembled to welcome us. But as I stepped on the platform I instantly recognized in the crowd, Dr. Wm. H. Grimes, an old acquaintance whom I had not seen for thirty-seven years, with whom I revived reminiscences of "lang syne" until the ceremony of reception was over. I also met another acquaintance here, Gen. B. F. Stringfellow, conspicuous in the Missouri raids some sixteen and more years ago, of which he had the reputation of being the life and soul. Yet here he was in a Yankee town of the most intense Yankee proclivities, thoroughly reconstructed, and as enterprising, energetic and progressive as any of them. I was not more surprised to find him here, than I was at the completeness with which he has yielded to the current that sweeps everything onward here with irresistible force. The peculiarity of Kansas society everywhere, is that the whole community is intensely in earnest, and seems to work as though it had but one mind and one purpose. This is a main reason, for that unexemplified progress and prosperity that marks all sections of the State. True, it requires intelligence to become master of the situation; and to see what is to be done; but when this is seen, then it requires, will, purpose, persistent and united effort to achieve it. Consequently Kansas will undertake and successfully accomplish, the most weighty enterprizes in less time than it takes the more sluggish and discordant elements of the older States to arrive at a conclusion of what were best to do. Major W. F. Downs, the General Superintendent of the Central Branch of the Union Pacific Railroad, had provided for us an extra train to take us to Waterville, the present terminus of the road, just one hundred miles west from here. We were accompanied by many of the principle citizens of Atchison, with whom we spent a most agreeable time going and returning.

For several miles the country is diversified by hill and dale; the hills rising but to a moderate height, and where not occupied by farms, have a dense growth of young oak, hickory, walnut, and other trees indigenous to the West. How the seeds from which they sprung got there, puzzles the citizens; for when the settlers first came these hills were covered with prairie grass with no sign of any other growth. I confess I cannot account for it, but it is an occurrence that happens everywhere; not only in Kansas, but in the West, wherever the fire is kept out of prairies contiguous to timber, a young forest growth immediately springs up. Many of the citzens of St. Genevieve, Missouri, recollect the time when the Illinois bottom opposite to their town, was a treeless prairie. Now it is a dense forest, with sycamore, cottonwood, walnut, linden, pecan and oak trees from thirty to forty inches in diameter.

The first village, Farmington, is twelve and a half miles west of Atchison. It is situated in a rich, undulating country, which is thickly settled, and well timbered. Three miles further is Monrovia on the south bank of Stranger Creek, surrounded by a rich country. It has a beautiful site, and is the oldest town on the road. Some three miles farther is Effingham, a new and thriving village. I will here state that all the towns' and villages along the road have good public school houses, and one or more churches.

The next town, one of the largest, is Muscoutah, handsomely located on the banks of the Grasshopper, which affords fine water-power. It is just on the edge of the Kickapoo Reserve, in one of the richest sections of the State. Senator Pomeroy lives here. He has a highly improved farm in the vicinity. Maj. Downs, the Superintendent of the railroad, also has a splendid farm near town. Both he and Mr. Pomeroy, have on their farms some of the best blooded stock in the State.

Here we saw the Kickapoo chief Parthe, who was in town with his squaw and papoose. He brought the latter up to see the engine, but it became so frightened, as to scream and struggle, and he had hard work to hold it; but when the band struck up it became perfectly frantic. He and his squaw were dressed in the costume of the whites. Poor fellow, he has since been murdered by a half breed. He was represented as a good man, had himself been naturalized, and was influencing his people to become both civilized and naturalized. At every session of the courts, from eight to fifteen, are invested with the rights, duties, privileges, franchises and responsibilities of American citizenship. They cultivate the soil to some extent, but are more generally engaged in stock raising. They have a system of public schools and good school houses, where all the children of the tribe are educated. They are entirely peaceable, and the whites deal honestly with them, and treat them with the greatest kindness.

Six miles beyond Muscoutah is Whiting; and five and a half miles beyond it is Netawaka, a prosperous town of six stores, two hotels; and a weekly paper, the *Herald*, is published here. Both these places are in the Kickapoo Reserve.

The next town is Wetmore, having four stores, a grain ware-house, etc., then comes Sherman, a railroad station at the fiftieth mile post from Atchison, surrounded by a most beautiful and rich agricultural country. Corning is a flourishing town seven miles farther West. Then comes Centralia at the sixty-second mile post, one of the largest and most prosperous towns on the line. Vermillion comes next, and then Frankfort, a large and thriving town. The Vermillion river close by, affords fine water-power.

Next comes Barretts, a thriving village, having a saw mill and excellent water-power, with plenty of timber in the vicinity. Elizabeth, another village three miles beyond, has a fine quality of magnesian limestone for building purposes. The next is Irving, ninety miles from Atchison; it is a most enterprising, prosperous town. A newspaper, the *Recorder*, is published here. Besides having the most commodious public school-house in Northern Kansas, it has the "Wetmore Institute," an excellent institution of learning. The town is situated just beyond the Big Blue.

Blue Rapids, five miles beyond, is a colonial settlement, from New York, about a year old. It has some seventy houses, two stores, sawmill, hotel, etc. It has fine water-power, and steps have been taken to make it available for manufacturing purposes. Waterville is situated at the present terminus of the railroad, one hundred miles west of Atchison. It is about five years old, has twenty stores, four hotels, gristmill, wagon manufactory, etc. It is beautifully situated near grassy bluffs, some two miles south of the Little Blue, which here comes in from the northwest skirted by a belt of timber. The citizens had prepared for us a sumptuous banquet, to furnish which every zone and climate on the globe, were laid under contribution. It was surprising to see here, on the outskirts of civilization, whither the first wave of immigration had rolled only a few years previous, the luxuries of the Old and New World, and of both the Indies, brought together to furnish a banquet that the proudest princes cannot excel. After dinner was dispatched then came the speeches, which were fully equal to the best effort that such occasions call forth elsewhere. But this is not saying much however; for postprandium speeches everywhere amongst us, show, that we as a nation are running more into *gab* than into *thought*.

After dinner we examined some beautiful blocks of magnesian limestone, and also an immense block of gypsum quarried out of the hills. Upon invitation we ascended the grassy bluff behind and south of the church. The sides, though covered with grass, were stony, apparently for the most part fragmentary chert; and amongst the grass the beautiful rose colored flowers of the Sensitive Briar (*Schrankia uncinata*) and the no less beautiful and large purple blooms of the *Penstemon grandiflorus*. A splendid carmine colored Phlox also abounded everywhere.

The soil on the top of the bluff is a deep rich loam, bearing a heavy crop of prairie grass. To the west, south and east is a boundless prairie; while north, beyond the fine valley at your feet, through which runs the Little Blue, the view is bounded by the timber belt along that stream. In other directions no timber was visible, though it is said to be abundant on a tributary of the Blue some ten miles off to the southwest; and also beyond that in the valley of the Republican, and its affluents. There are a considerable number of new houses dotting the prairies surrounded by the newly broken sod. The bluffs are mere swells rising to moderate elevations, say none exceeding a height of fifty feet. Though sometimes pretty steep, they are smoothly rounded off, and covered by the luxuriant green prairie grass. In fact so artistically are they rounded and dressed, that they look like immense sodded bastions around a fortification.

I will here state that the rural landscape along the entire route is not emotional as far as exciting the turbulent feelings of the wonderful and sublime are concerned; but on the contrary it inspires the quiet and soothing emotions of absolute peace, tranquility, contentment and repose. Looking at it until you imbibe its spirit, you think it almost an impossibility that men dwelling in such a quiet, peaceable Arcadia as this, would become, or ever could become ruffled, and show the stronger and rougher passions of the human heart.

Waterville is in the western part of Marshall county. Washington County lies west, and has already a considerable population, though all the settlements are of quite recent date. West of Washington is Republic county, crossed diagonally from its north-west to its south-east corner by the Republican river. This is, or was the western limits of settlement at the beginning of the present season. All these counties are bounded north by the state line, that is by Nebraska.

On board the cars again, we were soon on our way back, stopping at Blue Rapids, and paying a visit to the dam, constructed by the colonists across the Blue, just below the junction of the Little Blue, which has its sources to the north-west in Nebraska, and the Big Blue which heads north, also in Nebraska, near the Platte river. Blue Rapids is about a mile and a half from the railroad station. The citizens had come in wagons and other vehicles to convey us thither; but they had not calculated on quite so large a party, consequently all could not get accommodations, of which unfortunate class I happened to be one. Some however, walked; but as I thought a walk of three miles in such a sweltering day would not pay, I remained at the station. It was near sundown when the party returned. They found the citizens celebrating the completion of their iron bridge across the Blue on the abutments of the dam, by a pic-nic. The guests were invited to walk across by the colonists; on their return they were halted, a charge made along the whole line, (one dollar,) by an artist who had gone up on the train, and then photographed; a copy of which was to have been delivered to each, a condition that he has not yet been able to comply with.

These colonists have adopted the only plan of speedy success with such an enterprise, and at the same time avoiding the evils of non-employment, and consequent suffering and privation. They have selected as beautiful and as rich an agricultural location as there is in the West;

having at the same time a site furnishing any desirable amount of water-power. They have already completed a dam which makes that water-power available. A sawmill is in operation, and a gristmill of the largest size almost completed; woolen and other manufactories are to follow in rapid succession, and the colony will be more than a self-sustaining community before the end of another year. I did not learn whether the colonists own the capital invested or not.

Underway again; it was dusk when we crossed the Blue at Irving, reaching Atchison near twelve o'clock, where we found a special train to take us to Leavenworth, where we arrived at half past one in the morning.

The following may be taken as a general summary of the features, character, quality of soil, sanitary condition, etc., of the country between Atchison and Waterville.

The soil is deep and rich, even on the upland prairie. Timber abounds in considerable quantities, and is well distributed. Here the prairies are seen generally to be bounded by timber, while along all brooks and creeks the forest is heavy. In this there is a great difference between a landscape here and that of the great prairies in Illinois, Iowa and Missouri, where the whole horizon includes but one single continuous treeless plain.

The drainage is perfect, since the country is rolling, but only in gentle swells, while the river bottoms, several miles in width, are flanked by hills of considerable elevation. There is a strong current in all the streams, the water consequently is clear and pure. There are no stagnant pools nor low wet and marshy lands to poison the air with miasma. True, there are bilious diseases, but so there are everywhere, where new clearings are made, and virgin soil broken up and exposed to a midsummer sun. These diseases however are of a mild type, and decrease as the quantity of newly broken prairie diminishes from year to year, and almost entirely disappear when all the land is brought under cultivation. This conforms to experience everywhere, either east or west. That bilious diseases become milder and less frequent as the country settles up, is a well established fact. Time was when chills and fever were just as prevalent in the Genessee valley as ever they were in Illinois.

The bluffs that flank the valley often are stony, and some even expose ledges of rocks. They are so abundant in some places, that we saw quite a number of stone fences along the route.

Springs of pure cold water are numerous along the whole route, and are said to exsist westward indefinitely. On the highest prairies the best, pure and cold water can be obtained by sinking wells from 20 to 50 feet.

Wood is still generally used for fuel, costing from three to four dollars a cord. But it has been ascertained that extensive coal beds underlie the country, from two to four feet in thickness. At several places, these beds have been opened, and are now worked.

The Grasshopper, Vermillion and Blue rivers furnish a large amount of water-power, and sawmills are found along all of these streams. The price of native lumber is from $15 to $25 per thousand feet.

Besides, stone, board and wire fences, we saw quite a number of osage orange hedges planted, and some pretty well established. I should think the country from its abundant fresh water, large range covered with luxuriant grasses, and fine climate, well adapted to stock raising and dairying purposes. These no doubt now and for an indefinite time to come will be as remunerative as any other business whatever.

I could not obtain any reliable data of how much public land there remains subject to entry, homestead or pre-emption. The railroad has a grant of land of every alternate section for ten miles on each side of the road. They hold them from two to eight dollars per acre, with a liberal discount for cash. They will sell them also on a credit of three, four, six and ten years at different rates of interest, according to time. Full particulars can be ascertained from the General Superintendent and Land Agent of the road, Maj. W. F. Downs. The amount of corn, wheat and potatoes raised per acre, is equal to the highest figures attained in Missouri and Iowa. In fact the quantities reported seem like marvelous stories. But from the character of the soil and nature of the climate, there can be no doubt that the yield is enormous.

CHAPTER II.

After breakfast we found carriages provided by the citizens in readiness to give us a drive through and around the city. We drove up one of the main streets to the Military Grounds just north of the city. These grounds are very extensive, and are elaborately laid off into plots, on which are situated, surrounded with flowers and shrubbery, expensive mansions for the accommodation of the numerous officers always located here. This is the Headquarters of the Trans-Mississippi Military Department, where men and military stores are collected for distribution to the Upper Missouri, Colorado, Upper Arkansas and New Mexico. The barracks are very large to accommodate the soldiers concentrated here from the malarious Gulf States for recuperation, and from the Northwestern, Western and Southwestern Territories for relaxation. The military reservation is a most beautiful tract, containing 6000 acres. The part occupied is a level plateau on a high bluff, whence there is a commanding view of the city of Leavenworth to the south, which it entirely overlooks; the Missouri River for many miles both up and down and the rich bottom or valley east; and west a fine undulating country of hill and dale, as far as sight extends.

After driving through the military grounds, we drove south-east to the edge of the bluff, and dismounted to look at the structure, a stone abutment, in process of erection at the terminus of the bridge, on top of the bluff, for the Chicago and Southwestern Railroad, and also of the piers of the bridge, then ready to receive the superstructure.

The bridge is to be wrought iron, placed upon piers of cast

iron, the columns of which are now in position. As this was a novelty to me in civil engineering, I will briefly describe it. The sections of the columns are eight and a half feet in diameter, ten feet in length and one and three quarter inches thick, and weigh about ten tons each. With proper flanges at the ends, these sections are joined in the process of sinking, so as to form a continuous cylinder, reaching from the superstructure to the solid rock on the bottom of the river. The whole is then filled up with concrete masonry and grouting. Two of these columns placed side and side longitudinally with the current, form one pier. There are three of these piers, two in the river, and one on the eastern shore; the bridge to land on the western shore on a stone abutment. The elevation is ten feet above the high water line. Each of the three spans thus formed, will be three hundred and forty feet in length; and the bottom of the lower chord fifty feet above extreme high water, so that steamboats can pass at any stage of the river. The approach to the eastern end of the bridge consists of trestle work, 1500 feet long, and an earth embankment extending 2500 feet further, both of which are completed. It is contemplated to make this bridge a common union for the crossing of all railroads terminating here, both from the East and West.

Remounting our carriages, we were driven back through the military grounds, and west on and along the heights that surround the city. These were at some places quite stony, covered with a young and low growth of forest trees, interspersed with the many wild flowers indigenous to this section. We now for the first time realized the charming location of the city. We could look down the Missouri river south-eastwardly fully twenty miles, and both shores appeared one unbroken forest of gigantic trees. But right below us, on the banks of the river, in an amphitheatre of some three or four miles in length, two miles in depth, and gradually rising to our position, is nestled the city of Leavenworth, containing fully 25,000 inhabitants.

To the west, and at the distance of about half a mile, lies the valley of Salt Creek, a stream that debouches into the Missouri above the Fort. Our position must have been at least two hundred feet above this valley, apparently two miles in width, and surrounded on all sides by heavily timbered and high hills. It was one of the finest rural pictures I ever beheld. In the centre at the widest part arises a rounded hill, about sixty feet high, of perhaps eighty acres in area and heavily timbered; while all around it lay the most neat, tidy and thrifty farms in the highest tilth. It reminded me of the landscape and scenery of my boyhood's home in the Tuscaroras.

We now drove to the residence of Professor Percival G. Lowe, where we partook of some of his cherries and strawberries and some native wine. After walking through his garden and grounds of shrubbery, we drove to the southern limits of the city, and then returned towards its central parts, but were brought to a halt before the spacious mansion of Gen. J. C. Stone where we dismounted, and were received by the General and his estimable lady in the most cordial and hospitable manner. Ushered into his drawing room, we spent some time in admiring the fine specimens of art, both in painting and sculpture. Of the former but very few were fancy pieces, representing mostly noted wild landscape scenery in Europe and America.

The doors were now thrown open, and we found our host had with a munificence that would do honor to a prince, prepared a most sumptuous dinner for us. There were spring chickens, ham, buffalo tongue, pies, cakes and pastry of every imaginable kind, an exhaustive assortment of comfits and candies, together with ice cream Then there were the largest, finest and most luscious strawberries and cherries, all raised on his farm near the city, besides the choicest native wines.

Before leaving the mansion of our hospitable host, we were invited to inspect an upper room, completely decorated with military caps, and other German military paraphernalia brought home by the General's son, who has just returned after graduating in a German university. I never saw a native so completely Germanized as he; and so charmed was he with university life in Germany, that he spoke enthusiastically of it. We could not, however, admire or commend all the features of such a life, that for instance of the barbarous custom of resorting on every occasion to single combat, to avenge any real or fancied insult. Our young friend bears on his otherwise handsome face and manly brow, many ugly scars from sword wounds received in such encounters.

After taking a most cordial leave of our munificent host and his estimable lady, we returned to the hotel to await the departure of the evening train for Lawrence; meanwhile I took mentally a business review of the city and its surroundings.

Leavenworth has naturally one of the most favorable sites for a commercial city. Situated on the west bank of the Missouri river, it has water communication with all the states of the Mississippi Valley and the Gulf, and with the gold and silver producing territories of the upper Missouri. But in these days, no city has any hold on, nor security for permanent commercial prosperity, by having only water communication with the outside world. The arteries of commerce now are of iron, instead of water, as formerly. In foreign commerce, water communication will always hold an incontestible superiority, but it can no longer control the commercial movements within the interior of a continent. To concentrate and distribute the products of a continent and of the world, railroads have an unquestioned pre-eminence over all other modes of transportation. In casting the horoscope of any city's permanent growth and prosperity, her railroad accessability and facilities must be considered. Applying this principle to Leavenworth, it will be seen that the auguries for the future are most auspicious. She is now connected by way of St. Louis, with the East, the Centre and the South by the Missouri Pacific, and the Missouri Valley and North Missouri railroads; with Chicago and with the East and North, by the Chicago, Burlington and Quincy, the Hannibal and St. Joseph, and the Missouri Valley, the Rock Island and Pacific, and the Chicago and Southwestern railroads; with the North, the North-west and the Pacific coast, first, by way of Council Bluffs, by the Missouri Valley and St. Joseph and Council Bluff railroads; second, by way of Denver by the Leavenworth, Lawrence and Galveston and the Kansas Pacific railroads. The Leavenworth, Atchison and Northwestern railroad, now in process of construction, will connect it with Omaha, opposite Council Bluffs. The Union Central branch of the Union Pacific railroad, now completed to Waterville, will when completed, give it direct communication with San Francisco. With the South-west, with the Leavenworth, Topeka and Santa Fe railroad, now completed to Newton, within 20 miles of the Arkansas river; and with the Gulf and the South direct, by the Leavenworth, Lawrence and Galveston railroad. Besides these there are several railroads under contract and the work progressing, and several more projected. Amongst those under contract and in a state of progress, the most important is a narrow gauge to Denver, thence to Santa Fe, with branches through Middle Park to Salt Lake Valley, and to Helena in Montana, by way of Cheyenne. It will be thus seen that Leavenworth now is well supplied with railroad facilities which are annually extending. There are five daily newspapers, four in English and one German, published here, besides several weeklies and monthlies. There are about one hundred and twenty manufacturing establishments, the aggregate products of which are estimated annually to exceed $2,500,000.

At thirty minutes after four we left for Lawrence on the Leavenworth, Lawrence and Galveston Railroad.

The country between Leavenworth and Fairmont is generally heavily timbered with the varieties of trees that are indigenous to the country; such as Sycamore, Cottonwood, willow, elm, hickory, oak, hackberry, and walnut. The Kentucky coffeenut (*Gymnocladus Canadensis*) and two species of the honey locust (*Gleditchia triacanthos*, and *G. monosperma*) and the Red bud occurred occasionally. A young growth has also sprung up on what was formerly prairie, which has attained considerable height. The undergrowth is principally hazel and sumach. The different species of wild grape are also conspicuous everywhere. There are many fine farms along the line, but where man has not taken possession of the prairie, the forest trees have, so that east of Fairmont and for some distance west the prairies have practically disappeared. The country around Fairmont is rich and beautiful with a black friable soil. The surface undulates into gentle swells affording good drainage.

Westward the character of the country changes somewhat. The varieties of timber peculiar to the river bottoms appear no longer, being replaced by more valuable varieties, such as oaks and hickories. The undergrowth of hazel, sumach and wild grapevines continues in the forest, but there now occur small glades of grassy plain called "openings." These are enameled with the beautiful carmine Phlox already mensioned, the prairie, and dog rose, the *Tradescanthia Virginica*, *Schrankia uncinata*, white perennial larkspur, the purple Polanisia, blue Penstemons. etc. Amongst weeds I noticed an ash colored Artemisia, the daisy fleabane (*Erigeron annuum*) the Rosin-weed, or Compass-plant (*Silphium laciniatum*) and several species of Helianthus.

Tonganoxie, a small village, is situated on a fine rolling prairie, surrounded by beautiful farms. Westward the prairies become larger and the swells culminate in hills of moderate height. Reno is the next village surrounded by a rich farming country. The wheat crop generally along the route was heavy, and fully ripe on the 7th of June when we passed there.

A rather singular incident occurred here. While the

train stopped, some of the passengers got out and commenced caressing a colt belonging to a team standing at the station, and finally got it on the platform. When the train started, the colt got on the track and followed the train fully a mile, putting forth its best efforts to keep up, but of course was distanced. When we arrived at the railroad station at Lawrence, we found conveyances in charge of the Hon. I. S. Kalloch, President of the Kansas State Agricultural Society. He addressed us a few pertinent words, to this effect, that here were conveyances to take us to the Eldridge House, that we must consider ourselves as the guests of the State Society, who would pay all hotel and other expenses, and even for *medicine* while we remained in the city, and therefore, as he had captured and made prisoners of us, all we could do was to get aboard the 'busses, carriages, etc., as resistance was useless. Comprehending the situation, our party yielded with the greatest grace possible, and were rapidly driven over the bridge and up Massachusetts street, and set down at the Eldridge House. The Kansas Pacific railroad depot at which we landed, is on the north side of the river, while the city proper of Lawrence is on the south side.

The Kaw is a rapid stream some two hundred yards wide, and is spanned by a substantial bridge, which connects the northern suburb and the Kansas Pacific railroad depot with the city. The L. L. and Galveston railroad crosses the Kaw below, and has its depot near the eastern limits of the city on the south side of the river.

As the Eldridge House is the largest and one of the best kept hotels west of St. Louis, it cost us no effort to reconcile ourselves to our situation as prisoners. The kind treatment of the keeper and the attentive and obliging disposition of the servants, but above all the splendid supper, spacious rooms and elegant beds, rather made us like the operation of being "put through" in that way.

By the way this Eldridge House has a history. The abrogation of the Missouri Compromise, which excluded slavery from all territory north of thirty-six and a half degrees of north latitude, and the passage of the Kansas-Nebraska bill by Congress, actually initiated the conflict which culminated in the rebellion and the abolition of slavery. This of course could have been foreseen would the result of that illstarred measure. It actually was foreseen, and moreover predicted by such farseeing men as Benton and others who resisted the passage of the act, by all the power that reason, persuasion and parliamentary law and tactics afforded; but their efforts were powerless.

The syren, "Squatter Sovereignty" sang too charmingly to be resisted by a great many well-meaning and patriotic men; and the bill was passed under the delusion that settlement would be suffered to go on quietly and peaceably until State governments were to be organized in these territories. But the march of events from the beginning dispelled that delusion, if any one ever seriously entertained it. Emigrant societies were organized in most of the northern States, especially in Massachusetts, to settle these territories, particularly Kansas. These, though artizans and agriculturists, and coming with the intention of becoming *bona fide* settlers, came also prepared to meet any emergencies that might arise, hence the "Sharp's rifles" of which we heard so much, at that time. The extremists of the South in the Gulf States, and even in Georgia and other southern States, organized military companies and sent them to Kansas, not for settlement, but to prevent settlement from the northern States. A conflict at once ensued, which ended in a repulse of the southern military organizations, who retreated over the border, and there in conjunction with bad men in Missouri, organized marauding and murdering expeditions into the territory. One of these expeditions sacked and burnt Lawrence. The earliest colony from Massachusetts had selected Lawrence as a *point d'appui* for the settlers, and had built the Eldridge House, then the most expensive and commodious building in Kansas, for the accommodation of strangers and settlers while looking out suitable localities for settlement. The marauders came and first battered it down with cannon and then burnt it. It was immediately rebuilt, larger and more costly than before. It was a second time burnt in the murderous expedition of the infamous Quantrell. Phenix like, it again arose from its ashes enlarged and beautified; and is this day one of the best appointed hotels in the West.

Lawrence has many large and elegant buildings for business purposes, especially on Massachusetts street. Many of the private residences are expensive and elegant; especially on the knolls that surround the city to the west and south, which are covered with most costly and tasty mansions surrounded by lawns, shrubbery and flower plots. The churches and public schools are also large, tasteful and expensive. The State University on Mount Oread overlooking the city from the southwest, is one of the most elegant buildings in the West. It will cost when completed nearly half a million, of which amount Lawrence contributed $300,000. It is built of a yellow arenacious magnesian limestone half dressed; is four stories high, surmounted by two quadrangular domes and two turrets. Its style of artichitecture is the "Rennaissance."

Lawrence has a population of 10,000, and is rapidly increasing in all the elements of wealth and prosperity There are no idle heads nor hands here.

CHAPTER III.

At eight o'clock on the following morning, June 8th, we found carriages ready to convey us to the depot of the Leavenworth, Lawrence and Galveston Railroad, to take an excursion to the end of the road, at Thayer, one hundred and eight miles south of this point.* We were indebted for this pleasure to Maj. Charles B. Peck, the General Freight Agent of the road, who had a special train provided for the occasion. Nearly all the members of the Kansas State Agricultural Society had joined us now, to accompany us to Colorado. For the day's excursion, some one hundred of the leading citizens of Lawrence joined us, headed by Mayor Thatcher. Everything being in readiness we started towards the sunny South. A heavy storm cloud seemed to lay across our way some fifty or sixty miles distant. Otherwise the sky was perfectly clear, but the weather was sweltering, and the sun shone bright and intensely hot. The day previous a heavy rain had passed over this section, and there was, therefore, no dust to annoy us, but Nature seemed to have put on her gayest attire and brightest smile to greet and welcome us. To our right, and beyond Lawrence, lay Mount Oread, crowned by the superb edifice of the State University. The elevation slopes gently southward to the Wakarusa, some five miles distant. For several miles the sides and summit of this beautiful swell are covered with stately mansions, the sumptuous suburban residences of the wealthy business men of the city, surrounded by lawns, shrubbery, fruit trees, flower-plots, etc. Soon these are replaced by

---

*Since then it has been completed to Coffeyville, on the Virdigris river, where it enters the Indian Territory.

the neat and tidy farm house, surrounded by fields and meadows in the highest tilth, and threaded by osage orange hedges. The Wakarusa here runs about due east, and its immediate valley or bottom is heavily timbered. To the southeast, beyond the Wakarusa, is an elevation called Blue Mountain, a heavily timbered hill, rising perhaps six hundred feet above the plain. It is a beautiful feature in the landscape.

Passing beyond the timber skirting the last named stream, the road enters a beautiful rolling prairie, studded over with fine farms, but there are still immense stretches of unbroken prairie, covered with a luxuriant growth of wild grass, and at this season, enameled with wild flowers of every hue. The only new species I noticed, except an *Æsclepias* with immense dull greenish yellow blooms, was the *Œnothera Speciosa*, generally called by flourists, *Godetia*. Of these there were two varieties; one, the most abundant, was a pure white with a purple center; the other was a delicate pink. Sometimes both varieties were intermixed in large beds. Then, with their large blooms expanding fully two and a half inches, they were a most charming sight. For some eighteen miles, the rolling prairie was destitute of trees, except the orchards of the farmers and the young groves they have planted. As we approach the Marias des Cygnes, a tributary of the Osage, we enter a forest sometimes consisting of rich bottom land, and then again of rocky hills. The stream runs southeastwardly, and was much swollen by the heavy rain on the previous evening.

After emerging from the forest, a few miles brought us to the city of Ottawa, the county seat of Franklin county. I should estimate its population between three and four thousand. It has a bank, several good hotels, churches and fine public schools. Its principal street is substantially built up with brick and stone houses. It has various kinds of manufactories, and is a prosperous town. Ottawa University is located here, and for several years was opened and conducted with encouraging prospects of success. But its endowment failed on account of some defect in a treaty with the Osage Indians, by which it was to receive a donation of lands. It is now closed. The site of the town is rather level, but the surrounding country is one of the richest in the State. I should have stated that midway between Lawrence and Ottawa is Baldwin, the site of Baker University, but of whose history and endowment I could learn nothing.

Proceeding southward we passed several small streams swollen by the late rains, and skirted by belts of timber. Otherwise the country is rolling prairie until you reach the Pottawattamie river, flowing northeastwardly into the Marias des Cygnes. Here we again encountered heavy timber; that on the bluffs generally hardwood, and amongst that in the bottoms many large trees of black walnut. Five or six miles further brought us to Garnett, the county seat of Anderson county, on a considerable swell. The soil is pretty much the same as around Ottawa, but the country is more rolling, and on the sidehills and ravines I saw, in many places, ledges of magnesian limestone cropping out. This is characteristic of the country from this onward as far south as we went. I should judge that such portions as have only a few feet of soil overlieing this bed of magnesian limestone, are not well calculated to withstand droughts. Beyond Garnett, at a distance of some six miles, we crossed Cedar Creek, a tributary of the Pottawattamie, flowing about northeast. On the bluffs I saw a few cedars, and again the black walnut in the bottom. Beyond this the horizon encloses often but one expanse of prairie, which is, however, occasionally interrupted by a distant line of timber to the southeast, fringing Deer Creek. The country now slopes gently southwest to the Kansas Neosho river, and a belt of timber lining that stream, occasionally looms up in the western horizon. As we approach Deer Creek, the belt of forest we had occasional glimpses of in the southeast, crosses the path of the railroad, and we soon crossed the creek, a rocky turbulent stream, swollen and overflowing its bottom by a heavy rain in the morning, which fell from the cloud we saw as we left Lawrence. Deer Creek runs west and falls into the Neosho river, a short distance west. We were soon at Iola, the county seat of Allen county. The road now heads down the valley of the Neosho, the meandering of which stream brings it sometimes in sight. The prairie hence from Garnett was often yellow with the *Coreopsis Drummondii*, and occasionally a stray plant of the beautiful *Coreopsis Tinctoria*. A run of some ten miles further brought us to Humboldt, where an excellent dinner, especially prepared for us, was ready. It was soon despatched, and then came the inevitable postprandium speeches, which I escaped by taking to the prairies. I went to the southwest of the town, which stands upon a considerable swell. To the west, about a mile off, flowed the Neosho, having a general course nearly southeast. Its banks are heavily lined with timber, and its course can be traced by it for many miles from the northwest to the southeast. All the country east of it as far as could be seen, was a treeless expanse of prairie, but diversified by many newly opened farms, or by an immigrant's new cabin. The flora on the prairie I found the same as those already named, excepting a single plant of the *Callirrhœ Verticellata*, which we found abundant on the plains farther west the following day, expanding its purple-red blooms, often two inches in diameter. As the depot is east of the town, I made a detour around the latter to the south. The prairie was full of lupines, larkspurs, penstemons, *Godetias* and flowers already mentioned, but with the exception of the *Collirrhœ* I found nothing except a species of Sedum that was new to me. It was past blooming, and as I lost the specimen I put up for my herbarium, I have been unable to determine its species.

Returning to the depot I found quite a number of the company there already, waiting the arrival of those detained by the orators. When they finally arrived, it was announced that the day was too far spent to go to Thayer, twenty-two miles farther south, the then terminus of the road. This I regretted, not that I probably lost seeing any thing new, but I failed seeing a historical character, the veritable Eli Thayer, who, as a member of Congress from Massachusetts, in times anterior to the Rebellion, used to read with such gusto, the "Book of Martyrs," as he called the census of 1850, to the "fire-eaters." He also was the organizing spirit of the emigrant associations formed in the Northern States to settle Kansas in the days of "Border Ruffianism." A retrospect of the country passed over during the day, has satisfied me that a sight of it is sufficient to convince any reasonable mind, that it is one of the most beautiful and the richest agricultural districts in the world. The only drawback that I could discover, and which I have already mentioned, is the fact that the whole country is underlaid at no great depth with a bed of magnesian limestone, which often crops out on the banks of ravines, or the sides of gentle slopes. In case of droughts, which, however, have not occurred for several years, and it is contended that the climate has undergone an amelioration in this respect, land so situated cannot withstand them well. To this may be added the scarcity of fuel. For, although the bottoms along the streams are generally well timbered, yet there are long reaches of prairie, twenty and even thirty miles across, entirely destitute of trees. Dense settlement of the country cannot take place until a substitute for wood as fuel will be found; and this substitute must be found in an abundant and cheap supply of coal.

From indications it is fair to infer that it will not be long before an ample supply of excellent coal will be found throughout all this part of Kansas. At Carbondale, a mining town some 25 miles northwest of Ottowa, on the Topeka and Santa Fe railroad, there are immense fields of excellent coal. Again, at Osage City on the same railroad, about 30 miles due west from Ottowa, a bed of coal is worked, which is said to equal in quality the two best in the Mississippi Valley. Coal of a good quality is also mined at Ottowa and at Thayer, in Neosho county. At Iola there is boring going on with a view of striking the vein which is supposed to underlie the whole country.

In all its aspects the country passed over to-day indicates recent settlement. Neither farms, residences nor barns, have as yet assumed that solidity and permanence which mark those in the northern part of the State. There the original cabin and cottage have given place to the neat substantial and commodious farmhouse. But here evidently time enough has not yet elapsed to effect such great and permanent changes. I called the attention of some Lawrence friends accompanying us, to this difference, and asked for an explanation, since there evidently was no difference in the productive capacity of the soil. I then learned that the whole country south of Ottowa had been an Indian Reservation, and that only some six years have elapsed since the extinguishment of the Indian title. I also learned there was no government land to be entered in southeastern Kansas, excepting in the extreme southern tier of counties on the Indian Territory.

This railroad however has lands located in Anderson, Allen, Neosho and Labette counties, which they are offering for sale at from four to ten dollars per acre on a credit of seven years at 7 per cent interest. Lands contiguous to the road held by individuals, can be bought from eight to fifty dollars per acre, according to locality, or the amount and character of the improvements thereon. As in the northern part of the State so here the church and the schoolhouse are conspicuous objects in all the towns, villages and settlements, a sure index of the character of the people and of its dominant ideas. As already intimated the surface of the country is less diversified by hill and dale than that in northern Kansas. The swells are so gentle, and the elevation so moderate, that they cannot aspire to the dignity of being called hills; while in northern Kansas the elevations are considerable, and the slopes generally abrupt. The conformation of the surface therefore gives wide alluvial bottoms to all the southern rivers, which are admirably adapted for corn, while the uplands are particularly well adapted for small grain. The wheatfields passed on the route to-day, were not only riper on the swells, but far less affected by rust on the blade than those on the bottoms.

The return trip was not marked by any incident of note, except that we encountered a small thunder-shower south of Ottowa. On reaching Lawrence we found a large number of carriages waiting to give us a drive through and around the city. I took a seat in that belonging to Mayor Thatcher, driven by his son, a lad of some sixteen summers. Passing around the southern suburbs and westward until we reached the hill designated as Mount Oread, we were driven northward on the street that lines its side at some elevation above the plain below. This street is lined by tasty suburban residences, surrounded by shrubbery, lawns, winding ways, ornamented with the choicest flowers. To the north Mount Oread terminates before it reaches the Kaw in a well and prettily rounded hill, with a tolerable steep slope. We now drove westwardly until attaining the summit, and then southward till we reached the front of the State University where we were addressed by Mayor Thatcher in a very neat and pertinent speech. From this point the view is very fine. To the north and northeast is the Kaw, a beautiful limpid river, whose course the eye can follow for many miles down its valley. Between you and it lies the city of Lawrence, containing a population of some 12000, with its twenty churches, magnificent public schoolhouses, hotels, banks and other public and private buildings. There also is the bridge spanning the Kaw which connects the northern suburb where the depot of the Kansas Pacific railroad is. A few points south of east is Blue Mountain, a high knoll of but limited breadth, which deflects the Wakarusa to the north into the Kaw some six miles below the city. To the south and southeast is a campaign country, covered with fine farms and orchards, as far as the eye can reach. Through the centre of this campaign runs the Wakarusa. Westward is a succession of rolling hills, and northwest is the wide alluvial bottom of the Kaw through which its serpentine course can be traced for miles.

Remounting our carriages we were driven through some of the principal streets of the city, and finally through Massachusetts street, its Broadway, to the Eldridge House.

We have now been three days in Kansas, during which time we have traveled about five hundred miles, and seen the country from north to south, and from east to west; to be sure in the brightest season of the year, the flowery month of June; and we have met and become acquainted with its people and enjoyed their hospitalities. Retracing, mentally, the incidents and scenes of these three days, they appear more like a lovely dream than a reality. A richer and a more beautiful country the sun does not look down upon in its course around the globe; and in time it must become the seat of wealth and social and intellectual power and influence, that will make themselves felt even beyond the limits of our own nation. But a few years since and it was the pasture field of the buffalo, and the hunting ground of wild, roaming, hunting savage tribes of the plains. Then came the white man, and with him the fierce passions engendered in sectional strife, who made this their first battlefield. No crime that blackens the criminal code, but was enacted here, and that by people of the same lineage, speaking the same language, and hailing from the same nation. Fraud, violence, robbery, arson and murder were rife here, and roamed over and desolated the land unchecked by the civil authority, because of the imbecility, or rather servility of both territorial and national governments. But the men who came here to settle, stood their ground manfully, and maintained their position against unequal numbers backed, as far as they dared, by both civil authorities. Then to become an emigrant to, and settle in Kansas, was an adventure that required courage, firmness and resolution. None but men of positive and strong convictions dared do it; because it required taking their lives in their hands, with the resolution to die for principles if it became necessary. It was a winnowing process by which the dross was separated in the States from the pure metal, and by which cowards, neutrals, compromisers and temporizers were completely eliminated. Those that then came, learned the important lesson which has been, and is, the secret of their success, prosperity and unexampled progress, mainly that of unity of purpose and concentration of efforts. Whatever may have been, or is their object, whether to repel the aggressor, to organize industry, to establish schools and other institutions of learning, to build churches, and push forward enterprises of internal improvement, there has been no holding back, no division of council, no lukewarmness, but the united energy of the whole community has been, and is, always concentrated in the effort, acting as though it had but a single thought, and controlled by but one mind. In Austria or Russia, such unity of action would be effected by the use of despotic power, but here it is by intelligence and enlightened public opinion. The result is that in no State has there been such rapid material progress, and in so short a time such immense strides in all the elements of prosperity and greatness. In one decade they have done more towards the development of the natural resources of the State, to organize its industrial, social, moral, religious and intellectual interests, than is effected by the more apathetic and sluggish communities of the older States in a half century. During the border troubles it was customary to speak of "Bleeding Kansas." It is true she bled some, but with the light of to-day, we cannot but regard it to have been good for her health, and promotive of her constitutional vigor. It kept away from her the timid, the unenlightened, the thriftless and shiftless; in fact all those without enterprise and determination of purpose. Hence, in her social movements, and industrial enterprises, Kansas had nothing to clog the march of events, nor any dead weight to carry. Such material as that composing this infant State cannot be collected anywhere without developing its inherent tendency of pushing things that promote the interests and prosperity of communities. Hence originated that spirit of progress, and the adoption of those far-seeing and wise measures that have placed her in the front rank of States in the organization of her material, social and intellectual interests.

Our experience amongst them has convinced us that they are as kind, generous and hospitable, as they are brave, daring and resolute. In everything they do there is the ring of the pure noble metal. Be it doing acts of generosity and kindness, of extending hospitality to strangers, be it meeting the common enemy in a death struggle, or in attacking and overcoming the obstacles of Nature, the innate character of the people is never obscured or hidden. It is the embodiment of heart, will and purpose. Such is a true picture of Kansas and her people to-day, which must forever leave its impression on her destiny.

CHAPTER IV.

It was one hour past midnight on the morning of June 9th when we left, not without regret, the beautiful and enterprising city of Lawrence, the hospitalities of whose generous and liberal minded citizens we had shared for the last two days. Once on board of the western bound train of the Kansas Pacific railroad, our faces as well as our thoughts were turned to the great objective point of our excursion, the Rocky Mountains. Day overtook us at Wamega, 104 miles west of the State line, the initial point of the railroad, whence distance is measured west to Denver. The character of the country, both extrinsic and intrinsic, appeared about the same as at Lawrence. There were bold hills and gentle slopes, boundless prairies and hill encircled valleys, through the latter generally a line of straggling trees mark the windings of a small brook. The soil is a dark mould, and where cultivated, gives promise of an abundant harvest. On all sides were evidences that the country is fast settling up with immigrants.

New and unpainted cottages or the board shanty meet the eye in all directions, as far as sight can pierce over the plain. Some of these are yet surrounded with the primitive prairies, yet many stand within or beside the newly broken sod, but all are unenclosed. Often corn has been dropped in the furrow while breaking up the prairie, and where so, it is up with a tolerable fair stand five to eight inches above the sod. This often yields a third or a fourth of a crop, with no other labor than dropping it in the furrow while breaking up the prairie sod.

The older settlements exhibit unmistakable evidence of

that intelligence, industry and enterprise, and consequently thrift so characteristic of the people of Kansas. Neater homes, better cultivated farms, and more promising and finer crops, are hard to find, even in the best cultivated and richest parts of the older States. The aspect of the whole seems as though the people thought there were no enjoyments nor pleasures equal to the endearments of tidy, comfortable and pleasant homes.

The preceding day we had seen the wheat fields from Lawrence to Humboldt, along the Leavenworth, Lawrence and Galveston railroad. At Garnett and Iola there was often much disparity in the growing crop. Fields almost adjacent, with apparently no difference in soil, nor choice of location, differed so much in appearance that the owners of the poor fields must have made some great mistake or committed a grievous fault either in the time or manner in which they put the crop in, or in the quality of the seed sown. Be the cause what it may, one field promising 28 to 30 bushels of wheat per acre was fully ripe for harvest, untouched by blight, while an adjacent one, thin, green and rust eaten, would not yield one-half that quantity of a very inferior quality. Along the line of the Kansas Pacific railroad so far, although there were considerable differences in fields, there was nowhere such a contrast as we had observed in Southern Kansas. Corn from Wamega as far west as we found it planted, was very promising, of a dark rich green, since there had been through this section abundant rains, and most of the fields were in the highest state of tilth with not a weed to be seen.

Manhattan lies above and immediately west of the junction of the Blue whose upper valley, some seventy miles north from its mouth, we had traversed three days before as far as Waterville. Here is located the Kansas State Agricultural College and the experimental farm. According to pre-arrangement we were to have stopped here and spend a day in looking over the farm and studying its system and that of the organization of the college. The college and farm are located some two and a half miles northwest of the town. But finding that if we did so, our train arrangements would be interfered with, we kept on without stopping, with the intention to defer our visit until our return.

The railroad runs up the valley of the Kaw, or Kansas as it is sometimes called, a beautiful transparent stream with a rapid current. It is sometimes flanked by low hills, which now approach and then recede until lost from view beneath the distant horizon. The banks of the river are sparsely lined with trees, but with little undergrowth. Otherwise there is no timber except along the banks of some affluent whose devious windings can be traced over the plains until lost in the distance, by the line of trees that deck its banks.

The same species of mimosa observed yesterday in Southern and the day before in Northern Kansas, the *Schrankia uncinata* of the botanists, was still plenty, and occasionally the white and purple Œnothera, was still plenty. A new comer, however, made its appearance this morning, the white Mexican prickly poppy, (*Argemone grandiflora*) growing luxuriantly on the sides of the excavations and embankments of the railroad. Its enormous white flowers, often five inches in diameter, were the admiration of the whole party.

Some fifteen miles above Manhattan is to be seen on the south side of the Kaw the old capitol building now occupied if at all by hogs and other unclean beasts. Pawnee was to have been the capital of the nascent State; here the appropriation made by Congress for erecting Territorial buildings was expended, and here Governor Reeder convened the first Territorial Legislature, in midwinter on a bleak prairie one hundred and twenty-five miles west of any civilized habitation. This was too much for the practical good sense of the unsophisticated early settlers, and they rebelled against it. After many failures with renewed and energetic efforts, the ambulatory Legislature meanwhile meeting at other points, the capital question was settled by selecting Topeka, and the glory of Pawnee departed and with it visions of valuable corner lots, etc. On the surrounding prairies there is now nothing to be seen but droves of Texas cattle, remarkable only for their enormous uncouth horns. Such was the case on the morning we passed there.

Fort Riley is situated near the junction of the Republican Fork; and some three miles beyond is Junction City. A good idea of the topographical sloping of Central and Northern Kansas may be formed by studying its river system proper, which converges here. Southwestern Kansas, nearly one-fourth part of the State, belongs to another system, and is drained and traversed by the Arkansas, and the Cimmaron. But the system which forms the Kaw has its sources west in Colorado and north in Nebraska. The Blue rises in Nebraska near the channel of the Platte, and flows generally south, entering the Kaw at Manhattan. It is said to afford the best water power in the State through its entire length. It certainly does so in the northern tier of counties, as we saw three days before at Irving, Blue Rapids and Waterville. The Republican forms a junction with the Smoky Hill Fork just below Junction City. The Republican has its source in southwestern Nebraska and northeastern Colorado, flowing at first east, then southeast until it joins its waters with those of the Smoky Hill, forming the Kansas or Kaw. Thirty miles or so west, Solomon's Fork, rising in eastern Colorado, running at first northeast into Nebraska and then southeast, joins the Smoky Hill. Thirteen miles higher up, the Smoky Hill is joined by the Salina, which also rises in eastern Colorado. The Smoky Hill itself rises in eastern Colorado, and flows a little north of east in the general course. The line of railroad is up the valley of the Smoky Hill, but so level and expanded is its basin that the river is seldom in sight, flowing far to the south.

Some twenty-five miles above Junction is Abilene, 163 miles west of the State line. Being the point for shipping Texas cattle, it is quite a business place, but the concentration of the cattle trade here retards the growth, settlement and improvement of the rich agricultural country surrounding it.

At Abilene we saw the first subterranean habitations, which become more common further west. An excavation is made some ten feet wide, twenty feet long and six or seven feet deep. Timbers are put up like rafters over the excavation, and the whole is covered with prairie sod. Such were the houses of the railroad laborers when the road was built, and such still are the habitations of thousands of employees of the road, and of the poor on the plains from Abilene to Denver. An advance on this is the adobe, of which we saw several in the extreme western part of Kansas.

The first village beyond Abilene is Solomon, at the junction of that stream, and next is Salina, named so for the same reason. Salina is a thriving village, and the best wheat fields seen yet were in the neighborhood. It is a "meal station," consequently we took breakfast here—a very good one—for which the usual price along the line, one dollar, was charged.

Beyond Salina the appearance of the country changes. The hills, on the north side especially, become higher and steeper, with occasionally a rock cap. Some twenty miles above Salina, on the highest hill, there is either a natural or artificial stone column, about fifteen feet high, and perhaps three feet in diameter. Some people say Fremont set it up as a landmark to guide the wanderers of the prairies; others, that it is an Indian monument. It is a conspicuous object for miles around. Bavaria is the next Village above Salina. A good deal of newly broken prairie, and of new cabins were seen here. The town seems to be principally settled by Germans. Brookville, at the two hundredth mile post, is the next town, and has a very thrifty appearance. The machine shops of the Kansas Pacific railroad are located here. Between Rock Spring and Elm Creek, (207 miles west of the State line) we saw the first prairie dog village. It is, however, a libel to call this little fellow, the *Cynomys Ludovicianus*, a dog. There is nothing in his looks, manners, habits, disposition or nature that is at all currish. Why, to convince you of his *uprightness* he straightens himself and standing on his hind legs looks you in the face without winking; as much as to say "you may call me a dog, but you cannot accuse me of crookedness in my ways, for measure my acts by what rule you may, physically or morally, they will be found perpendicular to any base you lay down."

His defamers even admit that he lives in amity and peace with the jackass-rabbit, the burrowing prairie owl, and even with the malicious rattlesnake, sharing with them his house and bed. This ought to be sufficient evidence that he is not a dog, not even of "the dog-in-the-manger" sort. Moreover, in a life-time he never tastes meat, but being a true herbivore, he lives upon the luscious blades and roots of the buffalo grass. He indeed resembles a fox squirrel, being only a little larger and somewhat yellower, with a short, black, straggy-haired tail, like the groundhog or woodchuck.

From Rock Creek to Fort Harker, especially near Summit Siding, the bluffs and buttes are bold and picturesque, with lodges and crests of red rock. The soil is very dark and the subsoil a brown, ashy gray. At Fort Harker the hills again assume their wonted shape of gentle slopes, clothed in the light green of the prairies. Just beyond Fort Harker, we saw a caravan of about thirty ox-teams, on their way to Santa Fe.

Fort Harker has an altitude of 1,586 feet above tidewater. Here there is a summit, and at Ellsworth, five miles beyond, the altitude is only 1,440 feet. But from here to Gopher, 174 miles west, the average rise per mile is a fraction over ten feet; the altitude of the latter place being 3,220 feet above tide.

Ellsworth, the limit of western settlement, is a new, neat and thrifty village, standing on the north bank of the Smoky Hill, which here approaches close to the road. The country is rolling, rich prairie, but entirely treeless, except some straggling trees along the river and creek banks. Here the diminutive church, with a high, curious-shaped steeple, arrests attention. It looks more like a toy house than anything else. We concluded it to be the famous "little church around the corner," dispensing religious rites, privileges, consolation and charities on all alike as *poor sinners*, whether they claim, like the Pharisees, conventional respectability and righteousness or not. Seventeen miles beyond Ellsworth is Wilson's Creek, 1,586 feet above tide water. Here Mr. Elliot, the Industrial Agent of the Kansas Pacific Railroad Company, has located his first experimental station.

The existence of this agency is an historical sequence of events that took place more than half a century ago. When Missouri applied for admission into the Union, the same questions in principle, though not in form, were raised which forty years later culminated in a war that terminated forever the existence of the institution in whose interest these questions were raised, by submitting them to the arbitrament of the sword. It was evident from the heat and ardor with which conflicting, extreme, and at every point antagonistic views on the conditions upon which Missouri was to be admitted, were presented and urged, that an amicable compromise or an open rupture must ensue. Timidity counseled compromise; but compromise upon anything actual was out of the question; therefore it was made upon what was only prospective. The uninhabited territory hence became the matter of compromise; and to reconcile the extreme Southern men to a compromise, presented, urged and carried through by temporizing and timid men of their own section, an attempt was made to depreciate the territory in question. Hence, while all territory lying north of latitude 36 deg. 30 min. and west of Missouri was dedicated forever to freedom, the Southern people must be deluded with the idea that it was worthless. Hence there eminated from the War Department, then presided over by Mr. Calhoun, an aspirant for the Presidency, documents purporting to give a topographical description of the country, and of the nature of the soil and climate. These documents described the country as worthless; merely a vast, arid, treeless, rainless sandy desert; no springs nor running brooks, because there was no rain to supply them; and so sandy that the streams that flowed from the mountains were soon absorbed on the plains.

Hence there appeared in our school atlases, for the first time, that myth the "Great American Desert," shaded like the Sahara and other deserts to indicate sand, from the Missouri to the mountains and south beyond the Arkansas. The settlement of Kansas, up to Ellsworth, two hundred and twenty-five miles west of Missouri, has dispelled this illusion as far as the eastern half of the territory is concerned; but our geographers still represent the western half as the Great Desert, or the Desert omitting the sandy shading.

The Kansas Pacific railroad company having a large land grant, (the alternate, or more specifically all the odd numbered sections for ten miles on each side of the road,) from Congress given to aid in constructing the road, find it necessary to disabuse the public mind and root out the geographical errors that have been inculcated for two generations. They have adopted the truly logical way, which is to combat error by facts. Without facts and without investigation, and merely upon the dictum of some book compiler, the public yet take it for granted that practically, if not actually, there is a region some three or four hundred miles wide in Western Kansas and Eastern Colorado that is doomed to remain a desert and wilderness forever; and that the cause of this doom is natural sterility, imposed by a sandy soil and a rainless climate. To eradicate the belief in this sterility, the contrary must be shown, and not shown by arguments, but by facts which are incontestible. If crops actually grown there show that the soil is productive, then it cannot be a sandy, sterile plain; and if these crops are grown without irrigation, then the climate cannot be rainless. These are the problems proposed by the company to be solved and demonstrated by its industrial agent. Mr. Elliot selected three stations—Wilson's Creek, Ellis and Pond Creek—for his experiments. The distances from the State line, respectively, are 239, 302 and 425 miles, and their elevations 1586, 2019, 3200 feet above the sea. East of Wilson's Creek the demonstration of the inhabitability and fertility of the plains is *une fait accompli*. Up as far as and around Ellsworth, only sixteen miles east of Wilson's, the luxuriant fields of corn and the heavy fields of wheat, yellow and ready for the harvest, without any taint of disease, sufficiently attest the adaptation of the country for yielding the heaviest crops of cereals and of the best quality. But Wilson's is on a high bench, with a different soil, and with less black loam than the plains eastward. In fact, it is a different, a cretaceous formation, reaching clear to the mountains. Here, then, the test was to be made whether this formation was deficient in the elements of fertility, and if not, then under proper conditions the whole plain would be productive. Late in November wheat, rye and barley were sown, and the season being unusually dry, the prospect of success was not considered to be very flattering. The area sown was about one acre and a half of each kind. When we were there (on the 9th of June) the whole crop would be ripe within ten days. The stand, the hight, and the general appearance of the crop were equal to the best crops under similar circumstances in Missouri or Illinois, and in the rich yellow coloring of the straw and freedom from disease, far superior. Of the crop at Ellis we could not judge, since some nine days before our arrival a hailstorm had passed over, literally mowing it down and sweeping it from the field. At Pond Creek more than a thousand feet higher, the crop was very promising—not so forward, but of the healthiest kind of deep green. On our return, ten days later, the barley was here turning yellow and the ears very heavy. As far as the experiments of the present and past season are concerned, they have been eminently successful. The winter grains have not only succeeded, but succeeded most admirably, and the corn is promising. The only question, then, is, was the present an ordinary or an exceptional season? This it is impossible for me to decide; and further experiment and observation may be necessary to determine and settle this point.

It will be remembered that in Missouri the spring had been unusually dry. When we left St. Louis in early June, the spring crops were suffering for want of rain, and we found them still so when we returned on the twentieth, though there had been a few refreshing showers in the intervening time. West on the northern frontier of Kansas, as far as we went, some 100 miles northwest of Atchison, there had been abundant rains. The same remark may be made as disclosed by our trip to near the southern border. On the outward trip, west as far as daylight permitted us to observe, namely, to Fort Wallace, 420 miles west of the State line, and on our return from Aroya, 511 miles, there were evidences of not only abundant but quite recent rains; the excavations along the line and the buffalo wallows on the prairie were pools of water. At Denver, 128 miles further west, there had been no rain when we left. Now, these rains reaching away into eastern Colorado, and within 150 miles of the mountains, may have been exceptional and not the rule; but if they are as abundant and frequent every season as this, the crops will suffer less from drought on the plains than they have in southern and eastern Missouri this year.

Mr. Elliot also experimented in planting trees, both deciduous and evergreen. Of the former we saw maples, elms, ailanthus, chesnut, European larch, etc., which all appeared to do well. The larch had started finely and promised well, but my experience with it is that appearances are deceptive, and disappointment almost certain, being so liable to kill off during the summer heats. I think it will be found to do well on the higher, well irrigated and cooler plains of Colorado; but on the plains it should be planted sparingly until experiment has demonstrated that it can be done successfully.

The seedling oaks and walnuts looked thrifty, and of their success there can be no doubt. Of evergreens there were planted the Scotch and the Austrian pine and the Norway spruce. The latter so far appeared the most promising. It must also be stated that the planting was not done under the most favorable circumstances. It was done by the employees of the road, none of whom, perhaps, had ever set or seen a tree set before in their lives. The success in tree raising is of the highest importance, since incontestible facts prove that of all agencies within the control of man for the amelioration of climate, that of covering the earth with forests is the most effective. Of the progressive improvement in climate on the plains and the mountains, and the probable cause, we may speak hereafter. The supply of water is also a material question bearing upon the future settlement of the plains. There are more or less springs, but often at long intervals, throughout the plains; and then besides the living streams, such as the Solomon, Salina, Smoky Hill, Republican and their affluents, there are many "*aroyas*," that is beds of temporary streams with pools of water, which answer for stock purposes.

Suppose that the fall from the clouds is insufficient to fill the cisterns, the experience of the railroad company is that abundant and apparently inexhaustible supplies of water can be obtained in sinking wells of moderate depths. In sinking these wells no blasting is necessary. What the

4

approximate depth may be to which the wells have to be sunk will depend upon the elevation of the surface. The railroad company sank these wells where necessary, most generally on an elevation, since their road is on a divide. Their wells range from 48 to 130 feet in depth. Upon lower grounds the depth would probably be much less.

Fossil is a station village, in and around which some thirty families from Wisconsin are settled. They were very poor when they came here, soon after the road was opened. An employee of the road told me the company had brought them here at a mere nominal charge from St. Louis and set them down here, knowing they never could get away. They have comfortable cottages now, are breaking up considerable prairie, and have some cattle. I conversed with several of them, both male and female. They appeared quite intelligent and declared, notwithstanding the privations, hardships and trials they had to endure after coming here, they are now well pleased and quite satisfied with their situation. Some of the village boys had a horned frog they had caught, which they presented to Mr. Geo. T. Anthony, the editor of the Kansas *Farmer*. Here we saw the first buffalo, but it was a calf, tied with a long rope, and was quite tame. We could no longer doubt that we were within the range of the buffalo, not because we had seen the calf, but all along the railroad and over the plains, their dead carcases were strewn. This continued for 200 miles and how much further I cannot say, since, as long as there was sufficient daylight the same evidences of wanton slaughter and insensate destruction were visible. This is a fit subject for the attention of the Humane Society. I suppose I saw at least a thousand carcases lying as they fell, killed merely to afford amusement to the soldiers of Forts Hays, Wallace, etc. This is outrageous, and the strong arm of the government should be exerted to put a stop to it. These animals are and will be an important item to promote the settlement of the plains, furnishing an abundant and most delicious supply of meat to the pioneers. It is now served up at all the meal stations of the road, and is more relished by the hungry passengers than the best beef. Besides, our Indian difficulties always involve the wholesale slaughter and wanton destruction of the buffalo by the whites. Let the government rectify and prevent these outrages in the future, and let these thoughtless men be made to feel that humanity and civilization revolt against such wantonness and cruelty.

At Fossil there is a most beautiful white limestone in great abundance, admirably adapted for building purposes. Immense quantities of it are quarried and shipped from here and other stations along the road. Further west, near Wallace, there are softer limestones, some of beautifully variegated colors, so soft as to be as easily sawed as wood into blocks; yet when dried will bear the weight of large buildings. Near Junction City a similar soft magnesian limestone, called "Junction City marble," is found. Blocks from eight to twelve tons weight are quarried and sawed, like wood, into any shape desired. It is of a delicate cream color. Most of the houses in Junction City are built of it; and so is the magnificent State capitol, at Topeka. Its durability has been well tested for years at the government buildings at Fort Riley.

We are now fully on the plains. The short buffalo grass has supplanted the taller grasses, common to the prairies in all the Western States. This is a peculiar grass, not as long as, but standing fully as thick as the hair on a buffalo's back. Whether green or dried into a natural hay, it is equally well relished by wild and tame animals, and possesses most remarkable nutricious properties. It now would have complete possession of the plains where we are, were it not for the Patagonian plantain (*Plantago Patagonica*), which overtops it and gives to the plain a bluish-gray tint. This plantain is common to both North and South America, growing east of the Andes and Rocky Mountains, from the Straits of Magellan to the Arctic

Sea. The flora have also become fewer and scarcer. There are none to be seen, except the white Mexican poppy along the excavations of the road, and on the prairies occasionally a *Malvastrum Coccineum*, also the beautiful *Gaillardia Picta* and large plots of the *Callirrhœ Pedata* and *Callirrhœ Verticillata*.

On and on we go to the westward, passing a road station every twelve or fifteen miles, Walker, Hays, Ellis, Ogallah, Park's Fort, Cayote, Buffalo, Grinnel, Monument, Gopher, Sheridan, Wallace, Eagle Tail, Monotony, etc. Otherwise the scene is as monotonous as that viewed from a ship on the ocean. Varied, however, with the constantly occurring prairie dog villages. It was really amusing to see the dogs (?) scampering home, big and little, upon the approach of the train. Instantly they would disappear in their holes, excepting perhaps a veteran whose curiosity was greater than his sense of fear. Having arrived on his hillock, he sets himself upright, often raising on his hind legs, and stands unmoved like a statue, looking at the passing train. Some of the passengers in a forward car would empty their revolvers at them, but without effect, unless the ball struck near the hillock, when in a twinkle he would disappear in his hole.

On the hillocks were frequently seen the burrowing owl, the *Anthene Hypugœa* of ornitholigists.

We saw the first antelopes near Ogallah. As soon as they were discovered the shout of "Antelopes" burst from every car in the train, and all eyes were strained in a southwest direction to catch a glimpse of the novel sight. There, sure enough, at perhaps three hundred yards distant, were two fine ones, fleeting with the swiftness of the wind over the plain. As they seemed bewildered, and taking a direction almost parallel to the line of the road, they were some time in sight. Hardly had this excitement subsided before the shout of "Buffalo" broke out, with fingers pointing to the north. Away off at a great distance were three dark moving objects, which we were told were stragglers from the main herd.

A jackass-rabbit, the *Lepus Townsendii*, would now and then start up and scud away. He is as large as a four-month old fawn, with the color and immense ears of a jackass. Sometimes a very large old fellow, accustomed to the cars, would sit on a prairie dog's hillock surrounded by the dogs, and look unconcernedly at the passing train within fifty yards of it. The antelopes became so numerous as not to attract much attention, and twice or three times more we had views of a few buffaloes at a distance. Near dark there was a shout of "coyote," and a prairie wolf, as he is called in the Western States (*canis latrans*) was seen trying his "level best" to get out of the way of the "fire horse."

Towards evening the aspect of the plain changed. The "mesquite," a kind of vernal grass, was supplanting the Patagonian plantain. It is about four inches high, heads up like beardless barley, which are filled with a grainlike chess, and as it was past maturity, it was dry and dead, giving the plain, notwithstanding its wooly coat of bluish gray, green buffalo grass, a sere appearance. At Wallace we had fine buffalo steak for supper, and it was after sunset that we resumed our journey.

Conversing with Major Reddington, the paymaster on this end of the road, about the meteorology and climate of this section of the Great Plains, I received much valuable information respecting the periodic winds that sweep at regular seasons over this vast region. I may hereafter embody these facts, combining them with my own observations, into regular form, and explain their laws and meteorological relations to the climate of the Valley of the Mississippi.

Inquiring of the Major how long this wearisome monotony of plain and sky would continue, I received the welcome information that fifty miles west from where we then were, at First View Station, we would get the first glimpse at the mountains.

It was now getting dark, and a thick grayish haze had settled on the plain; it was therefore evident that we could not enjoy the "first view," even if at the station. The loneliness of the landscape, the sombre appearance of the sky, shut out by the thick haze, seemed to grow oppressive and to excite a vague, indefinite feeling of anxiety, akin to fear. I looked out, the pall of darkness had settled on the plain. In front was our engine, like a monster, breathing smoke and flame, giving a lurid tint to the thick haze, but all else was impenetrable gloom and darkness. I felt as though we had left the coasts of light, and Milton's description of the arch fiend's flight through the domains of Chaos vividly recurred to me:

> "On he fares, through a dark,
> Illimitable ocean, without bound,
> Without dimension; a vast vacuity, where
> Length, breadth, hight, time and place are lost."

Our weary company became silent, and one by one fell into the embrace of

> "Tired nature's sweet restorer,
> Balmy sleep."

And so I close for the present, leaving us asleep in the wide, wide plains.

CHAPTER V.

Our last chapter closed with the retirement of our party to rest, and left us asleep on the vast plains, in charge of the fiery steed, who, sure footed and fleet, and undaunted by storm and darkness, was, with unflagging speed, carrying us forward to our destination. Day overtook us at Agate, 572 miles beyond the State line of Missouri, and 57 miles east of Denver. Refreshed by a good rest, I was up at dawn to catch a glimpse of the great mountains, with whose description by Lewis and Clark I was charmed and captivated in early boyhood. But the same impenetrable haze of the preceding evening still rested on the plains and closed in the view on all sides. The morning was cold, and frost was observable on the plains, which looked more sere and desolate than before, since the dry "mesquite grass" was more abundant, and entirely hid the coat of buffalo grass underneath. But we were either running out of the haze, or else the rising sun was dispersing it, for it was growing thinner and more penetrable to the sight. Ah, there! the outline of something dark as a storm cloud appeared for an instant and then vanished. Was it fancy, or was it reality? Anon, and the same reappeared, this time like a series of black clouds, but hazy, and of no definite outline. Again they vanish and leave me in doubt. I hesitated making the assertion that I had caught a glimpse of the object that I had a life-long desire to see. I looked doubtfully at Mrs. T. who had been looking out for the same object on the opposite side of the cars. She beckoned me and whispered, "I believe I caught several glimpses of the mountains through the fog." I replied I thought I had too, but was not quite certain. Looking out again, in a moment they reappeared, this time quite distinct; and instantly a shout arose: "The mountains!" "the mountains!" that awoke every sleeper in the party.

In fifteen minutes more we had run clean out of the haze into an atmosphere of most crystalline transparency. There lay exposed to full view along the western horizon two hundred and fifty miles, at least, of the greatest, longest, and most remarkable mountain chain in the world, stretching from Terra del Fuego to Behring's Straits, a distance of some 11,000 miles, and containing more of the precious metals than the whole world besides. There they lay, sombre as cast iron, peak behind peak, duplicate and conduplicate, culminating in the far distance into snowy heads, peering over and dominating the whole. My observations on the plains had already satisfied me that in no particular whatever, either of general outline, formation, soil, climate, productions or meteorology, was the West a counterpart of the East; and that from an eastern standpoint, neither the appearance, character nor conditions of the West could be conceived or understood. From even this distant point, no one can look at the mountain system, spread out like a panorama before him, without having the conviction forced upon him, that though Nature operates everywhere by the same law, yet she never follows or passively copies the same pattern. In the eastern mountains the chains are parallel and separated by wide valleys. Moreover they are single and continuous, unbroken it may be, for fifty or a hundred miles. But here, even, the mountain wall that rises almost perpendicular to the height of two to four thousand feet, in a straight line along the edge of the plain, like the houses on one side of a street in our large cities, is severed from top to bottom, not unlike those houses, at intervals never exceeding two thousand feet. These immense rifts are the gulches and canyons through which the mountain streams, having their sources in the snowy range, fifty miles distant, pour their limpid, icy-cold water on the plains. These rifts do not strike in a single gorge directly into the heart of the mountains, but by more or less laterals, honey-comb the whole system. Hence, the mountain, instead of a monotonous range, as in the East, is a system of cones, oftentimes as sharp as the teeth of a saw. Most appropriately have the Spaniards called them the "Sierras;" that is, the serrated, or the mountains jagged like a saw. The great departure I had observed in the far West, from what Eastern experience would lead us to infer were the normal forms of Nature, had prepared me not to expect seeing the familiar forms of the East repeated, but I was totally unprepared, even in imagination, for the sublime, strange, and unique forms that greeted my sight that morning. East, and north and south lay the apparently illimitable plain, but to the west there loomed up from below the horizon what appeared at one time to have been an ocean of molten iron lashed into mountain waves; then instantly congealed and fixed motionless forever. The transparency and rarity of the air 5,700 feet above the sea, made it impossible to judge of their distance. They were fully eighty miles away, yet every one judging by ordinary experience, would not have assigned them a distance beyond five miles. Looking at them in this light, it required very little aid from the imagination to fancy that we were approaching a mighty city of cyclopean architecture, and that the mountain cones and peaks were domes and minarets, pyramids and pinnacles. Such reveries at least passed through my mind as I sat gazing at them from the car windows, which were uninterrupted till the announcement was made—"Denver." For once I was disappointed. It may have been from being so suddenly translated from the regions of fancy to those of reality; or it may have been that I expected in a region like this, where Nature operates on so grand a scale, and in so unique a style, that man would appreciate it, select his habitation at the choicest spot, and make his works correspond to the beauty of the surroundings. Be the cause what it may, yet the truth must be confessed, I never before visited for the first time any place that seemed so tame, humdrum, commonplace and unpoetical as Denver did that morning.

My subsequent observations did not improve or modify my first impressions. I believe such is a universal feeling experienced by travelers; and the first thought that finds expression is, the wonder why ever a city was located in such a point as this. The truth is, the selection of the locality was not determined either from the beauty or loveliness of the spot, from its primitive adaptation for a city, or from its prospective development for such, but by accident; and like most accidents, it was and is unfortunate, both for the commercial interest of the Territory and for public convenience.

The earliest gold hunters that went into the Territory found a few grains of gold in the sandy bed of Cherry Creek, an insignificant stream that flows, when it has any water, from the Divide in a northwesterly direction into the South Platte. This induced them to pitch their tents here and calling the place by the poetical name of Auraria. The news of the finding of gold here spread like wildfire over the States as well as over the mountains; and it became the objective point of gold-hunters from the States as well as from the mountains of New Mexico. This fact made it a good point to concentrate and distribute supplies. Here the miner of the mountains could go and replenish his stores of provisions, supply himself with tools and other necessaries; and the adventurers from the States, after their long wanderings over the plains, came here to overhaul and refit, and to complete their outfit for their mountain expedition. Numerous stores were opened, with full and complete assortments of mining implements, provisions, groceries and other necessities. Although the limited quantity of gold dust found in the sands of Cherry Creek were soon exhausted, Auraria still flourished and had become a respectable village. It still yielded gold to desperate adventurers who had large stocks of supplies to dispose of, and recklessly engaged in keeping up the delusion abroad of the fabulous richness of the mountain placers. But the bubble finally burst, and the poetical Auraria, (the golden land) shorn of its glory, became Denver, in honor of Col. J. W. Denver, the then Governor of Kansas, in which all this mountain region was then included. It is now a city lighted with gas, has a branch mint, several banks, and some heavy commercial houses. Its population is about 8,000. Johnny has invaded it some. On its business streets are conspicuously displayed the signs of How Chong, Ming Lee, etc., announcing that washing and ironing are done there. Besides there is what is called the Chinese quarter, near the bridge, entirely occupied by them. Like ancient Palmyra, the Thadmor of the Wilderness in Israelitish history, Denver is a mere entrepot of commerce, where articles produced in far separated regions, are taken to be exchanged and distributed, but where no article of commercial value is, or ever can be, produced.

Palmyra, however, was situated in a fertile oasis surrounded by shady palm trees, beyond which stretched an inhospitable sandy desert; but Denver is situated on an arid plain, with neither palm nor even the indigenous cottonwood to afford shade to the weary ox-teams that by scores are daily arriving with wool from New Mexico.

The articles of commercial value now furnished, and ever to be furnished, by Colorado, are the precious metals found in its mountains. The center of its mineral district, as far as now developed, lies considerably to the north of west from Denver. New discoveries, said to be very rich, are rapidly making in the northwestern part of the territory, while no extension of discoveries or in mining operations are being made in the southwest. Gulch mining is not prosecuted much in the Territory now, for it is not now and never was profitable here, excepting within very narrow limits. In the lodes, gold is mostly combined with pyrites of iron, a sulphuret; silver ores are also mostly sulphurets combined with baser metals, as copper, lead and zinc. There can be no combinations more refractory than those of the precious metals in this region; and no patent way of extracting them has succeeded in obtaining more than from one-quarter to one-third contained in the ore. Gradually all treatment of them has, and is returning to the old way of smelting. Regular smelting furnaces are now in operation in all parts of the mountains where the oldest lodes are located, and others are being erected at points convenient to the newly developed mines. But the talk now is of constructing narrow gauge railroads into the mountains at various points. As this is said to be entirely practicable, the construction of these roads is a mere question of time. Then, if coal of a suitable quality for smelting these ores exists at any point along the foot of the mountains, these ores will be brought there to be reduced. Geological explorations have established the fact that coal beds skirt the mountains through the entire width of the Territory. It is a rich lignite, differing much however in quality at different points. In some localities it is said to be of the best quality, being a pure anthracite.

It is not known whether any coal exists at Denver; but probably it does at considerable depth. The location of the commercial metropolis of this region is, therefore, still an open question, to be determined by future developments, with the chances decidedly against Denver, situated as it is on an arid plain, some eighteen miles from the foot of the mountains.

It is situated on the east bank of the South Platte, a bank-full and therefore canal-like stream which heads in South Park, and when it issues from the mountains, like all streams in this region, strikes out on the plain and then gradually tends towards the northeast.

After spending the greater part of Saturday in looking

over the city, visiting the United States Mint, scrutinizing its assaying rooms, examining all its appointments, and looking through the mineralogical cabinet, and then taking a walk down to the bridge, and from it admiring the limpid waters and beauty of the South Platte, rushing with a fearful rapidity past the western portion of the city, we concluded that we had about "done up" Denver, and that it would be a decidedly dull place to spend Sunday in. Besides, a view of the snowy range looked so cool, refreshing and inviting, that we could not resist the temptation of going there. Accordingly our party took the evening train of the Colorado Central Railroad, for Golden City, sixteen miles distant, and near the foot of the mountains, where we arrived at half-past six o'clock.

The railroad runs up to the mountains on the north side of Clear Creek, which, like all the streams here, is brimfull and rapid, running through the plain like a canal. Before reaching Golden, the railroad runs close under a range of basaltic buttes, jutting out on the plain at right angles to the mountains. They are crested with an immense wall of basalt, rising perpendicularly from one hundred to two hundred feet. This range is shown in the background of the engraving of Castle Butte, in which the appearance of the rock crest is well represented. Their altitude is from six hundred to one thousand feet above the railroad. They are very bald, extremely steep, rocky and destitute of vegetation, except in places sparsely covered with the short buffalo grass and a few flowers.

Golden City is cut in twain by Clear Creek, a large, dashing, icy cold stream, that comes booming from the mountains; the hum of whose noisy waters, of an evening, is a perpetual lullaby to the denizens of this unpretentious cozy town, nestled so snugly on its bosom. It is more than a mile to the mouth of the canyon, where the stream issues from the mountains; yet from the rarity of the atmosphere (for Golden is 5,700 feet above tide water) the apparent distance seems not to be more than a quarter of a mile. All visitors will learn, if not otherwise, by painful experience, that distance in this region cannot be measured, or even approximately guessed at by sight. This peculiarity, however, is not, as is generally supposed, due to the *purity*, but to the *rarity* of the atmosphere. Besides this, a change takes place in the form of the eye by being relieved by the altitude of so much atmospheric pressure. Several instances, illustrating this fact, occurred in our party. For years they could neither read nor write without glasses, yet here they did both unaware of the fact until from habit, when they got through, they reached for their glasses. The deceptiveness in regard to distance led me and others into several awkward scrapes. One of these occurred on the evening of our arrival at Golden. To understand it, however, a topographical description of the surrounding country is necessary.

West lies the rifted barrier of the Rocky Mountains, flanking the plains in a straight line north and south with a nearly perpendicular wall, from fifteen hundred to two thousand feet high. The light green of the plain contrasts beautifully with sombre brown of the feldspathic rocks of the mountain sides, or the dark green of the evergreens with which the mountain slopes, where not too steep, are covered. However on this plain, sporatic isolated mounts, or buttes, as they are here called, have been thrown up, mostly single cones, that stand on the plain looking like haystacks. They are often ten miles distant from the mountains, and twenty from each other, and attain altitudes from 500 to 1,500 feet. They invariably are crowned with massive columnar basalt, rising perpendicularly from the summit of the cone to a height of from 160 to 200 feet, while the slope of the butte below the crown is regular but very steep, say from forty-five to sixty-five degrees. They also differ from the mountain spurs and peaks in this; they are, without exception, bleak and bald, having no vegetation except a little buffalo grass. A series of these buttes, as already stated, occur north of Clear Creek, and flank the railroad up to Golden, where they terminate. Some of these, I would judge, have an altitude of 1,200 feet above the adjacent plain. South of Clear Creek and east of the main part of Golden, at a distance of about three-fourths of a mile, one of these buttes rises to some 800 feet. The basalt, crowning its top, appears as though it had been planed off, and hence has been named Castle Butte.

CASTLE BUTTE, AT GOLDEN.

Pulpit Rock, or Castle Butte, is represented by the accompanying engraving. The engraving is defective in this, that it does not show that the out crop of basalt crowning the ridge, behind the butte, is separated from it by Clear Creek, through which runs the railroad. The view is taken from the bench to the southwest, three-fourths of a mile from the butte; and only takes in a few houses in the extreme southeast of the town.

The height and isolated situation of the butte was so inviting that the larger portion of our party were tempted to ascend it to see the sun set behind the eternal snows. As the distance seemed so short, and the sun was still an hour high, they thought the thing was quite feasible. Some of the citizens suggested that the time was rather short, and cautioned them that distances were very deceptive here, but as they saw them bent on the achievement, they pointed out the only practicable way to reach the summit.

Well, to experience a new sensation, a number, both of ladies and gentlemen, started off for Castle Butte, while, accompanied by several ladies and gentlemen, I ascended a bench, or terrace, some fifty or sixty feet high, lying southwest of the town, the top of which, like all the benches, was a level plain lying against the mountains and overlooking the town and plain below, and Clear Creek, from where it breaks from its canyon until lost on the distant plains. This bench was covered with most exquisite flowers. Here were *Lupines* of every hue between snowy white to tyrean purple; red *Penstemous*; indigo-blue and crimson *Oxytropies*, (the reader must pardon the scientific names, as these plants, as yet, have no others) yellow *Mentzelias*; white and purple *Anemones*; the gaudy *Gaillardia aristata*, two or three inches in diameter; the white *Townsendia*; the purple *Cleome integrifolia*; the fragrant *Abronia*; the cream-colored, lily-shaped flower, large as a hollyhock, of the *Yucca angustifolia*; and the fragrant *Gaura coccinnea*. Hear we whiled away the time plucking the flowers, picking up pebbles, and occasionally casting glances at our friends on the other side of the valley to see how they were succeeding in their laudable efforts at rising in the world. But the sun went down before the foremost of them reached the precipitous basalt cliff crowning the summit. This could only be surmounted by a detour to the northeast of nearly half a mile. Twilight had set in before any of them stood on the summit, and most of them had to give it up in despair, after having achieved two-thirds of the task.

Returning to our hotel it was not long before stragglers of the unsuccessful ascensionists began to arrive. Seeing that failure was inevitable, they found compensation for their trouble in plucking the beautiful, and to them new and unknown flowers which covered the precipitous mountain sides. It fell to my task to classify and name them. Besides most of those found on the bench, there were three species of *Astragalus*, two of *Œnothera*, a *Vesicaria*, a species of *Castelegia*, and the beautiful *Calochortus venustus*, as large as a tulip, being, in fact, a three-leaved lily. It was nine o'clock before the last of the party returned.

At night there was a brilliant aurora, which, through the rare and pure atmosphere of the mountains, showed a rich display of colors and heavy waves of light. The view, however, was obstructed by one of the high buttes north of Clear Creek, which shut out everything in that direction that was not more than 35 degrees above the horizon.

CHAPTER VI.

As it was the ambition of some of our party on the previous evening to see the sun set from the top of Castle Butte, so it was mine to see him rise thence. Early dawn found me on the way up to the summit. Passing over the intervening plain between the town and the foot of the butte or mountain, in the gray dawn I espied coming towards me some animal, which I at first feared might be a wolf, but collecting courage I faced it boldly. It proved to be a large shepherd dog who had watched his master's cows during the night while they climbed up the steep sides of the mountain to crop the luscious herbage. Throughout the Rocky Mountains, I found it general, that it did not matter how rank and plentiful the grasses were in the valleys and canyons, nor how steep, rugged and dangerous the declivities, all animals, even at the imminent risk of their lives, would ascend the steepest acclivities to crop the scanty herbage of the cliffs and the mountain tops. The cows in question at Golden, like sensible animals, selected the coolest part of the day to get their tid-bit, and took with them a courageous and faithful guard. He seemed to be glad to see me and accompanied me until I returned from my mountain ramble. When I got back to the foot of the mountain he sat down, and on the plain I saw his owner coming with milk pails. Stopping to have a chat, he pointed his finger up the mountain and called to his dog to "fetch 'em, Jack." I told him the dog had been most friendly and had piloted me over the mountain. He said, "that he will do for any stranger, as long as he does not meddle with the cows."

Well, instead of following the advice I heard the citizens

give to the evening party, to follow the winding path made by the city for the benefit of visitors to the top of the mountain, I, like many an impatient politician, thought I would take a short cut for the attainment of my ambition. I saw a ridge, or "hog back," as it is here called, right before me which seemed entirely practicable for my purpose. As far as the ridge was concerned I found it so, but suddenly my "hog back" gave out, ending in a perpendicular precipice fifty feet deep, facing the mountain. I saw the trap, and also how I could get out of it. This was to go down the edge of the precipice, but before me there rose the almost impassible barrier of a slope up the mountain of an angle of about sixty degrees with the horizon, with but little foothold, and what was more important handhold either. Having determined to try it, after a most desperate scramble of about one hundred and fifty yards, I reached the winding path dug by the citizens. Thoroughly disgusted with short cuts, I gladly followed it. Looking down, I now first became aware of the risk I had run. It made my head swim to look down and see that one misstep would have sent me rolling and tumbling down the precipitous declivity five or six hundred feet. Though almost balked by the mistake made, I yet reached the summit fully twenty minutes before the sun showed himself above the horizon. Castle Butte or Table Rock, as it is sometimes called, from the plain below, appeared as though its truncated summit might be a square rod in area. I was surprised to find it about one acre. Approaching the edge of the precipice, one hundred and sixty feet perpendicular, there, apparently within a stone's throw, lay Golden. There, too, was Clear Creek, breaking from its mountain defile, nearly two miles west, 'rushing and foaming and roaring over the plain and through the village; clear as crystal, and like a stream of molten silver from its native mountains. It was a beautiful, quiet Sabbath morning scene. Sleep had not yet left weary eyelids, and all was silent save the ever murmuring noise of the limpid water. My eye ran up and down the vacant streets and across the bridge spanning this beautiful stream, but no living thing could be descried, except the ever-moving waters. Like a vast panorama the plain spreads out along the foot of the mountains until it dips below the horizon, though the view is somewhat interrupted by the buttes to the north. West lay the rifted yet unbroken chain of the mountains, terminating southward with Pike's Peak, which, like a mighty bastion, stands out from the mountain rampart in that direction. To the northward the mountains at length dip below the horizon, but far to the northwest the snowy summit of Long's Peak lies against the intensely translucent sky. To the west the scene is exceedingly grand and impressive. On the edge of the plain rises to the height of two thousand feet a mountain wall of rusty feldspathic rock, sometimes bare and sometimes covered with evergreen shrubs and trees, the whole crowned by fir, pine and cedar. Behind this wall, peak rises behind peak, until in the far West the whole are overtopped now and then, as seen from here, by a snowy pinnacle. As for the rising sun view, it was a failure and disappointment. Over all the plain to the east there hung a gray haze, and when the sun appeared he seemed to shine through a dull fog bank. This was singular, since overhead and through the whole mountain region the sky was of an intensely deep blue, and the air along the plain skirting the mountains extremely transparent. South on the plain, some three miles distant, is the large brick edifice of the Episcopal College, and some distance beyond stands the Territorial School of Mines. East could be seen several ranches whose irrigated fields of dark green contrasted beautifully with the dull gray of the buffalo grass on the plain. Beyond, just discernible through the haze, at a distance of sixteen miles, lay Denver, bordered on the west by the glistening waters of the South Platte; and from the north base of the butte through the intervening plain, like a silver band, Clear Creek could be traced until its junction just below Denver with the Platte.

Plucking a few rare flowers, amongst which was the *Erysimum asperum* of delicate orange purple; and taking up a *Melocactus* as memorials of the place, I reluctantly turned my back on the enchanting scenery and returned to Golden.

After an excellent breakfast, the major part of our company elected to go to the mountains and in the depths of their gulches and canyons, and from their high pinnacles to contemplate and admire the sublimity, grandeur and vastness of Nature's works. Clear creek canyon and Chimney gulch seemed both to be eligible points for our purpose. For two and a half miles up the canyon the track for a narrow-gauge railroad is graded. The scenery in the canyon is sublime, but we were assured there was no practicable route for ascending any of the peaks within a reasonable distance. A half a mile south of the canyon lies Chimney gulch, through which flows a mountain brook of clear and cold water. The gulch opens a vista into the mountains, and exposes to full view, in their third tier of cones, the culminating peak in this section. This was deemed most eligible for our purpose, and, therefore, was selected as the objective point of our mountain ramble for the day. To the summit in a direct line is only about three and a half miles, but the doublings and windings of the way leading to it, make it between six and seven. The sky was of the deepest blue, and from it beamed a midsummer sun, with an ardor and brilliancy unknown to other climes. But the craving desire to see and explore the most stupendous of Nature's works, was too strong to be repressed by the fiery beams of a vertical sun. Ascending the bench, or terrace, that here stretches out upon the plain and overlooks Golden and the valley of Clear creek, a walk of a mile and a half brought us to the mouth of the gulch, up which leads a path. Here it at once became evident that we had turned over a new leaf of the volume of Nature. Nor tree, nor shrub, nor flower presented familiar species, or greeted us as old acquaintances. All were new in form, in kind and in aspect. In pines, there were the *Pinus ponderosa, contorta, flexilis* and *Edulis,* the latter, *El pinon,* of New Mexico. Of firs or spruce there were the *Abies Douglassii, Engelmannii* and *Menziesii.* A maple, the *Acer glabrum,* so disguised in the form of its leafas to be unrecognizable except by its samara; a half a dozen new species of *Spirea;* the Nootka raspberry, with a bloom two inches in diameter; a shrub, the *Jamesia,* so called after Dr. James, a companion of Col. Long, an early explorer, whose name is perpetuated in Long's Peak; two species of shrubby *Potentillas,* and two species of evergreen barberries, generally known as *Mahonias.* The cornus and the rose families are also represented by new species; so also are the plum, cherry, serviceberry, huckleberry and raspberry. In fact, everything was new excepting the common juniper, the bearberry (*Arctostaphylos ura-ursi*) and one or two others. In addition to the flowers below on the plain, mostly repeated here, there were a yellow *Castilleja,* a large, snowy and splendid blue *Columbine,* two species of *Gilia,* the beautiful *Clematis ligusticifolia,* and her not less beautiful, and more than half sister, the *Atragene alpina,* the former expanding her snowy white sepals fully three inches and the latter two. Amid such a profusion and great variety of plants, gaudy as well as new, and surrounded by rugged cliffs, mountain precipices and overhanging rocks, that every moment threatened to fall and crush us or obstruct our way, the flight of time was unheeded, and we were ascending the steep acclivity up which our path led, without being conscious of weariness or exhaustion. The mountain air, though the sun was hot, was invigorating; and then at short intervals we turned aside to slake our thirst by dipping "the gliding crystal" from the little mountain stream that flows through the gorge, hid for the most part by ferns;

amongst which I noticed a species resembling the *Pteris aquilina* with an enormous leaf, (frond), from five to six feet high and three wide. Our path, made for bringing down ties for the railroad, was extremely rough and tortuous. The ridges or "hog backs" from opposite sides of the gulch continually forced the latter from a straight line; now forcing it almost at right angles to the left, and then back again to the right, so that its course is zigzag. The gulch finally terminates, and a huge "hog back" sweeps in from the south, terminating, only at the canyon wall of Clear creek. The road now slopes up to the north until the ridge of this "hog back" is reached, when it follows up the ridge southeastward, to a slight depression on the top of the mountain. West of this ridge is an immense chasm so steep as to be impracticable for any living thing except the mountain goat. At the bottom of this chasm runs Clear creek, the roar of whose waters are distinctly heard, though hid from view by the spruce and pine trees, on whose tops you look down from this point. Ascending the ridge, to the right rises our objective point, the peak, at some places almost perpendicular, to the height of between six and seven hundred feet more. Here we met some of our party returning, who had taken advantage of a steep cut-off up the great "hog back," and in about one hundred yards climbing had saved a mile of walking. Attaining the summit and taking a position on a projecting rock, they endeavored to attract our attention and to direct us where to go by firing a pistol as soon as we would come in sight on the "hog back." Accidentally the pistol was prematurely discharged, the ball passing through the hand of the party holding it. They therefore returned to the water to wash and tie up the wound. Persuaded by them that by going a little to the left the ascent of the peak was practicable from this side, besides saving a mile in distance, the last stated fact determined my course, so away I went up the acclivity, but soon had reasons to regret the choice I had made, for the soles of my boots soon became as smooth as polished marble, making it impossible to keep my feet on the dry leaves of the spruce and pine. As it was a question whether, under these circumstances, a retreat was preferable to an advance, so I chose the latter, and after the most desperate scrambling of all my mountain experience, attained the summit ahead of all my companions.

The summit is level, and covered by a pine and spruce grove. Walking in a northwestward direction beyond the skirts of the grove, brings you to a bare rock, the edge of the precipice. The view from this point is most enchanting, grand and magnificent. You stand on the top of the south wall of Clear creek canyon, a precipice that slopes down 2,500 feet at an angle but few degrees removed from the perpendicular. The roaring of the creek "like the sound of a rushing mighty wind" rises to your ear. To your left at the distance of about two hundred yards, for a part of the way down is a rugged perpendicular wall of naked rocks; but immediately in front the declivity is covered with young firs and pine. Since you overlook the whole, the side of the declivity appears not only covered with a mantle of everlasting green, but seems almost as even as if clipped by shears. But as you look down the chasm your eyes strain in vain for a sight of the bottom, or to catch a glimpse of the roaring waters that flow there. Down, far down as the eye reaches, the tops of gigantic fir or pine trees are the only objects visible; tops of trees whose heads are bathed in the light of noonday sun, but whose roots are fixed in the bottom of a gloomy, dismal chasm.

Lift now your eyes to the scenery beyond the chasm. You see you are looking down on the less elevated north wall of the canyon, beyond which rises gradually like a vast amphitheatre, mountain upon mountain piled against the northwestern sky, and the whole crowned by a rampart of everlasting snow. To the north this snowy rampart terminates in Long's Peak, some fifty miles distant, which rises fully two thousand feet above the average height of Snowy Range. Far in the southwest it culminates in Mount Lincoln. As intermediate bastions, rise James' and Gray's Peaks, each to the altitude of over 14,000 feet above the sea. The first is about twenty-five miles south of Longs' Peak; the last is about twenty miles south of James' Peak, and about thirty miles due west from here. Mount Lincoln is the Titan of the American Cordilleras, being estimated, according to determinations made by Prof. A. DuBois, at seventeen thousand five hundred feet above the level of the ocean. It is nearly ninety miles distant from here, standing at the northwest corner of South Park. West of it is the Upper Canyon of the Arkansas; north, Middle Park; and southeast, South Park. From its sides issue springs that on the southeast feed the South Platte; on the west, the Arkansas; and on the north, Blue river, which falls into Grand river, a tributary of the great Colorado of the West. Notwithstanding its great distance, there it stands majestically, towering high above all other peaks, unique and inimitable, a Titan among pygmies, like its prototype, whose name it perpetuates, did amongst men. Its base garlanded by evergreens, emblems of immortality, and its summit crowned with the symbol of spotless purity, the white, persistent snows of untold ages, it is a fitting monument to symbolize the towering intellect, and to perpetuate the memory of the devout patriotism and immaculate purity of the great and wise statesman and model President whose name it bears, and whose

> "One of the few, the immortal names
> That were not born to die."

Long's Peak and Mount Lincoln, terminating the extreme visible points of the Snowy Range, as seen hence, from their great altitude appear like immense bastions at the angles of an icy rampart, behind which stern winter lies intrenched forever. To the south the view is obstructed by a pine and spruce forest, but on the east there is a fine view of the plains for one hundred miles and more. At a point or two south of east and twenty miles distant, but apparently near the foot of the mountains, lies Denver. You look down into its streets, and from far south of it to down north of Greeley, where it meets the Cache a la Poudre, the sparkling waters of the South Platte are seen. The Plains are an unvaried gray, with nothing to give them variety excepting the irrigated fields along the South Platte and Clear creek, and the line of straggling cottonwood trees that skirt their brinks.

To the northeast, far beyond the Platte, appeared what seemed to be two beautiful lakes on the plains. One of our lady companions mistaking them for such, to undeceive her I told her they were only phantom lakes, the optical deceptions of mirage; giving the word the French, but also the only authorized English pronunciation. "And pray," said she, "what is *mirazh!*" To explain, I began by telling her it is one of those things

"For which the speech of England had no name."

In Italy they call it *Fata Morgana*. It was observed there in ancient times as is abundantly evident from both Greek and Roman records. Along the Straits of Messina then, as now, the coast and objects below the horizon sometimes loomed up above it; at other times seemed to approach the opposite shore, and what was more astonishing, oftentimes seemed to hang inverted from the sky. "Why," she replied, "that is *mi-rage.*" I then saw what was the matter and felt relieved, for I began to fear that if I attempted the explanation of special atmospheric conditions, different densities of adjacent superincumbent layers of air, and the consequent refraction of light, that I would succeed in making it plain that neither I nor the learned know a particle more about the true nature of the phenomenon than the common people do. Indeed, I made a narrow escape of exposing the fact that I was talking phylosophy, if judged by the Scotchman's rule, who always knew when a man talked metaphysics; namely "when you can'na tell what he means, and he din'na ken himsel."

As already stated I had reached the mountain top fully half an hour in advance of my companions. On the edge of the grove and near the brink of the precipice, there stands a perpendicular rock, some twenty feet high and about the same width. At the base, near its north end, there is about as beautiful a bench rock, some twenty inches wide, as if made by hand. It is a part of a huge rock which faces north-west, and for five feet this bench protrudes from the side. Where it terminates, there stands, with its trunk against the rock, a low headed spruce, completely shading for ten feet and more the ground around its roots. Breaking off some dry limbs that interfered with the use of the bench, I sat down to rest until the company would arrive, and to enjoy the magnificent scenery of evergreen mountains, bounded by everlasting snows in the distance that lay stretched out like a vast panorama before me.

Answering a call, soon brought the greater part of the company to the spot, where they gave vent to their enthusiasm at beholding the grand sight by a yell that would have done credit to the Utes themselves.

Appropos; why is this impulse for whooping so universal in all, even in the almost inexcitable, on reaching these elevated regions? Some think it is owing to the excitement produced by so great variety of novelty, or an outburst of enthusiasm at beholding so much grandeur and sublimity. Judging by my own experience I cannot conceive these to be the true causes. I felt an irrepressible desire to whoop long before I saw anything at all as extraordinarily impressive. Moreover, when I stood face to face before the shrine of Nature, and contemplated her inimitable beauty, bewildering grandeur and imposing majesty, I felt as though a whisper would be sacriligious profanity. I think the causes are physiological and not aesthetic. Dwellers in the Mississippi Valley or on the sea shore, breathe an atmosphere so dense that their average respirations are but sixteen per minute. But here on the mountains, the respirations are increased to twenty-four per minute; and the pulsations of the heart and the flow of blood in the veins are accelerated in like proportion. The effect on the system is an exhilaration almost amounting to intoxication, and hence that outburst of feeling which affects all, and which it is found so difficult to repress.

Resigning my seat on the rock to a lady, who made a sketch of the mountain scenery and the Snowy Range for her children, I sought shelter under the shade of a most magnificent Douglass spruce, whose pendant branches swept the ground for some distance around. Here I laid down on the dry fir and pine leaves that made a bed as soft as a mattress. Professor Kelsey, of Kansas, soon joined me, and we talked until we fell asleep. Awaking, we found our company all gone, and the mountain silent. Breaking a branch of the tree as a grateful memorial of the pleasant hours spent under its shade, we wended our way down the mountain towards Golden, where we arrived in time for supper.

CHAPTER VII.

Early on Monday, June 12th, we left Golden on the morning train for Denver, where we arrived in ample time to take the train of the Denver Pacific railroad for Cheyenne, in Wyoming Territory, one hundred and six miles north. By an amended act of Congress the Kansas Pacific railroad was released from its obligation to connect with the Union Pacific railroad at the 100th meridian, and the law so changed as to require it to connect with the Union Pacific railroad at a point not more than 50 miles west of the meridian of Denver. The Kansas Pacific consequently followed up the general route of the Smoky Hill to Denver, with the intention of ultimately connecting with the Union Pacific hence. As the land grant of Congress extends the whole length of the line, the Kansas Pacific encouraged the formation of a new company, whose initial point was Denver, to make this junction. Accordingly the Denver Pacific Railroad Company was organized, and by a subsequent act of Congress the Kansas Pacific was authorized to transfer its lands and the franchises of that portion of the line from Denver to the junction, to the new company. It was late in the fall of 1867 when the initial steps for the organization of the new company were first taken. The land grant amounts to 12,800 acres for every mile of the length of the road; or more specifically, the lands granted by Congress were alternate, that is odd numbered sections for ten miles on each side of the road. The work was commenced at Cheyenne; and on the 16th of December, 1869, the road was completed and opened as far as Evans, a distance of 53 miles; and on the 23d of June, 1870, the first passenger train arrived at Denver

The total cost of construction and equipment of the road is said to be $3,000,000.

At 8 o'clock the train started heading due north. The plain appeared dry and parched in consequence of the prominence and prevalence of the dead "mesquite" grass. But underneath this sere covering of mesquite is a thick coating of Buffalo grass (*Buchloe dactyloides*) possessing most extraordinary nutritive qualities. At short intervals we passed large herds of cattle feeding on this apparently arid plain in the best condition. Often these were accompanied by herdsmen. The road is straight, and its direction is down the valley of the Platte, but the river is generally several miles to the west and can be traced by an occasional cottonwood. It soon becomes evident that the direction of the road diverges from that of the mountain range; for the mountains apparently recede farther and farther to the west; whereas their course is due north and south. Long's Peak is now the central figure, towering far above all the neighboring peaks.

The first station, seventeen miles north of Denver, is Hughes', the junction of the Boulder Valley railroad; but the first town is Evans, the county seat of Weld county. Evans claims to be a St. Louis colony, but I could learn nothing of its organization, advantages nor investments. It seemed to me as though its inhabitants were singularly deficient in enterprise and energy, and that they have very little to do other than that of running to the station when a train arrives; at least such was the case each time *we* passed; and we can scarcely imagine that rumor had noised it abroad that in the coming train were great men worth seeing—yet such may have been the case, and a hoax played of on them may explain their conduct.

Four miles north of Evans is Greeley, about which there has been more written and published within a year than of any other place on the globe beside. Its history, in brief, is this: The colony was organized in the city of New York, on the 23d of December, 1869, by the enrollment of fifty-nine members. An executive committee was appointed to investigate what advantages and inducements were offered to settlers by Nebraska, Kansas, Wyoming, Utah and Colorado. After an investigation, the Executive Committee selected the site for the town between the Cache-a-la-Poudre and the South Platte, three miles above their junction, about fifty miles south of Cheyenne, and fifty-six north of Denver, on the Denver Pacific railroad. The distance from the mountains is about forty-five miles. But I must draw you a pen-and-ink sketch of the topography and scenery surrounding this famous place, that you may know how it looks: Suppose you take a position looking north, on the railroad bridge spanning the Platte south of Evans. Beneath you flows a mountain torrent one hundred and thirty yards wide, brimfull, yet clear as crystal, roaring and dashing down the plain. It is a noble, majestic and beautiful stream. No bushes encumber its edges, for banks it has none, because the level plain sinks down with its burthen of grass and flowers to kiss the silver wave. Like the shores of Loch Mary:

> "Just a line of pebbly sand
> Marks where the water meets the land."

The plain, level as a barn floor, is covered with the persistent, but now dry mesquite grass, and has, therefore, the color of a newly harvested oat-field. Some eight miles distant, and stretching to the northwest until lost sight of in the distance, is a very straggling line of low cottonwood trees, the only sign of living vegetation. The plain extends west to the mountains, forty to forty-five miles distant, and rests against them. It has a regular ascent from here to the mountains of fifty feet per mile, but is entirely destitute of vegetation excepting the hidden buffalo grass and the dry mesquite. Far towards the east the plain seems to culminate in a ridge, probably merely mirage, which often on the Plains seemingly raises up the edges of the horizon like the rim of a saucer around you. Before you is the village of Evans, and four miles further is Greeley, beyond which sweeps the Cache-a-la Poudre, marked out over the plain by the aforesaid line of cottonwood. In the far north rise elevations of a whitish greenish gray, indicating that the mesquito has been supplanted by some other vegetation. Down, northeast, after the junction with the Cache-a-la-Poudre, some three miles below Greeley, the course of the Platte can be traced by the cottonwood, until it sinks below the horizon. There you have a picture of Greeley and its surroundings, which in all conscience is monotonous enough.

The colony purchased of the Denver Pacific Railroad Company and from individuals 12,000 acres of land. The preliminary steps, that is, by pre-emption, etc., for the occupation of 60,000 acres of government lands, and also a contract was made with the Denver Pacific Company to purchase within three years 50,000 acres more, at from $3 to $4 per acre. The colony thus has control of some 125,000 acres of land, all of which can be irrigated from canals from the South Platte and Cache-a-la-Poudre.

The town is subdivided into 520 business lots, 25 by 190 feet; 673 residence lots, ranging from 50 to 200 by 190 feet; and 277 lots reserved for schools, churches, public buildings, etc. The adjacent lands are subdivided into plats from 5 to 120 acres each, according to distance from the centre of the town, and each member allowed to select one of these under his certificate of membership. The town now contains about 350 buildings, from board shanties to brick fronts. It has some seventeen stores, three lumber yards, three blacksmith and wagon shops, and one printing press. It has an Educational Board, Farmers' Club and Lyceum and Library Association. As far as the eye can reach the plain is dotted with new shanties of the homesteaders and pre-emptioners. Some of our party stopped over until the return of the train from Cheyenne.

They interviewed the citizens, but the latter seemed so reticent and averse to communicate information or answer questions, that nothing of importance, either concerning the progress or prospects of the colony, was elicited. It is not possible for any one merely looking from the car window of a train to form any accurate opinion of the condition and capabilities of a soil, or to form an accurate judgment of the art and skill with which it is handled. If it were, then, I must confess that the opinion so formed is not of the most favorable character as to Greeley. In this case the opinion of those who stayed over, and had better opportunities than I had, not only coincide with my own, but are even more unfavorable. In the first place the land is very gravely, forming naturally graveled streets, and certainly not of the first quality for agriculture; and then it seemed as though those who had the management of it knew next to nothing of the way things have to be done in this climate. Gardens were flooded and literally drowned out; and of the thousand of trees planted, both evergreen and deciduous, not hundreds were living from the same cause. It would have paid the colonists well if they had hired some New Mexican to have taught them the art of irrigation, and some expert tree-planter who would have shown them how to plant and to take care of a tree. It seemed as though the greater part of the colonists were mere theorists, and were for the first time in a situation to reduce their theories to practice. But we have hope they will profit by their mistakes, and guard against their recurrence. As a matter of course it could have been anticipated that dreams and expectations of enthusiastic natures, who are most likely to engage in such an enterprise as this, would not be realized in a day, nor even in a year. Moreover they may be so *outré* as not to be realizable. Consequently, disappointment is to be expected, and, necessarily dissatisfaction and grumbling. Perhaps the management has not at all times been the wisest; and there may have been over-reaching on the part of some managers for self aggrandizement and personal ambition; but still the enterprise seems to have the elements of ultimate success, notwithstanding the hardships it imposes on its pioneers and the many present discouragements.

At present the prospect of finding a market for its surplus productions, is not of the most flattering nature. It is sixty-five miles to Boulder, by rail, the only inlet into the mountains at this point; to Cheyenne it is fifty, and to Denver fifty-six miles. To be sure there is some talk of constructing a railroad direct to Boulder, forty-five miles distant. But in that case the citizens on the Plains around Boulder will have the advantage of them, to the amount of freight and charges.

After passing the Cache-a-la-Poudre, another of those bold, limpid and rapid mountain streams, the plain ascends rapidly 1,675 feet in the forty miles to Summit Siding, and then descends into a valley, whence it rises to the ridge on which is Cheyenne. Cheyenne is 6,041 feet above the sea and 375 feet lower than at Summit Siding. Soon after crossing the Cache-a-la-Poudre the character of the plain changes. The mesquite grass disappears, the soil becomes a lighter color, it even appears whitish, and the only vegetation on hill and plain is the short buffalo grass and prickly pear or cactus. The latter in full bloom, extending its yellow blossom fully to the size of a holly-hock. Hitherto the only color was yellow, but now a brownish purple is intermixed with the yellow, and often alone occupies large patches. The prairie-dog villages also are more numerous, and there is a lively time in them when the train approaches. Hundreds of the dogs, big and little, can be seen running for dear life to their holes. But there stands the stolid burrowing owl on the hillock, fixed as if he were a brass statuette, unmindful of everything that passes around him.

The hills occasionally show caps of rocks, frequently assuming the shapes of low pillars, pyramids and occasionally of ruined castles. In a valley on the plain is a most singular one of the latter. It stands within fifty feet of the railroad. It is about forty feet square with an extension eastward for half the length of the east wall, say twenty feet more. The wall is about thirty inches thick, and its average height is about four feet. Facing the road at the southwest corner is a space of about four feet wide, making an opening in the enclosure which is covered with grass and looks for all the world as though it had been the doorway. The sides of this open space are perpendicular rock, weatherworn and rounded as with architectural design. The wall also has angular depressions that resemble openings for windows. It simulates the work of man so closely that it would be mistaken for such did its exposure not disclose that it is a single rock

With the exception of these castellated rocks protruding, for the most part, from the hilltops, the scenery for the fifty miles between Greeley and Cheyenne is extremely monotonous. The rolling plain is covered with a coat of buffalo grass of unvaried greenish gray, enameled now and then by a stray plant of the deepest blue perennial larkspur (*Delphinium azureum,*) a red *Penstamon*, an indigo blue *Oxytropis*, and occasionally a spot covered with *Cactus*.

At Cheyenne your eye sweeps in vain around the horizon for an object to rest upon, nor shrub, nor tree, nor rock is visible at any point or in any direction. Alone, the mountain tops are to be seen, seventy or eighty miles away, protruding their icy pinnacles above the southwestern rim of the horizon; all else is vacuity except plain and sky. Such is the weary monotonous scenery of the plain in and around Cheyenne. Again, as in the case of Denver, the question rises spontaneously, why was this point selected for a city? and again the answer is, by accident; that accident was the arbitrary choice of the managers of the Union Pacific railroad locating their machine shops here. Like Denver, it has streets graveled by Nature, which never need repairing; but unlike it in this respect, that the gravel rests upon a solid foundation and not upon quicksand. Cheyenne, unlike its sister city, Denver, will, therefore, never be afflicted with a periodical paroxism of treasure seeking, looking for the city safe. Even our eastern cousins are not exempt from similar attacks of more or less severity and frequency, during which they vigorously hunt for the mythical treasures hid by Captain Kidd. But the gravelly streets of Denver, or rather the pebbly bottom of the South Platte, hides a real treasure, which occasions the outbreak of the mania in Denver; for on an ever memorable morning in 1864, Cherry Creek being "on a bender," the glory of Denver, the City Hall, containing the city's safe and its treasures, took its departure down stream, and finally disappeared in the quicksand like a dissolving view, leaving nor wreck nor trace behind.

Forbidding as is the appearance of the landscape around Cheyenne, and oppressively monotonous as is its scenery, yet there is the demonstration being made of the value of these apparently arid plains, for grazing and stock-raising. Here are men who own cattle by thousands, and who are realizing from ten to twenty thousand net profit annually from their flocks. More than 6,000 feet above the sea level, and forty-one degrees and more of north latitude, yet cattle here need no shelter or feeding the year round, subsisting upon the natural hay of the country, the dry buffalo grass, and going through the winter in better condition than cattle do in the States upon both food and shelter. And then if you desire to know what a tender, juicy and savory beefsteak is, let me commend you to try that raised and fattened upon the buffalo grass of the western plains. I have abundant statistics on hand to show the number of the flocks of different owners and their annual profits, on the plains along the foot of the mountains hence to south of Denver, which I must here omit. Sheep do splendidly, and are entirely exempt from diseases. Large flocks are being introduced annually; a Boston company alone has a herd of 25,000 head.

After an excellent dinner at Cheyenne, we took the return train for Denver, where we arrived at half-past six o'clock. Finding carriages in waiting, we hastily drove through Denver, crossing the fine bridge over the Platte, and ascended the plateau beyond from which there is a fine view of Denver and the surrounding country. The plateau is in high tilth, being irrigated by canals brought from the Platte on the south, and Clear creek on the north. The crops looked fine, but we had no time to make a critical examination of their mode of cultivation and irrigation, as the sun was setting. Finally turning in at the gate, we found ourselves in Mr. Perrin's strawberry patch, and were abundantly supplied with fruit. But without halting we drove down the plateau and across Clear creek, here one hundred and fifty feet wide, three feet deep, and running with such fearful velocity as threatened to sweep carriage and horses down with the torrent.

On the plain north of the creek, and within fifty yards of the brink, stands Mr. Perrin's residence. Alighting, we had just time to inspect, before dark, his highly cultivated and artistically irrigated vegetable garden of about three acres. We were both delighted and surprised at the large size and vigorous growth of every kind of culinary vegetables. As we are promised samples of beets, turnips and cabbages for exhibition at our next St. Louis Fair, our citizens will have an opportunity of seeing for themselves what Colorado can do in the way of vegetables. Supper being announced, but as the distance was about five miles from Denver, the major part of the party who were going away with the eastward bound train, left, which was to be regretted, as the vexed strawberry question would have been settled by the best proof in the world—the eating. Larger, finer-flavored and more luscious strawberries I never tasted than were furnished for desert that evening. I soon deserted the company and went out on the verandah. It was now quite dark, and I sat down to be soothed by the ever-murmuring waters of Clear creek, which sweeps around on two sides—west and south—of Mr. Perrin's place. Oh, it is a place for night-dreaming, and day-dreaming, too! Leaving, we drove leisurely back to Denver, in the splendid equipage of Mr. Byers, of the Denver *News*, where we arrived before the departure of our friends.

At half-past nine we took leave of the major part of our party, who were returning home; but there were twelve of us, who thought that it would not be entirely satisfactory to come 1,000 miles to see the great temple of Nature, and then turn back after having only entered its vestibule. Besides the Boulder County Agricultural Association, the only one in the Territory that had acknowledged our presence, had extended to us, by a committee on the day of our arrival in Denver, a cordial invitation to visit Boulder City. This invitation a few of us had at once accepted, and consequently the committee had gone back to make the necessary arrangements. This engagement we now determined to fulfill, and this incident determined the point of our mountain excursion and movements while we remained in the Territory. Boulder City, in a direct line from Denver, is but twenty-eight miles, but the railroad traversing two sides of a triangle, makes it forty-seven. The Boulder Valley railroad meets the Denver Pacific at Hughes, seventeen miles northeast of Denver; thence to Erie is seventeen miles more—as far as the road is now completed—and thence twelve miles by stage to Boulder City.

At Erie is a vein of excellent coal, twelve feet thick. The Kansas Pacific railroad tapped this coal by a road from Hughes', but the grading is now done, and the ties are being rapidly laid up to Boulder City, the road to be completed by the time of the Boulder Fair, in September

This vein of coal continues up to Boulder twelve miles, where it is thirteen feet thick, and where four other veins exist, namely: one twenty, one four and a half, one five, and another seven feet thick. The next day when we arrived at Erie, we found our Boulder friends waiting with spring wagons, hacks, buggies and carriages to convey us to Boulder City, a distance of twelve miles over the plains.

The road is on a plateau or terrace, south of, and slightly elevated above the plain, through which runs Boulder Creek. Far down northeast as the eye can reach towards Greeley the shimmering waters of Boulder Creek can be seen, or their direction traced by a straggling line of cottonwood and a dark green belt of from five to seven miles wide, of wheat, rye, barley and corn fields, irrigated by its waters. Midway between you and the mountains, and some half a mile north of the creek, is White Rock, looking like a huge snowbank, a conspicuous object from all the plain around; and immediately opposite, on the south side of the creek, is Valmont, one of those sporadic buttes of erupted basalt occasionally found on the plain along the foot of the mountains. It is 300 feet high, rising somewhat in the form of a haystack, and at its base occupies about an acre in area. It terminates in a curious basaltic column, curved somewhat like a horn leaning northward. At its foot is the village of Valmont. Valmont Mill stands a few rods northwest, and beyond the Boulder is White Rock Mill. As soon as the mill is passed Boulder City, on the Plains at the foot of the mountains, and five miles distant, comes into full view. Here also the South Boulder joins the main stream. The country between here and the mountains is all under cultivation, covered with farmhouses surrounded by the finest farms, irrigated by the waters of the two Boulders, which issue from their mountain defiles at points about five miles distant from each other.

We soon pass the Agricultural Fair grounds, forty acres

with the necessary buildings, the whole inclosed by a tight fence. Just northeast of Boulder is one of those remarkable benches or terraces already spoken of, surrounded on all sides by a plain rising about thirty feet high. It is an oblong ellipse, having its transverse diameter at right angles to the mountain chain. It contains about fifteen acres, and has been selected for the site of the State University when Colorado becomes a State.

Arriving at Boulder we were received at the Colorado House by the citizens *en masse*, and addressed in their behalf by Judge Berkley, tendering to us the hospaliites of the city during our stay, and offering to place at our disposal conveyances to visit any points of interest, either around the city or in the mountain canyon, that we might desire. I, by arrangement, responded to the reception speech, as the Denver *Tribune* reporter, flatteringly no doubt, said, "in very appropriate terms," thanking the citizens for the distinguished honor conferred upon us, but declining in behalf of the Missouri and Kansas delegation the generous offer of free rides *ad libitum*. In a country where, to us, there was so much novelty, so much to interest, and such sublime and magnificent scenery, the offer was entirely too generous and the inducement too great. "to ride a willing horse to death;" we therefore most gratefully declined it, and placed ourselves at their own disposal, to visit only such places as they might deem most interesting.

After a dinner, sumptuous enough for princes, we were driven around the suburbs, visiting some of the adjacent farms, examining the condition of the growing crops, the canals and ditches for, and the method of irrigating, picking the most luscious strawberries we ever saw, and ending by a drive up to the mouth of Boulder canyon, to see the head of the irrigating canals which begin in the canyon.

and branch off both right and left from the creek as soon as it enters the plain.

> The weary Sun had made a golden set,
> And, by the bright track of his fiery car,
> Gave token of a goodly day to-morrow.

The citizens now had settled that on the next day they would give us a picnic up in Boulder canyon; and so we retired to rest with bright anticipations of to-morrow.

CHAPTER VIII.

From peculiar meteorological causes, which it is not necessary here to state or explain, dew never falls on the Plains adjacent to the mountains. A morning's walk therefore, can be enjoyed without incurring the drawbacks of wet feet and soiled garments, and without having the specter of chills and fever flitting constantly before your eyes. Then, too, the sky is always so bright, the air so pure and exhilarating, the songs of strange birds so charming, the murmuring of the mountain torrents, dashing headlong down the plain, so soothing, and the scenery so bold and captivating, that ears and eyes are never satiated. Stolid and phlegmatic must be the nature of that man, or woman either, who here can act the sluggard, where Nature puts on her gayest attire and most majestic mien, as well as displays her wildest and most phantastic forms.

Under such influences and impulses, even at the risk of disturbing the tranquility of our host, the Rev. Nathan Thompson, and his estimable lady, whose hospitality we were enjoying, Mrs. T. and I were up early, and out for a morning's ramble up to the mountains and along their base, to drink in health from the pure, invigorating mountain air, and inspiration from the scenery surrounding us.

Mr. Thompson's house stands about one-third of the way up the slope of a terraced plateau that lies against the mountains, extending from Boulder canyon to the first gulch north, distant from the mountain at this, the farthest point, about 400 yards. Like all these elevated plateaux, it is perfectly level on the top; but the slopes are as neatly and as smoothly rounded off as if done by hand. These benches, as they are here called, are unquestionably the remains of abrasions, records of events long anterior to the existence of man, when the pent up waters of mountain lakes broke through the rocky barriers, and issuing from the gulches and canyons with irrisistible force degraded the plain to its present level. The slope rises with an angle of about thirty degrees with the horizon, and the summit of the bench is about forty feet above the level of the plain. Mr. Thompson's house stands near the north end, and his church (Congregational) on the south end of a five acre lot, lying against this bench on the east side. Above and higher than the top of his house and along the edge of the level summit of the bench is an irrigating canal carrying from Boulder canyon a rapid stream of water five feet wide and thirty inches deep. Up to this canal and along its margin northwestwardly lay our morning walk.

From the plain on the top of this bench the view is charming, and in any other country than this would be entitled to the terms grand and magnificent. West and northwest the precipitous walls of brownish porphyritic rock rising from the edge of the plain to the height of from 1500 to 4000 feet;* mostly nude, but incidentally at many places there are narrow terraces, bearing evergreen shrubs and dwarf pine, cedar and spruce trees. Southwest is Boulder canyon, an immensely deep, narrow rift in the mountain; and beyond it rises a most singular protuberance, oblong, rugged and imposing, to an altitude of 4000 feet and more. Its roof-shaped top starts from terraces on both the east and west sides, and runs up as steep as the steepest roof of a gothic church for some 600 feet, the ridge running north and south. But what is most singular, along the eastern terrace rise no less than six abutments, looking for all the

---

* "The scenery along the flanks of the mountains is wonderfully unique, and I have not seen a similar example in the Rocky Mountain region. The uplift is on an unparalleled scale. The mountain wall, a tremendous uplift of metamorphosed sand-stone rises 4000 feet above Boulder Valley on the plains below, and their rugged summits project far over on the granitic rocks westward." *Prof. Hayden's Geological report of 1869.*

world like pilasters, extending above the terrace and terminating in sharp quadrangular pyramids, some three hundred and fifty feet high. South of this singular mountain is Bear Gulch, a correct engraving of which can be seen in "Views from Nature." Beyond Bear Gulch rises another high mountain, round-topped and dome-shaped, ending in a narrow peak like a sow's teat. This closes the mountain view south from this point.

BOULDER.

Turn now your face towards the east. To your right, southeastward, you see a bench about four miles distant; there is Marshall's coal mine, and near this bench on the plain are seen the sparkling waters of South Boulder creek. That building beside it is Marshall's iron works. Then, on the intervening plain, are seen farm-houses and green fields up to the main Boulder creek, a dashing mountain torrent, hastening down the plain to embrace her sister stream. At your feet, between the elevation on which you stand and the creek, is Boulder City, which you entirely overlook, extending northward on the plain between you and the University plateau, which lies immediately east. Down on the plain eastward in the distance, is seen Mr. Day's and other ranches, on the South Boulder. Then there is the fine lake between the two Boulders, formed since the plain has become irrigated, now well stocked with fine fish—mostly perch and redhorse. Nearer still, the house in that dense coppice is the residence of Judge George Berkley, the oldest and most enthusiastic tree-planter in the Territory; and nearer still come the fair grounds, with its inclosed buildings. But over all, and beyond, is seen that singular butte or basaltic dyke, Valmont, raising its isolated cone on the plain; and to the left of it, that white object like an immense snow bank, is White Rock.

In the northeast, at a distance of about ten miles, is seen Haystack Mountain, another of those isolated basaltic cones, that at long intervals are found protruding from the level plain. Those buildings near its base are the villages of Burlington and Longmont—the latter a new colony from Chicago—organized somewhat on the principles of that at Greeley. Around these, and extending up to the mountains, are seen ranches and green fields, and the uncultivated plain covered with cattle. This gives a somewhat faint idea of the scenery from this point, to which must be added, to complete the picture, the light green color of the plain as compared with the sombre evergreens which deck the porphyritic sides of the mountains.

As we were strolling leisurely towards the mountain, plucking flowers and examining the pebbles for moss agates, our attention was suddenly drawn to the thrilling notes of the skylark (*Eremophila cornuta*); notes which for compass and silvery sweetness of tone are inimitable and unapproachable by any other songster. There he sat on the fence half way down the slope, and again and again he would pour out his silvery, ringing notes on the morning air, that almost awoke the sleeping echoes of the mountains. As we walked on, he would fly ahead and take his position on the fence, and pour out his matin song as if in triumph. When we returned he followed us, and

MOUTH OF BOULDER CANYON.

repeated more and more rapidly his charming song, seemingly striving to excel his first efforts. At last his notes seemed mingled with the sadness of despair, becoming louder, sweeter and tenderer, but touched, as it were, with the anguish of a heartrending sorrow. At this moment I spied his mate dodging through the grass; and now I understood his strange conduct, and the cause of his alarm and distress.

Our host now appeared in sight calling us to breakfast, so we hurried on, greatly to the relief of our feathered friend. May he live a thousand years and raise a brood of songsters every month!

After breakfast, returning to the hotel, we found carriages, buggies, spring wagons, etc., collecting to convey us, and baskets and trays filled with luxuries to add to our enjoyment, and minister to our comfort during the excursion up the canyon. When all was ready the train of some twenty wagons and coaches moved off toward the mountain defile, up which lay our route, into the heart of the Cordilleras. The mouth of the canyon, where it opens on the plain, is about one hundred feet wide, and the ascent of the canyon walls on either side exceeds but little fifty-five degrees. The acclivities are sparsely covered with stunted pine and cedar trees, growing on huge rocky angular terraces, that jut out all over the sides of the walls. On the top of the wall, amongst evergreens, occasionally stands a tall pine or spruce tree blasted by the lightning. The scenery is rugged and wild in every imaginable sense. The creek, a stream discharging fully three times the quantity of water our Meramec river does;* flows rapidly *through* not *over* its rocky bed, for the sharp rocks project in every direction from one to four feet above the water. The water purls and frets, and foams as if in a rage at the obstruction imposed by the rocky barriers, but otherwise it is dark, being prevented by its rapid flow and agitation from reflecting either the canyon walls or the narrow strip of blue sky above. The road and the stream mostly occupy the full width of the canyon, but occasionally a large rock crowds the stream into narrow limits and against the opposite wall; then there is a little headland used for turnouts, where ascend-

---

*Meramec river in Missouri.

ing and descending teams pass each other. When not so used, these headlands form a nestling place for numerous mountain flowers. Amongst entirely new flora, I here found a splendid red lily, as large as a cup, (*Lillium Philadelphicum*,) and the most showy of all the mountain flowers, the *Epilobium angustifolium*, forming plots of brilliant rosy purple flowers.

As the course of the canyon is zig-zag, it often narrows so as scarcely to afford room for the waters to pass; the roadway is then blasted out of the perpendicular side rock of the canyon wall. If this side rock (as is generally the case) is a projecting promontory of a mountain peak rent in twain, then there is left a fissured rock from one to two thousand feet high hanging overhead, that any moment may tumble down, or from its sides send down an avalanche of rock into the abyss below. You instinctively hold your breath until it is past. Now you come to a bridge, (for there are thirty-one of them in twelve miles), leading to the narrow beach, eight or ten feet wide, on the opposite side, while the river dashes its foaming waters against the perpendicular cliff three thousand feet high, on the side you are leaving. All you see of sky is now reduced to a narrow band overhead. You look up the sides of the canyon, and in crevices in the flank of the walls, or on protruding rocks, grow shrubs of pine and spruce, while their summits are crowned with sturdy evergreens, who for centuries have battled with the storms and defied the artillery of heaven, not with impunity, however, as many a lightning scarred or dead one attests. High over all is seen, wheeling in his airy flight, the golden eagle, who finds his congenial home here

"On the mountains that proclaim
The everlasting creed of liberty."

Miles are thus passed, the scenery becoming grander and more imposing at every step, and the flowing of the water, now all foam, also more impetuous. Suddenly the canyon walls for an instant recede, for man has invaded and profaned the sanctity of the place. There stands his puny, busy mill turning into plank, shingle and lath the brave old giants of the mountain forest. On the right, too, there are indications of his presence; for from the rocky chasm of a cleft mountain issue the turbid waters of Four-Mile creek; turbid because miners are washing the auriferous sands of the gulch in its limpid waves.

But this interruption is only temporary. Coy Nature, that fled the contaminating presence of man, returns with more commanding presence and majestic mien than ever, to avenge the interruption by displaying sublimer forms and more imposing and awe-inspiring grandeur and wildness. The river roars and pitches more furiously than ever; there hangs the beetling cliff, higher and more threatening than before; and there, too, the graceful fir lifts high its head into the light of the sun, 250 feet above the roaring, foaming waters that rave at its roots.

It seemed now as though Nature must have exhausted her stores of wonders to astonish, amaze bewilder and overwhelm, and drawn upon her last resources for exciting enthusiasm and exalted emotions; but not so. The magic panorama moves on, and we enter a mountain defile, sundered by some great natural convulsion, of perpendicular walls, scraggy and naked, three thousand feet high, overhung by pines and cedars. It can easily be taken for a huge stair-case walled in, such as might have been built by Titans and Cyclops for ascending Olympus, the residence of the gods; and that the jets and fountains in which nymphs and goddesses disported themselves, fallen into decay, were pouring down their waters over the dilapidated steps; for the river here descends a steep, rocky declivity. The waters are no longer foam, but spray, and their roar is deafening. You look ahead whence they come, but the canyon is closed up by a transversal perpendicular wall, with no sign of an outlet, forming appar-

7

ently a complete *cul de sac*. Again and again is this repeated. The walls, when perpendicular and solid, are always naked; but when full of fissures and crevices, they are completely hid by evergreen shrubs, and decorated as evenly and as neatly as the ivy decks the dilapidated castles of Europe.

Turning the angle, the scene now changes. The acclivities of the walls, instead of perpendicular, are but 75 or 80 degrees, then the sides become a thicket of spruce sapplings thirty or forty feet high, and completely hide the side rocks, forming a green wall as you look up the canyon. Immense spruce trees also stand in the bottom of the canyon, sometimes alone and then in groups. Thus at every turn, and in every instant of time the scenery changes and new and startling forms present themselves. You are now opposite the embouchure of the North Boulder. You look up a dark deep rift in the mountain side, overshadowed by trees and partly hid; you see at the distance of ten rods a white sheet of water pitched westward across the chasm. This is the rebound of the falls of the North Boulder from a shelving rock. We will visit them on our return.

Up, up we go (for the acclivity up which our road leads, or rather the declivity down which the river flows, ascends for twenty miles at the average rate of 210 feet per mile, but here it is 469 feet per mile). The chasm now for a short distance becomes heavily timbered with fir and pine, and its sides very rugged, then intermits and becomes narrower and bolder. Huge rocks obstruct the passage of the water. It pitches over some and forms a series of cascades, others deflect it and dash it against the perpendicular wall of the canyon, whence it rebounds. Closer and closer the canyon contracts, and higher and steeper arise its walls. A dense grove of spruce trees, narrow and tapering as church steeples, and two hundred and fifty feet high, crowded each other so closely as to fill up the entire chasm between the walls, completely shut–

ting out the light, and shrouding everything with twilight gloom at noonday. The imposing grandeur of the appearance now may be fairly conceived, but not realized, when to this solemn, almost dismal scenery, is added the milk-white waters of the river rushing down the rocky declivity, dashed hither and thither by the obstructions, roaring and casting their spray in your face.

EAGLE CLIFF, BOULDER CANYON.

Anon, the scene changes. Light breaks in and disperses the gloom; and the canyon is clear again of trees, excepting the long, tapering spruce sapplings that run up and seem to lay against its walls. But look! twenty rods ahead a perpendicular mountain, three thousand feet high, is thrown across the canyon at right angles, and there seems no possible outlet from it. But soon a break is seen to unfold itself towards the left; and on turning the angle, the canyon walls, instead of continuous rock, are composed of dissevered mountains, crowded against each other, varying from 1,500 to 3,000 feet, sometimes exposing large, craggy, naked rocks, and at other times clothed with evergreens to their summits. To the left is what appears as the half of a huge red granite mountain, vertically cleft from top to bottom, whose perpendicular wall rises fully 2,000 feet high. About six hundred feet from its top is seen a small speck which we are assured is an eagle's nest in a cavity. Mr. Fitch, from Boston, who accompanied us from Denver, had with him a field glass, which was brought into requisition, and lo! sure enough, there is the eagle upon the nest.

But on we go silent, abstract and thoughtful, now entranced by an overhanging crag, then startled by a beetling cliff, and spell-bound by the stupendous vastness, inimitable grandeur and awful sublimity of Nature's works around us. Suddenly our revery is broken by a commotion in the advance. The men rise to their feet and swing their hats, and the ladies are waving their handkerchiefs; there is shouting, but it is drowned by the roar of the waters. To make us understand what was the matter, fingers are pointed to a culminating cliff to the right. Turning our eyes in the direction indicated, upon a prominent rock, and under a pine leaning over the precipice, stood a bighorn, or Rocky Mountain sheep (*Ovis Montana*) against the blue sky, and fully 1,500 feet above our heads. It was a large buck, and he gave us side views, both by turning his head to look at our advance, and rear. We found the attempt vain to make noise enough to frighten him from his commanding position.

Finally we reached the objective point, as far as the party was concerned, this was Castle Rock. Here our picnic was to take place in an alcove in the rock. This recess is some forty feet wide and sixteen to eighteen feet deep. Cloths were spread on the sandy floor, baskets and trays were unpacked. There was boiled ham and buffalo tongues, roasted chickens and turkeys, together with any amount of cakes, pies, custards and tarts, and all washed down with lemonade made from the icy waters (for the snows are but three miles distant) of the Boulder, which sweeps by within twenty feet of our retreat.

CASTLE ROCK.

But what of Castle Rock? Why, of this it is enough when it is said that it is an object worthy a trip across the continent to see it. It stands right across the direction of the Boulder coming down from the snowy mountains. When within fifteen feet of its base, the stream deflects southeastwardly, until it strikes the south wall, which it follows until it meets a perpendicular rock 1,800 feet high, standing at right angles to the south wall. It is then deflected back to the northwest striking the northeastern base of Castle Rock. Here the bridge crosses from the opposite side, and the road winds around the base of this wonderful rock. On the northwest side is a gap, through which, at a former period perhaps, the Boulder flowed. It is, perhaps, a hundred feet wide, reaches to within one hundred and fifty feet of the base, and separates Castle Rock from the north wall of the canyon. This wall is here hardly more than 1,200 feet high, while the southern one is fully 1,500. This latter is nearly perpendicular, but the evergreens with which it is covered from top to bottom, make it look as smooth and regular as though it had been trimmed with shears. The perpendicular rock that meets it at right angles, is red granite, and entirely bare.

The area of the base of Castle Rock is less than half an acre, but its altitude is over 800 feet. The Court House in St. Louis, from the pavement to the ball on top of the dome, is 196 feet. The imposing appearance of Castle Rock can, therefore, be imagined. Standing on a base not 150 feet square, yet rising to the enormous altitude of more than four times the distance from the pavement to the brass ball on the St. Louis Court House. Its distance from Boulder City is thirteen miles.

The engraving from a photograph taken at a point up the canyon, gives a good idea of the appearance of this singular rock. It is, however, only a view of the upper part of it, commencing say 300 feet above the base.

But we must here terminate our vain and futile attempt to describe Boulder Canyon—an object that is absolutely indescribable. No language can do justice to its awful, sublime and grand scenery. Here is immense variety and stupendous vastness combined with all the elements of the grand, the beautiful and the sublime, which no mortal pen can describe or pencil delineate; yet the whole presented with such rugged and austere, yet lovely simplicity, that it strikes every beholder with awe, delight and amazement. We have read of Alpine scenery, and of the Yosemite Valley, and we have both read of and seen Niagara Falls, Delaware Gap and the passage of the Potomac through Blue Ridge; and we pronounce Niagara Falls, Delaware Gap and the passage of the Potomac as tame and common place, when compared with the scenery of this fearful and wonderful canyon; and unless writers on Alpine scenery and of the Yosemite Valley lack command of the resources of our language, they, too, will suffer by the comparison. We, therefore, assert confidently, that for majestic presence to excite powerful emotions of veneration and awe; for wild, stern, and startling ruggedness to impress fear, and for sublimity and grandeur to fill the soul with inspiration and enthusiasm, Boulder Canyon stands without a peer or even a rival in the world.

I will only relate one of the many incidents that show its magic effect upon visitors, though many might be related that occurred to our own party. Soon after entering the canyon, my attention became completely absorbed and spellbound by the immensity, sublimity and wildness of the scene that was unfolding to view. The ladies occupying the open barouche with me thought I was listless, and was missing it all. Hence there was a continual call on me of, Oh! look here! O, there, etc., which I must confess annoyed me not a little. But the grandeur soon became so sublime and overwhelmingly powerful that they were filled with unutterable emotions and awed into silence. Abstract and staring wildly at the magic scenery, grander and vaster, that was constantly unfolding itself, they were incapable of any effort except to wave the hand slowly in the direction of the object on which their eyes were fixed spellbound.

Here we took leave of all our Kansas friends, who returned home, while the Missourians pushed on to the mines and snow fields, higher up and deeper in the recesses of the mountains.*

---

* Since this was written I have received the levellings of the railroad survey made up the canyon during the summer which is as follows:

1st mile from Boulder City, 184 feet; 2nd mile, 126.1; 3rd mile, 98.8; 4th mile, 175.8; 5th mile, 128.3; 6th mile, 180.9; 7th mile, 205.1; 8th mile to Falls of N. Boulder, 331.3; 9th mile, 469.4; 10th mile, 188; 11th mile, 95.5; 12th mile, 129.6; 13th mile to Castle Rock, 150.21.

CHAPTER IX.

As already stated, we took leave of our kind Boulder for the present, and of our Kansas friends, perhaps forever, at Castle Rock. The latter expressed themselves satisfied, yea, more than satisfied at having seen what it falls to the lot of but few, the most varied, picturesque, grandest, most imposing and sublimest work of Nature, and of having experienced such sensations and emotions as only such a work can excite and inspire. If the Italians can say, "See Naples and then die," they felt that with emotions of a higher order, they could say, "See Boulder canyon and Castle Rock and then die, for the world holds nothing besides that combines so much of every element of beauty, grandeur and sublimity as they."

We Missourians hired conveyances to take us up to the top of Caribou mountain, to inspect the silver mines there. Our party was now reduced to Judge Moore, of Franklin county; B. Smith and wife, of Crawford county, and myself and wife, from St. Louis.

It was about four o'clock when we started, and the distance about seven miles to Caribou. The canyon soon widens, and instead of bare perpendicular rocky walls, the stream is flanked on both sides by mountain ranges, sometimes running parallel with the banks of the stream, but generally the ridges or "hog backs" abut on the stream at right angles to its course, and have the general trend north and south, of the Cordilleras at this point. They are heavily timbered with pine and fir, and rise but to a moderate height, say from 700 to 1000 feet above the valley. Occasionally a high cone is seen in the distance protruding from one to two thousand feet above the surrounding peaks. Were it not for these sporadic cones, the scenery otherwise would remind one of the wildest portion of the Alleghanies, except that the "hog backs" (a very expressive and descriptive term) never have a length of more than five or six times their width. The canyon now has become a valley, with from five to forty rods of arable land on one or the other side of the stream, and the mountains measureably give way to high hills covered with evergreens and buffalo grass.

Signs of beaver now appear. Here on both sides of the road stand the stumps of trees, six to ten inches thick, gnawed off last fall to build their winter dam, which is here close by, as you see, cut through recently by the accumulated waters of the melted snows of the present season. Yonder they had

"Reared their little Venice;"

lodges from 16 to 18 feet in diameter and from 6 to 8 feet high, resembling huge mud ovens. Their interior is said to be about seven feet in diameter and from two to three feet high. Their beds, separated from each other, are made of grass or fibers of bark, and are placed around the walls of lodges, leaving the space in the center unoccupied. That deep ditch around the lodges is the moat made so deep that water never freezes, giving egress and ingress to the lodges. In it also they lay up a store of wood, the bark of which serves them for food in winter, while the wood after the bark is gnawed off is used for repairing their dams when needed. The lodges are covered with boughs of evergreens woven and matted together, lined and well stuffed with moss and grass, and the whole covered with mud. It is said that even amongst the beavers there are lazy fellows who will not work, refusing to assist in building lodges or dams or to cut wood and peel bark for winter provender. The industrious ones beat these idle fellows and drive them away; sometimes even disgracing them by lopping off a part of their tails. Those *"Paresseux"* as the French trappers call them, that is, "lazy fellows," are more easily caught in traps than the others, because, I suppose, being more in want, they are more reckless.

New flora also appears. The *Thermopsis montana* with its large raceme of papilionacious yellow flowers, dwarf *Dodecatheon*, with intense purple blooms; the delicate *Iris tenax*, and the *Polygonum bistorta*, with its white oblong head, are abundant on the grassy glade, or along the banks of spring branches flowing from the mountain sides. Birds were quite numerous. Amongst old acquaintances I noticed the silent lark, the chipping and tree sparrow, the robin, red-headed woodpecker, common dove, some warblers and fly catchers. The following are the principal ones amongst the new species: the mountain song-sparrow, green-tailed and Lincoln's finch, two kinds of grouse (the gray-mountain and dusky), the long-crested and Woodhouse's jay, both much larger and handsomer than our blue jay, the Rocky Mountain magpie, etc.

The first dwelling is that of Abel Goss, a young couple from New Hampshire, who have here a pleasant mountain ranche; and a few miles beyond is Brown's, now called Middle Boulder, where a large new tavern is nearly finished. Here we met Col. B. O. Cutter, superintendent of the Caribou Mining Company, who is here engaged in erecting smelting works to cost about $150,000 for the company. Here there is a cross road leading from Central City to the Ward mining district, north, near the base of Long's Peak. The Colonel gave us a letter of introduction to Mr. Martin, who superintends the mining operations at the lode, requesting him to give us every facility for inspecting the mines, and that he himself would be up in the morning if he could leave.

The valley now spreads out to a considerable distance and the bottom land would be as level as an Illinois prairie, were it not for the ridges of the old beaver dams that every fifteen or twenty feet lie across it from one mountain flank to the other and the old beaver lodges. These ridges are made of trees and sapplings cut down and dragged into place by these animals, the upper limbs all cut off and woven in below, and then the whole filled in with small stones, bark and moss, and covered with earth. It is only where the water has broken through them that you can see their structure. They are even yet from two to five feet high, and four to eight feet wide. Their length varies with the width of the valley, but some of them are fully two hundred yards long.

As we were leaving the valley to ascend the Caribou Mountains to our left at the head of the glade and south of the Boulder, we saw a high rugged mountain, some half a mile distant, whose side was covered with a field of snow of considerable size. The mountains on the north also crowd in on the creek above, and as the sun had descended behind their peaks, the dark green of the pine and firs that cover their sides gave the scenery a sad and gloomy appearance. Above and over head, coming in from Long's Peak, on the north now also appears a narrow storm cloud, from which at intervals dart forked lightning, and the roar of the thunder with its reverberating echoes from peak to peak is as grand as it is terrific. I gazed up at the low cloud with wonder and amazement. Instead of a hazy, ill-defined outline and enveloped in fog, it looked so pure and crystalline that I could not help imagining it carved out of solid ice, so distinctly were all the outlines of its involutions and convolutions marked, and then it was almost rendered transparent by the sunlight. I observed this same appearance on other occasions while in the mountains. It is only in case of terrific storms that anything at all resembling it can be seen "in the States." With this difference, however, that the cloud is dark and gloomy, instead of crystalline and almost transparent as here.

The road is very steep from where it leaves the valley

of the Boulder to Caribou City, rising at the average grade of five hundred and fifty feet to the mile. It slopes up westwardly along the south side of a mountain whose declivity is impracticable for anything except a Bighorn. Yet so dense is the spruce forest on the side that for some hundred feet below the road the forest has been felled to let in the sun to melt the winter snow from the road in the Spring. A few days before we passed there, a fire had swept up the mountain side amongst these felled trees leaving nothing but their blackened trunks, and doing immense damage to the beautiful forest. Soon Cardinal City is reached, a hamlet of some dozen of houses, mostly built since the fire of the blackened trunks of trees, and some of them covered with nothing but spruce branches. Here are two very rich and promising lodes; the Trojan and the Boulder county lode. The former averages $160 per ton, about equally divided between silver and gold, sometimes one predominating, sometimes the other. It is not yet fully developed being only one hundred feet deep. Boulder county lode is owned by Colonel Cutter and Mr. Conger. Shaft twenty-five feet deep, its ores are zinc-blend and argentiferous galena. More specimens of native silver have been taken from this mine than any in the district. Some eight or ten other lodes in the vicinity, we were told by Mr. Adolphus Livernash, an assayer who has his log cabin here, assay from 132 to 243 ounces of silver per ton. They are mostly argentiferous galena.

After leaving Cardinal, we ascend another mountain spur which lies to our right, while to our left lies a mountain gorge perhaps 1000 feet deep, beyond which rises an extremely steep mountain. The gorge and mountain are covered with a dense forest of spruce trees, in which a fire is raging, the flame often rising high above their tops. Near the western terminus of this mountain is a snowfield reaching from the top to its base. We had now ascended to sunlight again, for through a gap between two bald heads in the Snowy Range, about four miles distant, the sun poured a flood of Golden light. The spent storm-cloud now showered down a few large drops. I looked up, and from the nearness of the cloud could see the drops from the time they left the cloud. They looked like a shower of pearls, ruby, opal and amethyst; but when they hit, made one wince by their icy touch.

CARIBOU.

The mountain spur we are ascending now deflects north; and west beyond the narrow valley lies a hog-back, heavily covered with spruce, whose culminating point is at the head of the valley, northwest. This hog-back is Caribou mountain. Against this culminating point, and in the head of this valley lies Caribou City, of some 250 houses. The town has been built since spring set in. The houses are frame, many two stories high, made of spruce and pine plank sawed by the mountain mills. Not a brush of paint had been applied to any of them when we were there. There are two streets well built up running longtitudinally with the direction of the valley. Above the town from under a bluff issues a fine mountain spring, in which is a spout, and from which the greater part of the citizens obtain water. In the accompanying engraving the log house in the foreground is just below the spring. The view is down the valley and taken from the road leading to the Caribou lode on top of the mountain.

We put up at the Planters' House, kept by Capt. W. O. Logue, a former steamboat engineer, a captain in the Union army, and long in the employ of the McCord Brothers, of St. Louis. As soon as we had stowed away our luggage, all of us belonging to the masculine gender, started north over the mountain, to the nearest snowbank. As an evidence of the rejuvenating effect of the mountain air and climate upon the human system, I will state that though we were all on the shady side of sixty, yet we indulged, boy-like, in a real hearty snow balling.

We went over the mountain ridge in a northeastern direction, but the culminating point on which is the Caribou lode, is northwest, and about a third of a mile distant from town. Where we crossed we found the whole top of the mountain perforated with shafts and prospecting pits. All the shafts sunk last fall were filled with the drifting snows of the winter; some were yet even full of snow, and undisturbed. At others the miners were engaged in cleaning out the snow, and in others this had been done and the work of mining was progressing. Within a circle one-half mile from town there are no less than seventy lodes; fifty-six pay well, and all would pay if there were means for reducing the ores. But the nearest reduction works are at Black Hawk, twenty miles distant. They are owned by Prof. Hill, who buys ores at his own price. He also buys only the better grade, because the supply is abundant.

For this reason the lower grades are neglected and many mines fail of being developed because the miners cannot dispose of the ores. I have heard it stated no ores will pay that do not yield eighty ounces of silver per ton, because the mill men will charge some thirty-five dollars for reducing them, to which is to be added at least ten dollars for hauling, making altogether forty-five dollars, which leaves thirty-five dollars to the miner. Two men working together in sinking on a pay-streak, will raise on an average two tons of ore per week, making their wages thirty-five dollars per week, from which, however, must be deducted the wear of tools and powder for blasting. The average cost of mining per ton, with proper facilities, where the lodes are fully developed, including wages, etc., is about $5 15, and when operations are carried on on a large scale, 30 per cent. less. Colonel Cutter thinks the actual cost of reducing a ton of ore, ought not to exceed $7 50 per ton. At present the mines can be made to produce five times the quantity that can be reduced at the reduction works when completed.

The reduction works already spoken of as in process of erection at Middle Boulder, two and a half miles below, will not afford any relief to the Caribou mines, since the Caribou and other lodes owned by the company that is erecting the works, will alone supply all the ore it can work. There are more than ninety lodes open in Boulder county, but there is not a single mill nor reduction work in it, while in Gilpin county there are twenty-six, and in Clear Creek county some twenty mills and reduction works in operation. The result is that mines are well developed there, and ores reduced of such low grade as only yield from $20 to $24 per ton. The reason there are no facilities at Caribou for reducing the ore, is because all the lodes have been discovered within the past year, except the Caribou, which was discovered in September, 1869.

The Caribou mines alone can furnish ore enough to run

a dozen stamp mills; and here is a fine opening for an immense fortune, by erecting a first-class smelting furnace at Boulder, where the best quality of coal in the Territory exists in unlimited quantities.

Prof Hill, of Brown University, R. I., went to Black Hawk a comparatively poor man, some three or four years ago, and invested some $8,000 in a smelting furnace. He is now a millionaire. He reduces the ores to what is called "matte," which is packed up and sent to Swansea, in Wales, where the precious metals are separated from the base. Prof. Hill receiving all the gold and silver, and the English company retaining the copper and lead obtained from the "matte" for their pay.

Our evening ramble took us around the Caribou mountain westward, and then over its top back to town. In this ramble I performed the feat of gathering snow with one hand and plucking flowers with the other, which I had often heard could be done, but about which I was somewhat incredulous. The flower, which I preserve in my herbarium as a momento of the fact, is that of the *Vaccinnium myrtillus*, a species of blueberry. We found the northwest side of the mountain to be the wall of North Boulder canyon. We could hear the roaring of the waters about a thousand feet below us, but could not see it, the view being obstructed by the dense grove of spruce that line the declivity.

The north wall of the canyon is the southeastern side of a peak of the Snowy Range. The trend of the peak is a little west of north, and on its eastern side lays an immense snow field, reaching to the summit. This is caused by the west winds drifting the snows, as they fall, to the leeside of the mountain. Up to the hight of the Caribou mountain, this wall was densely covered by dwarf spruce and pine, some even standing within the margin of the snow field. Above the "timber line" and on the west side, the peak was bare; and being covered with the velvety buffalo grass, it looked like an ordinary, smoothly rounded, grassy but steep hill. No rocks can be seen protruding from its sides above the timber line.

Its apparent distance from us seemed not to exceed a stone's throw, but we were assured in a direct line it was more than a mile; and to get to the point *opposite* some three miles had to be traversed. Being now tolerably posted as to the deceptive appearances of distance in this region, yet while we were looking at it, and following with the eye the margin of the snow line toward the summit, some one jestingly proposed to ascend it. I replied, "No, we will leave it for to-morrow, and do it up before breakfast." At this a miner, hid in the spruce thicket, and whom we had not noticed before, volunteered the kind advice: "You had better take your breakfast first, and your dinner along, for you'll have a late supper."

This incident recalls another. While standing on the summit of Caribou mountain, I said to Judge Moore, "Judge, have you observed with how much ease and freedom you can talk here, and how sonorous and ringing the voice is?" No sooner were the words out, than Mr. Smith, who was fully one hundred yards distant, replied, "I expect that is the reason you talk so much nonsense here." The explanation is very simple. In the caissons of the St. Louis bridge, those persons who went down in them remember the difficulty there was in speaking, or making yourself heard. There the air was compressed and consequently the effect was the reverse of the effect here, where the air is expanded by the altitude. The barometer here stood 19:52, showing that the atmosphere had only about two-thirds of the density as on the sea shore, or in other words, that the mountain was over two miles high. Its hight, as received here, is 11,300 feet.

On the following morning the barometer stood 19 52 inches—the boiling point of water was 191.8 degrees. Following the usual formula for deducing altitude from these *data*, the hight of the mountain would be 11,286 feet. It must, however, be stated that at the time the electric tension of the mountain was great, as was evinced by the bushy appearance of the tails of the horses, and also by the hair of our heads having a tendency to stand out straight. This electric condition was followed by a mountain storm in the afternoon. Probably an allowance of one inch in barometric pressure should be made for this electric condition at the time; still, it would leave the mountain over 10,000 feet high.

Apropos, this rarity of the atmosphere makes itself felt in the breathing of all animals. We had to give the horses, on ascending the mountain, their own time, for if urged they soon commenced panting for breath, and had to stop. The miners here walk slowly, and never feel any inconvenience; but "greenhorns," like ourselves, in trying to rush up the mountain, soon find their "wind" failing. I felt no inconvenience, until walking rapidly up a steep terrace, only some six or eight paces, and then found I had either to sit down or fall down. A miner gave me this direction: "Whenever you find your breath failing, stop and turn your back to the mountain. Two or three breathings, and you are all right again." I found, in following it, invariably an almost instant relief. When we reached the tavern, a little after dusk, I found Mrs. Y. sitting by the stove and fanning, complaining she could get no breath. The landlady assured her it would be all right by morning. It is said that the few who are thus affected by the rarity of the air, find themselves entirely relieved of the difficulty after a stay of a few hours.

CHAPTER X.

As we were to return to Boulder by evening, we resolved to utilize the earliest beams of light in pursuing our investigations of the mines, their character and method of working them. Accordingly we were up even before twilight had completely dispersed, and out on the mountain amongst the mines. At all the well developed mines the ores had been separated by an expert and classified, and all the first class taken away or locked up. Where they had facilities, the second class were also locked up in houses to prevent depredations. We found many excavations just commenced; these we examined critically, to ascertain by what signs and appearances the miners were guided in their prospecting. We had taken with us samples obtained at the mines of the rock carrying the lowest grade ores; with these we compared the surface rock at the newly opened prospecting pits, and came to the conclusion that signs of metaliferous veins were either very obscure, or that it required a cultivated and experienced eye to recognize and detect them. Some of the new pits we found, were developing well defined metaliferous veins. At these we found small piles of rock showing the progress of development, from very faint signs to well-defined crystals. Comparing these with specimens of rock from the well-developed mines, we were satisfied that though surface indications to "greenhorns" were undistinguishable, yet the metal bearing rocks had well-marked characteristics to distinguish them from the non-metaliferous. We examined some thirty or forty paying lodes and any number of prospecting pits.

After passing through the mining ground, we went around the peak westward, to take a look at the snowy peak opposite, seen the evening before, now that it had its snowy side bathed in sunlight. It was really a charming sight to see the white snow apparently piled against an intensely blue sky.

Pushing on still further, but southwestwardly, we entered a dense pine and spruce forest, full of long-crested jays. (*Cyanura macrolopha*,) larger, and having no resemblance in color to our blue jay.

From here we ascended to the top of the mountain to take a morning's view of the scenery. West at from a mile to two miles distance lay the Snowy Range, running a little west of south and east of north. The range separated us from Middle Park, only eight miles distant. But the only practical route thither is by Boulder Pass, some fifteen miles southwest. To the south and east lay what appeared a hilly table land covered with a dense evergreen forest. At various distances a few isolated cones protruded above the surrounding hills from one to two thousand and perhaps more feet. A little north of east the peak of Sugarloaf Mountain, some nine miles distant, was a prominent object. I did not learn the name of a very large, high cone some fifteen miles southeast. It had really a majestic appearance. In the northeast was another cone, but at some distance, and apparently not as high as Sugarloaf, some seven or eight miles south of it. The town of Caribou lay at our feet on the east side of our look-out in a scooped-out valley between two mountains. We now went to Caribou Lode, entirely closed in and under cover, which lay to our left on the northeastern point of the mountain. Northwest of the mine are the large stables of the mining company well stocked with provender, including corn. As we approached a large number of little vermin were seen running from the stable which I supposed to be rats. But seeing one dodge behind a large rock, I kept a lookout for him as I turned the corner, and there he sat erect on a small rock, and handling a grain of corn in the most graceful style while eating it. He proved to be a chipmunk. (*Tamias quadrivitatus*), or the four-striped ground squirrel, fully as beautiful but not so large as the chipmunk or ground squirrel (*Tamias lysteri*) of the Eastern States. The four-striped ground squirrel was discovered by Prof. Say, attached to Colonel Long's expedition to the Rocky Mountains. Audobon gives its comparative size at five-sixths that of the Eastern chipping squirrel, from which it differs by having four stripes instead of three.

Finding that I had ample time before breakfast would be ready, I made a detour to the left, and coming in front of what I had taken to be a pile of spruce boughs, I found it to be a miner's lodge, made of a few poles laid over the gap between two large rocks and covered with the fan-shaped boughs of the *Abies Englemannii*. His bed consisted of a buffalo robe and some gray army blankets. He was just rising, and from his cordial "good morning" I knew he was a "whole-souled fellow," and therefore stopped to have a talk. He soon had a hot fire to get his breakfast. He put on his coffee pot, and from a pouch drew some ground coffee. Slicing his bacon, he put a sharp stick through it, held it in the flame, and when right hot would pour cold water on it to "freshen it," as he said. He gave me a history of his wanderings for the last twenty years, when he left Pennsylvania for the mines in California. Had made a half dozen of fortunes and lost them all, but had now ample means laid up for old age, whenever it might undertake him. I asked him why he did not take the world easy and enjoy life now? "I do," he replied; "I think there is no enjoyment like the wild, free, dare-devil life of the miner on these mountains. "Here," he continued, " we have no classes nor ranks in society, but every true and honest man we meet is at once and forever a friend and brother." I asked him how long he had been here. "About three weeks," he replied.

"I had just got," he continued, "into Denver from a very successful prospecting tour through New Mexico, when Mr. —— met me and offered me 'grub' and five dollars a day, and half interest in what I might find, to come here and prospect Caribou mountain over for him." I remarked that I had made his employer's acquaintance in Denver, and that he bore the reputaion of being "very sharp." "That's so," said he "and I got things so fixed before I left that convinced him I was sharp too, and knew my man." "Well, my friend," said I, "ever since daylight I have been tramping over this mountain and trying to find out what signs governed the prospectors here in their search for mineral, and have failed. Can you tell me?" "Well," said he, "in my twenty years' experience I have not seen a place where prospectors have to work so much in the dark. We have almost to go it blind here, for the surface indications are so indistinct. Our experience tells us in what rocks we need not look for minerals, and also what rocks may have them, but here there are often no surface indications whether they carry mineral or not; yet this is the richest silver region in these mountains."

I here rose and left, with the cordial invitation extended to me to come and see his prospect after breakfast, which I accepted, but had no time to keep my promise. After breakfast the whole party, accompanied by the landlady and several other ladies, walked up to the Caribou lode. Here we met Mr. Martin, one of the original discoverers of the lode, who had sold the west half to Mr. Breed, of Cincinnati, for $50,000, still retaining his interest in the eastern half, and superintending the mining operations. He received us cordially and showed us all over the works, their arrangement and operation, the separation and classification of the ores, and liberally furnished us with rich specimens. The ladies then left for a ramble to the snow banks on the north side of the mountain, while the men descended the shaft, then 186 feet deep. The shaft, following the lode vein, is sometimes perpendicular, then slopes at an angle of about 80 degs. east, which is the general dip the strata here of all the lodes, and the vein runs northwest and southeast. In Clear Creek, Gilpin and other counties south, the veins run northeast and southwest. The descent is by ladders, and the place was damp from the dripping water of the side rock above, and gloomy, notwithstanding the star candles we held. It possessed no particular interest nor attraction, and we were glad when we returned to daylight.

The Caribou is the great silver mine of the mountains. The Colorado *Gazetteer* says: "It is not only one of the most valuable silver mines in Colorado, but amongst the richest ever discovered in America." Prof. Hill bought a ton of choice ore for which he paid $13,000. It assayed $16,498,95. About one hundred tons of ore were taken out per month when we were there, but it was not worked to its full capacity. Besides the company are now mainly engaged in extending levels east and west so that when their smelting works go in operation they can keep them running from this mine alone, if necessary. The assays show the following results:

	Per Ton.
First class ore	$1,054
Second class ore	634
Third class ore	145

The ladies soon returned accompanied by quite a number of miners, and loaded with specimens given them. We now left, following the lead of the miners to a small black swell on the mountain consisting entirely of black magnetic iron, which the miners said "the clouds kissed every time they passed." We found the ore strongly magnetic, often suspending a string of watch keys. The miners proposed to find me a real good one, and at last succeeded in finding one weighing about three pounds that suspended a chain of no less than six watch keys. Instantly I saw a hammer descending on it, shivering it into half a dozen fragments. "Oh!" I exclaimed, "you have spoilt it now." "O, no," said he that struck it, taking up the largest fragment and applying it to his key, but the key fell to the ground. "O," said another, "you did not get the magnetic part," while trying another fragment, but with the same result; and so on till every fragment was tried, but not one showed a trace of magnetism left. This astonished them. One of them asked. "What did you mean when you said you have spoiled it now? and how did you know it was spoiled?" "Why," said I, "it is a well known fact that no magnet can be struck without loosing its magnetism." They looked at each other as though they thought, "he is trying to poke fun at us;" but instantly the thought struck them of verifying the assertion by experiment. Strong magnets were selected and struck with hammers, and then tried, but every trace of magnetism had disappeared. "Well," exclaimed a half dozen of voices at once. "that's a new wrinkle."

As they saw I knew *some* things they went to the usual extreme of believing I knew *all* things; and as their curiosity had been excited they demanded to know "what magnetism was, how it got there, and whether the struck stones would again acquire their lost power?" "Well," I rejoined, " to answer your first question were to tell a long story of what it is imagined to be, because I don't know, nor does anybody truly know, what magnetism is; but you can find out the answers to your second and third questions for yourselves. Lay all the stones that you have struck, and which you know are not magnetic now, on a pile, and wait until after the lightning has struck here, or, as you say, "a passing cloud has given them a smack," and you will find them all right again. "Is that so?" said some of them. Try and see, said I, and if it is not so let me know it. They then piled up the stones for trial, and as I have not heard anything from them, I infer that the experiment has succeeded to their satisfaction.

We now returned to the tavern, and at eleven o'clock started to return to Boulder. But it is due, before breaking off this narration here, to bear unequivocal and unqalified testimony to the order and quietness of Caribou, and to the sobriety, intelligence and manly bearing of the miners, not only here but elsewhere. Liquor of every form is for sale here, but there are no drunken broils, rioting, wantonness or profanity.

This is at variance with the common idea of the habits, customs and condition of society in mining villages, which are regarded as only a synonym for any amount of drunkenness and rowdyism, because desperadoes, roughs and bullies are fond of congregating at such places. But I saw nothing of this kind here, nor in any of the mining villages I visited in Colorado.

We stopped long enough at Cardinal to examine the Trojan lode, one of the most promising new lodes in the Grand Island district, as the mining district enclosed by the North and Middle Boulder creeks is called. It receives its name from a mountain fully one thousand feet high a few miles below Caribou, forming an island in the North Boulder which flows around it on all sides. This mountain is called the Grand Island, which has been transferred to the adjacent mining district. The Caribou and Pugh mountains and other metaliferous cones are in this district. Silver and lead are the predominating metals in the district, the mines being what is called argentiferous galenas, though silver in some localities is found combined with copper. Gold has not yet been found to any great extent, though just south of the Middle Boulder, and a short distance southeast of Middle Boulder Post-office, rich lodes have been discovered. It is probable that further explorations of the lower part of Grand Island district will develop the existence of this metal in paying quantities, since it is surrounded by rich lodes, three of which are located at different points on the south side, Gold Hill on the east, and the Ward mines on the north. Besides, on Four Mile creek, which has a course parallel to the North Boulder, north and east of the latter, gulch mining is carried on, paying daily from $8 to $15 per hand. Some miners were at work on a placer on Beaver creek, a branch of Middle Boulder, just south of the mountain on which the road ascends to Caribou; they quit because the water gave out.

The Trojan lode yields on an average of $160 to $240 per ton, half gold and half silver, sometimes the gold predominating and then the silver. The vein increases in riches as great depths are reached. We did not go to the Boulder county lode, also located here. Prospecting is also going on vigorously and quite a number of paying lodes have been discovered here. Between here and the village of Middle Boulder the fire was still raging as on the previous day in the tall spruce forest that lined the mountain acclivity on the farther side of the gorge to our right, the side we were descending having been completely swept by it several days before. Its distance from us was less than a quarter of a mile, and its crackling noise and roaring was terrific, the flames leaping up in large sheets over the top of the forest. It was a sad sight to look at. Here were forests destroyed and wasted, that for several generations would have furnished ample supplies of lumber for building purposes and for fuel for smelting the ores, and all for what? Merely to clear away the fallen leaves so as to expose the naked rocks to the observation of the prospector. This wantonness has no parallel except the folly of killing the goose that laid the golden egg.

The penalty for firing the woods is severe, and there were fifty-one indictments found against persons and pending for the offence in Boulder county alone. It is to be hoped, if found guilty, that the full penalty of the law may be meted out to them. On our descent we met a burly mountaineer on a spirited horse going up to Caribou. Mr. Smith recognized him as Major John Q. A. Rollins, an old Illinois acquaintance, but whom he had not seen for many years. Hailing him, and a mutual recognition taking place, the Major insisted that we should pay a visit to and take dinner at his mountain ranche, some two miles south of Middle Boulder, offering to accompany us back. This we gratefully declined, as we had in the morning sent down word to Goss's to have dinner for our party at two o'clock. At Brown's, or Middle Boulder, as it is now called, we again met Colonel Cutter, another mountain specimen of physical development, robust in health, and manly vigor. He is a New Yorker, an educated and intelligent man, and from his long residence in the mountains, an expert in mining affairs. He considers this as one of the richest mining districts yet discovered, and that investments judiciously made and managed here, either in mines or reduction works, cannot fail of being remunerative. The reduction works he is erecting for the Caribou Mining Company, of which he is managing director, will be completed by the 1st of September. But the present activity in the mining district and the extent of the discoveries making, indicate that the works will be, when completed, entirely inadequate to reduce the ores that can and will be supplied.

Arriving at Goss's, and having a few minutes to spare before dinner was ready, I followed the mountain branch up to the gorge whence it issues, in search of new flowers. I was rewarded in finding the *Dalea laxiflora*, the *Thaspium montanum* and a new and perhaps undescribed Gilia; besides any number of the dwarf purple Dodecatheon, *Polygonum bistoria* and *Thermopsis montana*.

Mrs. Goss had a large collection of mountain *cacti* from which she invited us to help ourselves to such as we might fancy, but we were not provided with means to transport them. She also had a Woodhouse jay (*Cynocitta Woodhousei*) which she presented to the ladies, but which, to our regret, we had to leave at Boulder, for want of facilities to bring it away. It was a most magnificent bird of brilliant bottle green plumage.

After a most excellent dinner, to which our mountain appetites did ample justice, and for which we were charged a very moderate price, we started and were soon at Castle Rock, where we stopped to survey it once more, first from the west, then from the east side. A mile or two below we descried a pair of bighorns, (*Ovis montana*,) or Rocky Mountain sheep, with a lamb under an overhanging cliff on a terrace of the canyon wall some 1200 feet above us. There they stood immovable as statues, looking down upon us. We shouted, whooped and yelled, making all the noise we could, but it had no effect upon them. The lamb, however, became alarmed and kept dodging from one side to the other of the pair.

Still further down we stopped to see the son of our Caribou host, Willie Logue, a St. Louis boy, fourteen years old, who was working on a very promising prospect of his own discovery. He was in a very great glee, and assured us that the assayer had just sent him word that a specimen sent had analyzed at the rate of 140 ounces to the ton. He sent a specimen of the ore to the Missouri State Cabinet, where it can now be seen at the Washington University. We have since heard with regret that the same discovery had been made before and recorded in 1862. It seems, however, by the latest news from there, that Willie has been in luck, and made a very promising discovery on the north side of Caribou Mountain, in the canyon of the North Boulder.

We were next halted by one of our Boulder female friends, the excellent wife of Major Buttles, who is one of the principle stockholders and managing directors of the Boulder canyon road, which I ought to have stated before, was only completed three weeks before our arrival there. The Major having some business in connection with the completion of the road in the upper part of the canyon, Mrs. B. had accompanied him to stay a day or two; and here we found her in the wild, gloomy, mountain canyon, beside the noisy stream, occupying a cabin made of poles, with a ground floor, covered with the wing-shaped boughs of the spruce. She said she had just finished catching a fine mess of mountain trout, and pressed us to wait and she would fry some for us. Old Roman etiquette would have required us to take an emetic to get rid of our dinner, that we might accept the invitation. But modern politeness, foolish, heartless and exacting as it is, deviates not quite as far from the path of common sense as the ancient did. Suppose it did, what judgment would Mrs. Cross form of our estimation of her cookery?

Our next halting place was opposite the embouchure of the North Boulder. The road here crosses a bridge to the south side of the main canyon, where we drove because here was one of the few turnouts to pass ascending teams. After alighting, we walked back over the bridge and then clambered along the precipitous sides of the north wall of the canyon, down to the mouth of North Boulder. I soon found that I had as much as I was able to do to take care of myself, and therefore had to abandon Mrs. T. to the care of Mr. Corson, the President of the Boulder County Agricultural Association, who had accompanied us to Caribou. The canyon of the North Boulder was even more difficult than the first. By running any number of risks of breaking our necks, or of a cold bath in the stream, we stood at length on a very narrow gravelly beach facing the falls. The canyon runs northwest, but suddenly becomes a *cul de sac;* a perpendicular wall, a thousand feet or more high, lies right across it. The falls meet the canyon from the northeast and therefore at right angles. To the right of the falls the northeast wall of the canyon consists of red granite, and is apparently a mountain peak cleft in twain perpendicularly and rising to an altitude of from 1,500 to 2,000 feet. Between this peak and the mountain closing up the canyon the water has cut down through the granite a trough some 300 feet deep and 20 feet wide. This trough is of the same width throughout, and perfectly symmetrical. It is the only instance I saw in the mountains of erosion, the canyon walls invariably being cleavages made by convulsions of Nature. The falls are about 20 feet wide and 70 feet high. They strike a slanting rock inclining to the northwest, which lies on the east side of the canyon. The rock is about 12 feet high; it therefore pitches the water, the south half of the cascade that falls on it, against the northwest wall, which closes the canyon. The other half goes without any obstruction to the bottom behind this deflected sheet and boils up at our feet white as milk with foam. We are standing within 30 feet of the falls and facing it, and occasionally a whirl of air carries the spray into our faces, but the roar is terrific and the ground trembles beneath our feet. Behind the falls is a large cavity extending to within ten feet of the top, so that the falls pour over a projecting rock, leaving a deep recess. What was singular a Rocky mountain blue-bird, the *Salia arctica*, had its nest in this recess, and it had evidently "not learned the fear of man," for it would come down to the beach on the opposite side and within fifteen feet of us, without seeming to notice our presence. It would hop about, and after finding an insect, often a grasshopper that had come over the falls, it would rise, and after a little suspension would dart in through the thinest part of the falling sheet, close by the north wall. A moment after and it would re-appear at the same point to repeat the performance. There is a second fall a short distance above the lower, of some 45 feet, which is said to be extremely grand, but it is inaccessible from this point. After an equally hazardous scramble, we got back to our conveyances, but now we found ourselves in trouble. Some teams had come up from below carrying a part of Col. Cutter's machinery, but our vehicles blocked up the way, so there was neither a way to retreat nor advance for either party. After mutual consultation, it was discovered if we unhitched and took the horses across the bridge, and then piled up the vehicles, room could be made for the wagons to pass, which being done, all of us went on our way rejoicing. It was about sunset when we issued from the mouth of the canyon, upon the plain where stands the city of Boulder.

CHAPTER XI.

The next morning, Friday, June 16, I was up with the dawn and out on the streets. They were yet deserted and silent. Not a living thing was to be seen nor heard, except the ever purling murmur of the waters hastening down over the plain. Instinctively I was drawn to their side and up their brink and on to the bridge that spans the Boulder opposite the centre of the town. It was yet twilight and I stood on the bridge for some moments musingly looking at the flow and listening to the murmur of the waters; and then raising my eyes to look at the aperture in the mountains whence they issued. Oh, those mountains how dear to me now that I have made their acquaintance! When I recalled the gloom and solitude of the rifted canyon in the Cordilleras through which these waters have flowed, and the overpowering and magic grandeur of the scenery of which they had formed a part, I felt sad. I thought that they, like I, had left forever scenes of inspiration that give birth to thoughts and emotions too high and holy for utterance, to mix hereafter with the low, groveling, commonplace humdrum of every-day life. Purling and dancing and singing so joyously as they glided along over their rocky bed, I could not help sighing: Ah, little do they know of what is before them! I felt like apostrophizing them thus: Ah! well may ye of so little experience be light of heart and dance and sing and prattle with glee as you hasten from your mountain home. Soon the merciless iron of experience will penetrate your bosom and your joy will flee forever. You will enter into the great throng, and falling under its benumbing influences will lose your identity forever. With them, you will pursue a sluggish career amid fens, bogs and sandbars to obstruct your way, till you finally fall into and are lost in the great ocean of which you are an emanation. Were ye sentient, and had ye the faculty of prevision to see the low career before you and its final end, like the dying Swiss boy, ye would entreat and cry:

"Oh, carry me back to my mountain home."

But fate has set its seal upon me as well as you, and from you I can learn the lesson to be cheerful, and not repine while obeying his behests.

Breaking from my reverie, I crossed the bridge and followed the pebbly margin of the stream up to the mouth of the canyon, examining the endless variety of size, color and material of the boulders and pebbles of which its bottom and margin are composed. Then turning south and following the base of the mountain, I soon ascended one of those terraced plateaux that invariably lie against the mountains between the mouths of canyons and gulches. The plateau I followed till it terminates at Bear gulch, and thence down till I reached the road leading to town. The view from the plateau is most charming, even finer than from that on the north side of the stream already described, since it brings the valleys of both the North and South Boulder under nearer view, and for a greater distance the valley below their junction at Valmont. The lower plain and that of the plateau were densely covered with flowers, all of which have been mentioned before except the *Mertensia paniculata* and the *Campanula rotundifolia*, which I found in the mouth of Bear gulch, and the beautiful *Lippia cuneifolia* of the lower plain.

After breakfast at the Colorado House, where we put up, the proprietor called my attention to some stones used for flagging the pavement, which he said were "photograph stones." I found several large slabs fringed around with images of miniature trees and forests. While I was examining them, Mr. J. A. Carr, a grocer, but formally a miner, and a true lover of Nature, passed by; and seeing what had attracted my attention, said if I would go to his store he would show me, and make me a present of very fine specimens of these stones. Complying with his invitation, I accompanied him, and he gave me a specimen of great beauty—two miniature trees, more than six inches in length, imprinted on a fine white sandstone. He said about two miles north of town, the top of the first hog back was entirely composed of these stones. These, however, were of a red sandstone, while the white specimen he gave me was from a hog back two miles west, in the recesses of the mountains.

He very generously got a carriage and took me out to the locality. In driving out I noticed on the edge of the plain, near the mountain, and running parallel to it, a dark-looking rocky ledge, rising sometimes to a height of 80 feet above the plain. This is a bluish semi-crystalline limestone, from which excellent lime is made. It occasionally appears along the foot of the mountains, but nowhere else on the plains. Arriving at the foot of the spur, on the summit of which the "photograph stones" are deposited, we found it consisted of red sedimentary sandstone, upheaved to a hight of some 1,200 feet above the plain. Against its sides lies a steep bank of earth, through which the rocks protruded, and which is carried up to a hight of some 500 feet above the plain. Then comes the rock split into lamina from less than one-half to six inches in thickness. This upheaval is very steep and can be ascended only by using both hands and feet, a dangerous performance, however, since often you get on a slab which will slide down the side of the mountain with you. After ascending about one-third of the acclivity, we commenced splitting the slabs, and wherever there was an indication of a seam, we always found the "photograph tree" and sometimes a picture representing a forest. All the handsomer ones we slid down the sides of the mountain to take with us, but they were generally broken into fragments by the operation. However, we secured a fine lot, which we brought home with us. Different explanations had been given of the nature and origin of these pictures of trees and forests in the seams of these stones. One is, that as these are sedimentary rocks, annual freshets brought down from highlands silicious matter which would be deposited on the bottom of some pool or pond of still water. During the interval between freshets, mosses would grow and spread themselves out on the bottom of these pools, which in turn, were submerged by the sediment of the succeeding freshet. As these lamina were often not more than a fourth of an inch in thickness, this account for their origin and nature appears quite plausible. But the fatal objection to this theory is that the cleavages in which these figures occur are always perpendicular to the sedimentary stratification.

Another theory to account for them is this—that they are of electric origin, and that the figures are the photographs of trees or forests that once stood around the pools in which these sedimentary deposits took place; that a flash of lightning, after night, had photographed the images of these trees upon the bottom of the pools, which was supposed to have been sensitive to such an impression—in other words, somewhat similar in condition to a photographic plate. In support of this theory they advance the well-observed and indisputable fact that persons killed or shocked by lightning often have the image of a tree, leaf or branch intervening between them and the main electric discharge imprinted on their bodies. This theory also assumes that the lamina in which these figures occur are identical with, or at least parallel to, the sedimentary layers, when the fact is, they are at right angles to them —a fact likewise fatal to it.

The true explanation of these figures is as follows: If we put some mercury in a phial filled with a weak solution of nitrate of silver, in a few days, if not disturbed, the silver will be found precipitated, the crystal constituting a beautiful tree-like form, called Diana's tree, (*Arbor Dianæ*). Similarly the lead tree, (*Arbor Saturni*) is precipitated from acetate of lead by zinc. They are therefore simply arborescent mineral figures, that is, crystalizations of some solution of manganese which had been carried by the water into the fissures of these rocks, and there precipitated and crystalized by the reaction of iron, or perhaps potassium. They are known to geologists as *dendrites*, that is, stone trees.

After dinner, accompanied by Mr. Corson and 'Squire Dabney, we drove out to the South Boulder, some four miles, to inspect the iron works of Langsford & Marshall, adjacent to their coal bank. A mile or so from town we passed the limits of cultivated fields, and found the plains covered with cattle. There are again fine farms on the South Boulder, though they occupy but an insignificant area when compared with the scope that can be reached by irrigation. The South Boulder we found a limpid, turbulent, rapid creek, like all the streams issuing from these mountains, though less in size than the main Boulder.

On its south margin are the iron works, where considerable ore is smelted and castings made; but they were not in operation when we were there. The iron ore is obtained on the terraced plateau in which their coal bank is situated. A good strata overlies the coal, but is not fully developed. Most of the ore heretofore used has been gathered by collecting the loose nodules on the plateau and the adjacent plain. The nodules are often several feet in diameter, and are red hematite of varying richness. Judge Moore, who has had some experience in such matters in Pennsylvania, says if they would assort their ores and not use them indiscriminately, more satisfactory results would be attained, both in the quantity and quality of the metal. In fact, that the ores generally are rich enough to make the enterprise eminently successful. The coal mine is situated some two hundred yards southeast of the iron works. It is a drift running southwardly under the bench or plateau. The coal is metamorphosed lignite, being but one remove from anthracite. It is light, and does not soil the fingers in handling. The vein is thirteen feet thick, and often stumps of petrified pine trees are found in it. What is most singular about it is that it is permeated in all directions by seams of resin; and often lumps of pure amber colored resin varying in size from a hazelnut to a hen's egg, are found embedded in it. Analysis give about 50 per cent as the amount of fixed carbon contained in it; ashes under two per cent, and entirely free of sulphur. It is found to answer most admirably for smelting all kinds of ores, the only drawback being its tendency of breaking up into parallelopipeds and then fusing into a mass, thus choking up the draft.

We explored the mine as far as worked, some three hundred yards in a straight adit. It is under the superintendence of Mr. Henry Wrigley, a Welch miner, formerly of St. Louis, and who at once recognized me.

This is unquestionably not only the largest, but the best deposit of coal on the western plains. There are no less than eleven distinct veins with but small intervals between them. The aggregate thickness of eight of these, ascertained by working them, is sixty-three feet; the thickness of three being unknown. A vein 12 feet thick of the same deposits is worked at Erie, twelve miles from the mountains, and extends south towards Golden City, but thins out before reaching there; it also depreciates in quality, as shown by Professor Hayden's Geological report of 1869.

We then visited other mines farther down on the plain; and among them the shaft on the 16th, the school section, which some malicious persons had set on fire, and which was banked up with earth to smother the fire. Strata of the best fireclay are interposed between the veins of coal varying from 4 to 8 feet in thickness. These will be invaluable for furnaces hereafter in smelting the ores of the mountains.

On our way back to town we inspected some of the principal irrigating canals, and examined the method of applying the water. We found main canals away out on the highest benches of the plain, conveying water to ranches from five to eight miles distant. The general regulations here respecting irrigation are, that proprietors of land join and excavate an irrigating canal along such line as will supply water to the greatest scope of territory compatible with their own interest and convenience. After the canal is so constructed, any one entering land "under ditch," as they call it, that is, that can be irrigated from any completed canal, is required to pay the proprietors of the canal at the rate of fifty dollars for every quarter section of land so entered, or acquired, which had no water privileges. This secures to him forever the privilege of free use for all the water required for irrigating his land; the number and size of the sluices, however, are regulated by law. He is subject, however, to such annual assessment as may be necessary to keep the main canal in repair, which is found on an average never to exceed four dollars per year. This, added to the interest on his original investment, makes the cost of water from four to five cents per acre annually. About Denver irrigating privileges have become a monopoly; and the monopolists charge outsiders one dollar and fifty cents per acre annually for water.

We passed fields of oats, barley, wheat and corn, all under irrigation, of the darkest green, and in the most thrifty condition. We also passed a meadow of splendid promise. Finally we came to the ranche of a farmer from Pennsylvania, the largest wheat grower in the territory, whose name I have unfortunately forgotten. He has been here nine years, and for the last seven years has not raised less than 5000 bushels annually. This year he expects between 9000 and 10,000 bushels. He was in his wheat field, about 190 acres, with his hoe, attending to irrigation. We stopped and had a long conversation with him. From him we learned, as we did from others, that their crops never suffer from insects, because they drown them out; that there is never any rust on the blade, nor smut on the berry, because the aridity of the climate prevents all fungoid growth. The wheat I examined at the mills gave testimony to the same effect. It had the plumpest kernels I ever saw. No imperfect, diseased or shriveled kernel could be found. I asked him what effect the extension of railroads will have upon the price of wheat, oats and barley. He said none whatever; we fear no competition here, because the quality of our wheat, and consequently of our flour, is so superior that it will always command a higher price than any that can be brought here from abroad; and then with irrigation, and with our exemption from disease, our crops never fail; while we raise fully between two and three times as much per acre as you average in Missouri. To the inquiry what he had obtained for his crop last year, he answered, three dollars and forty cents per cental, (that is, $2 04 cents per bushel) which was about New York price for prime white wheat.

I asked him about the grasshoppers. "Well," said he, "we had them here one year. They came over the mountains and eat us out, and then left for eastern Kansas and Missouri, and would have eaten you out, too, had the season been longer." I asked him what he supposed was the average yield per acre of wheat, oats and barley. "Wheat," said he, "taking all that receives respectable cultivation, will yield on an average of thirty-five bushels per acre. But, by the best cultivation, this can be increased from twenty to thirty bushels more per acre. A premium field of five acres averaged seventy-one bushels per acre. Oats and barley," he said, "would yield from 90 to 120 bushels per acre; corn, ordinarily, about thirty-five bushels, but as high as eighty bushels has been attained.

Meadows will yield two and a half to three tons per acre, but the hay is not of the first quality." But this is the case everywhere. No hay of prime quality is made anywhere, where the growth is rank. I examined some timothy (*Phleum pratense*) that had spikes from six to eight inches long, and was coarse in haum in proportion; and this is the cause of its inferior quality. There is a wild timothy in the mountain parks which I did not see, which is said to yield heavily and to make a better hay than the tame on the plains below. It may prove indentical with the *Phleum alpinum*, found on the White Mountains in New Hampshire, and on the mountains of Europe.

It will thus be seen that though the natural climate of Colorado is such that agricultural pursuits, for lack of moisture, could not be conducted successfully, yet wherever the soil can be irrigated the agriculturist is practically independent of the weather. In its season the sun pours down a flood of light and heat from an intensely blue sky, and through a perfectly transparent atmosphere. Though the clouds withhold their rain, yet their remissness is retrieved by the abundant water that flows from the melted snows which the mountains collect during the winter. No worm or other insect devours the succulent grain, while growing, nor is it ever smitten by blight, an abundant harvest therefore never fails to reward the agriculturist, nor is there little variation in quantity and none in quality.

All this is indisputably true; but still the picture is too highly colored. There are some drawbacks, which are patent to every close observer. In the first place, when the water is withdrawn the soil becomes as hard as a brick, and there is no stirring it until the rains and winter frosts have mellowed it again. For this reason, but little winter wheat is or can be sown unless there are heavy rains in the latter part of summer, which is sometimes the case. Then, the waters coming from the melted snows in the mountains, only 20 miles distant, and from the short time it takes them, because of the rapidity of their descent, are yet intensely cold when they reach the plains. Hence there is an unevenness in the ripening of the grain, the coldness of the water keeping back a strip just below every ditch, while that portion of the field which receives water that has flowed over a considerable surface and become warmed, comes earlier to maturity. But the coldness of the water is the most serious drawback in irrigating corn, which is a lover of heat. This is partially overcome by letting the water flow over a considerable extent of plain or pasture land until it has become warmed, and then gather it into ditches again and apply it to the corn. But the fact is, corn can be raised about as well without as with irrigation, and sometimes, in favorable seasons, produces crops fully as heavy as the average crop in Missouri.

It must also be stated that occasionally there occurs a season when the rains are sufficient to mature all crops without irrigation. Thus in 1868 the irrigating canals were not opened at all. A season of thunder-storms commencing in the mountains in June and continuing to September, often extends to the plains along the foot of the mountains. Then corn yields an abundant crop.

Spring wheat is almost universally raised; but the flour and bread made of it have no resemblance to those of spring wheat in the States. The flour contains less gluten, and consequently is not sticky like flour made of spring wheat in the States. The bread made of it is as white as that of the choicest St. Louis brands; and then it is so light and spongy. I actually believe it also has medicinal properties. Why should it not? The soil on which it grows, when the water is withdrawn, becomes encrusted with the carbonate of soda, white as if a flurry of snow had passed over it. Cattle lick this crystalized soda, and never need to be salted; in fact, they will turn up their noses, if you offer them salt, and walk away. Soda springs and lakes abound throughout the mountain region; and since the soil on the Plains is almost exclusively formed of *debris* from the disentegrated rocks of the mountains, it is peculiarly rich in phosphates of lime, soda and potash. The grain that grows upon such a soil must partake richly in these phosphates, especially that of soda. Hence the chemical action taking place between the soda and the gastric juice must give rise to electric currents in the system.

Since then the Colorado Fair has been held at Denver, and the Boulder county, at Boulder; the following amongst other awards were made: At Denver to John G. Lilly, of Arapahoe county, in which Denver is situated, first premium for largest yield per acre of wheat, on entire farm. Amount of acreage being 90 acres, yield 4,968 1-2 bushels, or a fraction over 55 bushels per acre.

At Boulder, for best field of corn raised in Boulder county; first premium to M. G. Smith, being 70 bushels, less 19 pounds, to the acre. Second premium, Mr. Walker, 64 bushels to the acre.

First premium for largest yield of potatoes per acre to David Hersham, being a fraction over 305 bushels to the acre. Seventeen of these potatoes made a bushel by weight. First premium for best half-dozen beets, to G. F. Chase, the average circumference being 31 inches each.

The best half-dozen heads of cabbage; first premium to Mr. Smith; average weight of each head being 54 1-4 pounds. The rival competitor's average was 53 1-2 pounds per head.

The extent of arable lands is the limit to which irrigation can be carried. How far east of the South Platte this may be done I am unable to say definitely, but so far as the supply of water holds out. Between the Platte and the mountains there extends a triangular plain from the debouchure on the plains of the Cache a la Poudre to that of the South Platte, whose longest side along the foot of the mountains is about 90 miles. From the mouth of the Platte canyon until it receives the Cache a la Poudre the distance is about 80 miles. The course of the latter stream from the time it leaves the mountains until it meets the Platte is about 40 miles. The following are the mountain streams proceeding south from the Cache a la Poudre in the order in which they occur: Big Thompson, a tributary of the Platte; Little Thompson, a tributary of Big Thompson; St. Vrain's Fork, a tributary of the Platte; Left Hand Creek; and then Boulder, both tributaries of the St. Vrain; South Boulder, a tributary of Boulder; Coal Creek, a tributary of South Boulder; Clear Creek, a tributary of the Platte; and finally Bear Creek, which falls into the Platte above Denver. Besides these there are numerous branches which issue from mountain gulches, but whose sources measurably fail before the summer is over.

This triangle included between the mountains and the Platte covers an area of about 1,800,000 acres of land, four-fifths, at least, of which can be irrigated; and the whole is one of the most desirable grazing regions in the world. To substantiate this I quote from Professor Hayden's United States Geological Report of 1869, page 144:

"Snow sometimes, though rarely, reaches a depth of twelve inches; yet it passes off as rapidly as it comes, seldom remaining longer than twenty-four hours. Even in the valleys which penetrate the first range of mountains in the northern section this is the case. Some winters but little snow falls during the entire season. As conclusive evidence of this statement, cattle are herded out during the entire winter in all parts of the Territory, such a thing as preparation for winter feeding being almost wholly unknown. And yet in the spring they will come out in as good order as those of the States which have been housed and fed day by day. The Mexican horses, or *bronchos*, will also winter out during the winter like the cattle."

This, however, is only true of the plain immediately along the base of the mountains, say a strip from 15 to 20 miles wide. Lower down on the Plains, it does not always hold good. There are exceptionally cold winters, when the depth of the snow and the intense cold are fatal to stock unless fed and sheltered.

The herds in Boulder county are not very large, ranging from 400 to 1500 head. Wm. A. Corson, the President of the Boulder County Agricultural Association, is one of the principal stock raisers in the county.

It will be seen, from what is said elsewhere, that those vast parks, formed of the table-land on the summit of the mountains, possess an agricultural value that cannot as yet be estimated. That they are admirably adapted for dairying purposes there is no question. Butter made there, in quantity, quality and delicacy of flavor, surpasses that of the famous land of Goshen. They are also well adapted for stock-raising. Hay, oats, barley, rye and even wheat can be raised in all of them notwithstanding their great altitude above the level of the sea. Of hay, oats, turnips and cabbage, no country yields more abundantly, area for area, than the three most elevated of these parks. Their value for agricultural purposes was early acknowledged, not because their soil was richer and more productive than that of the mountain lands east of the Snowy Range, but because their lands lay in compact bodies; while those of the elevated mountain plains east of the Snowy Range are broken up and dissevered by sporadic peaks, and cleft asunder by gulches, deep chasms and impassable canyons. The difference in the quality of the soil, if any, is in favor of the mountain lands. It is no unusual thing to find a black soil of *humus* or vegetable mould from four to six inches thick underlaid by a rich subsoil of ochreous clay. Notwithstanding the broken character of the mountain table-land, fully one-fourth of it is arable, and three-fourths of the remainder is well adapted for grazing purposes both for sheep and cows. This is contrary to the generally received public opinion, but it is nevertheless true. Potatoes of the largest size, weighing as much as four pounds apiece, and of the best quality can be raised on these hills and mountain plains without irrigation. The yield often approximates 300 bushels to the acre, which is larger than is generally obtained in the rich prairie lands of the Valley of the Mississippi.

These lands indeed are often rough, but I have seen thousands of acres cultivated in the Eastern States not only rougher and steeper, but poorer and far stonier than these.

CHAPTER XII.

Colorado seems to be regarded as a favorable ground for trying colonial experiments. I heard, while there, of no less than three locating committees that were exploring the Territory for the most favorable location for a colony. One of these represented a Boston colony, another a Western, and still another a Tennessee colony. I have not heard whether they have finally fixed upon their sites, or at what conclusion they have arrived.

To those affected by this colonizing mania, and who think of acting a personal part in carrying out such a scheme, I would address the admonition,

"'Tis distance lends enchantment to the view."

The most rugged landscape viewed from afar looks charming and roseate, but it is otherwise when we meet face to face the stern realities of Nature. Then the path that promised to lead easily and gently over a smooth and level plain, shaded by trees, enameled by flowers and enlivened by the songs of birds, is found to be rugged, obstructed by rocks and floods, full of yawning chasms and insurmountable precipices, a real "howling wilderness," the roaming ground of the wolf, the tiger, the panther and the bear, exacting resolution, energy, courage and daring to make way through it successfully. So it is with these colony schemes. It would be a nice thing if a hundred or a thousand persons of small means, but large hearts and noble aspirations, could locate upon a territory now of no intrinsic value, and to all of which their very presence would give a marketable value of ten, fifty, or even a hundred dollars an acre. How easily and rapidly people would then pass from straitened circumstances to competence, and even affluence.

There is no doubt that after years of patient endurance, and hoping against hope in many instances, this will be the case, but the sanguine colonists see all this realized at once, without any trial of waiting and tiring of patience; with no hardships to be borne, nor any privations to be endured. He supposes that in a new country labor is scarce, and therefore must be in demand, and that the products of his industry and skill will find a ready market. All this is a delusion which sad experience will dispel. If a vacancy for a colony, with all these advantages, could be found in the heart of a civilized community, all these dreams and expectations would be speedily realized; but out on the vast Plains, surrounded by a domain only inhabited by the wolf, the cayote, roaming beasts of prey and wild animals, and where the only towns and villages are those of the prairie dog, the conditions forbid such instant realization. There a man with the inventive genius of a Watt or Fulton, with strong arms, willing mind, and skillful hands, is practically reduced to inaction, because there is no use for their skill or talents and no demand for any article they can produce. Such a community necessarily is without money because it produces nothing that brings money; and all cash that accidentally finds its way there is sent abroad to obtain necessaries. Trade within the community is thus reduced to bartering and its industry diverted to doing "chores." Such ever has been and always must be the case of isolated communities beyond the pale of civilization. Greeley now is an example that may be quoted both for proof and illustration. It started with seventeen stores and no customers except the colonists. These for a while may have had money brought with them, but when that was exhausted none came in to supply its place, because nothing was produced that commanded money, and there is as yet no market or anything that can be produced.

Even in the new mining communities of the mountains the same evils are felt, but not in such an aggravated form. They produce something that has a commercial value in the markets of the world; but it is only the prime article they can make available; and from that they hardly realize more than one-half of its intrinsic value. The other half is absorbed by expenses in taking it to market, and by middle men. Take Caribou for illustration; it has the richest silver lode in the Territory—in fact, one of the richest ever discovered in America; and the whole mountain seems to be argentiferous. There are now more than one hundred lodes opened that would, at localities provided with proper facilities, be sources of immense wealth to their owners. These lodes could furnish three hundred tons of ore a week, that will on an average, assay $80 to the ton. But as the locality is isolated and too new for reduction works, they have to carry their ore, the richest only bearing the expense, twenty-two miles to a smelting furnace, where they receive just what the proprietor of the works chooses to give them. Thus that community is working along and kept from stagnation, hoping and praying for better times. Yet if they had reduction works, the mines now open would furnish ore that would yield at least $35,000 in silver per week, besides the gold, copper and lead. Now, perhaps, a thousand dollars is the limit received per week by the miners in that locality, which is only about 40 per cent. of the actual value of the ores sold. Then this community, while its labor is actually adding $2,500 per week to the wealth of the world, does so at an expense to itself of $1,500. Not only so, but the labor there that would add from $40,000 to $50,000 per week to the common wealth, is idle and unemployed from necessity. New discoveries carrying only ores of a low grade, but rich enough to pay the expense of opening them and leave a margin to the miner besides, are left undeveloped, because these low grade ores are without value under present circumstances.

The great Comstock lode of Nevada has yielded upwards of one hundred million dollars of bullion, yet the average yield of its ores does not exceed twenty-five dollars per ton. Why has it been so productive and profitable? Simply because San Francisco capitalists provided reducing works, which have enriched both the miners and themselves. Now, furnish the new discoveries at Caribou, hardly a year old yet, with facilities for reducing all classes of ores that will pay for reducing, and Boulder county in one year will have one thousand lodes that will furnish ores as rich as that yielded by the famous Comstock lode, which has enriched all connected with it.*

These facts make it clear that colonists, whatever the object of their settlement may be, should be either well provided with cash to last till the advent of their expected golden age, which will only be when civilization overtakes them, or that they should fix definitely the main pursuit to which their industry is to be directed, and go provided with all the appliances and appointments to insure success.

The want of foresight to foresee the inexorable conditions of isolated communities, and hence of providing for meeting them, now press heavily upon the colonists of Colorado, and is the cause of that dissatisfaction, bickering and crimination which more or less prevail in all of them.

I make these remarks because there is scarcely a State east of the Mississippi but has colonization schemes, and is excited by colony excitements. In fact colonization schemes are now the rage, and the rage intensifies as time advances. I give results as developed in Colorado; and volunteer unwelcome but wholesome advice to those about

---

*This estimate is not mine but is that of an experienced miner, perfectly familiar with the silver mines of Nevada, Utah and Colorado. My opinion is, the estimate is too low.

entering upon such enterprises. Then if we must have such enterprises, and as they are forewarned of what they have to expect, and of the stern realities that will confront them when they get there, let them go prepared to meet the exigencies that must arise, and overcome in the shortest time possible the obstacles in the way of success.

I have already sufficiently spoken of Greeley to give an idea of the condition of things there. On the South Platte, some twenty-five miles below Greeley, and below the island in the river covered with cottonwood, known as "Fremont's Orchard," is the location of the Southwestern Colony. It was initiated at Memphis, but its members are from Tennessee, Kentucky, Ohio, Indiana and Illinois. Its town has been named Greensboro, in honor of its chief projector and patron, Col. D. S. Green, now a citizen of Denver, a gentleman well and favorably known in Colorado. Lost Spring debouches into the Platte just above the town site. Its valley, about two and a half miles wide, has a soil of deep alluvial loam, as light and pliable as an ash heap, covered with a most luxuriant growth of a peculiar kind of perennial grass, resembling, it is said, the famous blue grass of Kentucky. At least 15,000 acres of this valley need no irrigation, and the same may be said of thousands of acres of the Platte bottom. The broad expanse of uplands away from the streams furnish excellent and unlimited range for pasturage; and the colonists are principally engaged as yet in stock-raising. Of their condition, progress and prospects I could learn nothing. From the articles of association I ascertained that the organization of this colony is different from most of the others located in Colorado. There are no restrictions or obligations imposed on its members, no communism, nor co-operative interests provided for. Each member has to pay a moderate fee of membership—one hundred dollars—which entitles him to special rates of transportation to the colonial site, a share in the division of the town property, and such other privileges as inhere in similar organizations. Each one is then left free to make his own selection of vocation, and to pre-empt lands, claim as homestead or otherwise, as he may elect. There is a railroad talked of to run from Boulder, by way of Longmont, Greeley and Greensboro, down the valley of the South Platte, to connect with the Union Pacific railroad at or near the mouth of the stream. In that case, the colony may become a thrifty settlement.

In the spring of 1870 there was organized a German colony at Chicago, under the leadership of Col. Carl Wuesten. This colony made almost as much noise in the world as did the Greeley, or more properly, the Union colony. It found its way into the high valley of the Sierra Mojada (wet mountains), in Pueblo and Fremont counties, in the southern part of the territory. The valley is south of Canyon City, located at the mouth of the canyon of the Arkansas, which there breaks through its mountain barrier and passes upon the plain. The valley is shut in by spurs of the mountain ranges. It is well watered, abundantly supplied with timber and has excellent and extensive beds of bituminous coal.

There is a good deal of disaffection in this colony, and charges of corruption and dishonesty have been made against some of the prominent men of the organization. Some members have left in disgust; and in conversation with them both at Denver and Boulder, they represented the elevation so great and the valleys hemmed in by bleak mountains, that most of the crops fail to mature before the frost nips them.

I have no doubt that much of this is exaggeration, proceeding from disappointed expectations. My own observations rather would discredit the statement of the failure of the crop in consequence of elevation. I saw as thrifty potatoes as I ever saw, in the upper part of the canyon of the Boulder, at least 9000 feet above the sea, and was told that the average yield was upwards of 200 bushels to the acre. Hill's ranche, on the North Boulder, about three miles east of Caribou, yields him $5,000 net profit from hay and vegetables, and he says winter wheat can be successfully cultivated there. There are three ranches, Orvis', Jones' and De Land's, all within five miles of Caribou, and at an elevation of nearly 10,000 feet, which are extremely profitable to the proprietors, who make a business of raising hay and vegetables, and who have never sustained any serious loss from frosts and storms. In Gilpin county, south, and also at the foot of the Snowy Range, Hall & Banta's ranche has averaged them $19,000 profit per annum from 62 acres, chiefly in potatoes, turnips, cabbage, and other vegetables. Then the success of Queen, Cochran, Hickox, Conner, etc., are well known facts. Therefore, I think the statement of frost destroying the crops in a more southern latitude, and most probably at a lower elevation, must be taken with many grains of allowance.

There is another of these colonies, yet in its infancy, located in Boulder county, about 15 miles northeast of Boulder city. It is called the Chicago Colorado colony. We had an invitation to visit their location, but we had no time for that purpose. Their town, located about a mile north of the village of Burlington, is called Longmont. I think the location the best of any colony in the territory, since it is contiguous to the mountains, where it must eventually find a market for its products, and adjacent to the settlements that extend along the mountain range the entire width of the territory. It is convenient to coal both at Erie and Boulder; is supplied with lumber from the mountains, and is well watered. It has selected and obtained control of about 60,000 acres of land lying longitudinally across the valleys of the Boulder, Left Hand, Little Thompson and St. Vrain's Fork. The soil is as good as any in the territory, has all needed facilities for irrigation, good water power, and being so near the mountains has fine scenery; the snowy crest of Long's Peak rises majestically above the surrounding peaks, almost due west. It will, from its location perhaps, realize its expectations in a shorter time, and with the endurance of less privations and hardships than any colony in the territory.

The colony only commenced its agricultural operations in the spring of the present year. It sowed considerable wheat, to what extent I did not learn; it has constructed many of the principal irrigating canals, and was busy in building. A Mrs. E. Thompson, a wealthy lady from New York, made the colony a donation of forty thousand dollars for purchasing a library, and she had a building put up that cost her five thousand dollars more to put the library in. Some of our party that stopped at Greeley met her there on her way to Longmont on a visit; she came over to Boulder to join our party in our excursion up the canyon, but arrived too late, and went on to Denver. It will be remembered that there is also a colony at Evans, four miles from Greeley, of which I could learn nothing, except what I saw, and my impressions have already been given.

From the altitude of Colorado a rigorous climate would be inferred. The plains in the eastern portion of the Territory, along the State lines of Kansas and Nebraska, are more than 4000 feet above the sea. At Denver the elevation exceeds 5100 feet, and along the mountains it is 6000 feet and upward. Between the Snowy Range and the Plains there is a gradual ascent; the table-land attaining an elevation on an average of a little over 8000 feet. The North, Middle and South parks, encircled by the Snowy Range, have an altitude of about 9000 feet on an average, while the highest peaks attain an altitude of from 14,000 to 15,000 feet. It is claimed that Mount Lincoln is 17,500 feet; and Silver Heels 17,000 feet above tide water. The elevation at which timber ceases to grow, "timber-line," as it is called, is various; on the Eastern slope it is 11,800 feet; on the Western, 11,300, and on the isolated peaks it is over 12,000 feet.

Scientists have given us mathematical formulas for determining climate from altitude. It is unnecessary to state these formulas, and the reasoning by which they have been arrived at. It answers every purpose by merely stating that in them, it is assumed that an elevation of every two hundred feet above the level of the sea deteriorates a climate as much as the displacement of the locality of one degree of latitude from the equator towards the pole would do.*

Now, while these formulas may give approximate results when applied to the Atlantic coast and to Europe, yet, when applied to the continental plain and mountain system of Colorado they give results so egregiously erroneous as to show their utter worthlessness for that purpose.

I have already stated that in no way do our Eastern standards of comparison serve us when applied to Nature's operations in this great mountain system, and these scientific formulas prove the truth of the assertion. According to deductions drawn from them, the table-land of the Cordilleras would have the climate of northern Greenland, and the Plains along their foot even more rigorous than that of the coast of Labrador. But observation has established it as an incontrovertible fact that the Plains along the mountains in Colorado have the climate of the same latitude along the Atlantic coast, and that the climate of the most elevated table-lands of the mountains corresponds with that of three degrees higher latitude on the Atlantic sea-board.

Another error in regard to the climate of Colorado is that its aridity is owing to the want of precipitation. Now, the fact is, the amount of annual precipitation on the mountain is nearly thirty-four inches, and that of the Plains a fraction over twenty. The aridity, therefore, is due to other causes than want of precipitation. First it takes more vapor under a given pressure to saturate a *rare* than

---

*See article, CLIMATE, in Cyclopedia of Physical Sciences.

a *dense* atmosphere; great elevation, producing rarity of atmosphere, is, therefore, the controlling cause, since it not only rarifies the air, but reduces also the boiling point. I ascertained at Caribou that the boiling point of water, that is total evaporation, was 191.8 degrees Fahrenheit, while on the seashore it is 212 degrees. Now, since water evaporates at all temperatures, even when frozen, therefore, in the elevated regions of Colorado, a given amount of water, at any degree of temperature, evaporates as much as the same quantity does at the seashore with a temperature twenty degrees higher. Consequently vegetable and animal substances are more speedily desiccated there than in less elevated regions. Hence it is that fresh meats hung up in the free air never putrify, but dry up sweet. Hence, also, there is so little decay of animal and vegetable substance that no noxious effluvia arises from the one, nor miasma from the other. To the aridity of its climate Colorado owes its remarkable exemption from all kinds of bilious diseases. The thermometer often in Denver indicates a greater heat by five degrees than we experience in the trough of the Mississippi Valley. Yet sunstrokes are unknown; because it is impossible for a dry atmosphere to become sultry, sweltering, smothering and oppressive. It matters not how warm it is, the air is always elastic and exhilarating, because evaporation is constant from our bodies. Climate unquestionably exerts an immeasurable influence on every living organism in both the animal and vegetable kingdom. To a nation of invalids, (for such we must be taken to be, if our sanitary condition is measured by the amount of medicine we consume), it will be welcome news to be told that within our own borders there is a climate that produces almost as marvelous effects as the Spanish cavaliers expected to realize from the fabled Fountain of Youth which they sought in vain in the malarious fens and bogs of Florida. The influence of this atmosphere is remarkable, as is testified by general experience. It is entirely free from humidity, wonderfully clear, exhilarating and health inspiring. Mists and fogs, except when rain and snow are falling, are unknown. The absence of clouds, the clear intensely blue sky, and a brilliant sunshine are remarkable, the year round. Colorado has a wide spread celebrity already for releaving and curing tubercular and pulmonary affections, general debility, scrofula, dispepsia, asthma, bronchitis, enlargement of the liver, splenetic diseases, etc., and not without cause, for at least one-third of her present population are reconstructed individuals.

Dyspeptics soon recover their lost power of assimilation and become vigorous and more robust than ever. There are many there who had been afflicted with bronchitis and other throat affections, who had tried Minnesota, the West Indies, California and sea voyages without effect; who, as a final resort, took up their sojourn in Colorado, and are now sound and well. Consumptives who come here before the ravages of the disease have wasted the recuperative vital energy, almost certainly recover; others become comparatively comfortable, even regaining a considerable degree of vigor. Many, however, come too late, that is in the last stages of the disease. In such cases a crisis ensues at once, followed in a few days or weeks by a fatal termination. The cause of this is self-evident. They are brought here from a dense atmosphere in which all the demands of vitality are satisfied by using from one-half to two-thirds of the capacity of their lungs, while here in this rarified air the full capacity of every lung cell is taxed, and then cannot satisfy the demand; for to make up the deficiency the respiration is accelerated fifty per cent, that is, from sixteen to twenty-four times per minute. The full inflation of lungs and the accelerated motion must produce ruptures in diseased cells, hence the fatal crisis that speedily ensues. Before railroads penetrated here, when it took thirty to forty days to make the journey, more desperate cases were cured than now; because the strain on the lungs, caused by the increasing rarity of the air, was so gradual that the slight lesions had time to heal. I would therefore give this advice to all consumptives: Make the journey by easy stages; say first stop over ten days or more at Abilene, Salina or Brookville on the Kansas Pacific, all of which points are from 1,000 to 1,200 feet above the sea. Then, if no unfavorable symptoms have made their appearance, go to Hays, nearly 1,000 feet higher; thence to Wallace, some 1,200 feet higher still; thence to Kit Carson, about 1,000 feet higher than Wallace; thence to some of the towns at the foot of the mountains; and not to ascend the mountains until a decided improvement has intervened. By following these suggestions, many will be permanently cured, others relieved, who would rush in the very jaws of death if they go there at once, as many now do, as fast as steam can carry them, which is in about two days from the Mississippi.

It is now generally conceded by physicians and physiologists that the phosphates possess great medicinal value in the treatment of tubercular and other diseases involving enfeebled vital functions. The soil on the Plains, adjacent to the mountains, is the *detritus* of feldspar disintegrating slowly, through myriads of years on the mountains, and carried down and deposited by floods. The constituent elements of feldspar, which is a silcate, are silex, soda, lime, potassium, magnesia, etc. Hence, the soil is rich in these alkalies. In fact the first crop of wheat, raised in some localities, was so much embued with alkaline matter that the flour made of it would effervesce with an acid and would almost make "suds" by adding lard and water; and the bread could not be eaten at all.

Dr. Chambers, an eminent English physician, in his lectures on the "Renewal of Life," gives this sensible rule on this subject:

"In choosing a home for your consumptive, do not mind the average hight of the thermometer, or its variations; do not trouble yourself about the mean rain-fall; do not be scientific at all; but find out from somebody's journal how many days were fine enough to go out forenoon and afternoon. That is the test you require, and by that you may be confidently guided."

Judged by this standard Colorado is one of the most favored spots on the earth for a home of the consumptive. There is not a score of days in any year that invalids may not sit out of doors, ride or walk forenoon or afternoon without any discomfort. Then the nights are always cool so as to ensure refreshing sleep, an essential condition for the restoration of shattered nervous systems and broken down constitutions.

Another favorable condition is the dryness of the atmosphere. There is no such thing as "damp night air." There is no "taking cold" if you sleep with doors and windows wide open summer and winter. Invalids can sleep on the open plains or mountain recesses, wrapped in a pair of blankets without incurring any risk. The new, varied and sublime scenery inspires to activity, and the pure exhilerating air and mild climate invite to outdoor life. In obeying these impulses lies the great secret of the many wonderful cures a residence here has effected.

CHAPTER XIII.

The founding of new communities on the frontier of civilization, whether done individually or collectively, is accomplished at the sacrifice of temporary ease and comfort. The hardships and privations it imposes are longer or shorter in duration as the location has been judiciously made with regard to favorable surroundings. A main point is to secure a location in the direction that the current of migration is strongly tending; and the next point is not to make it too far in advance, unless overruling considerations determine it otherwise. Immigration can very aptly be compared to the movements of those large flocks of wild pigeons in their migrations from higher to lower latitudes and *vice versa*. Invading a grain field, the rear is constantly flying over to the front. Therefore the front soon becomes the rear, and the field in a short time is cleanly picked over and crossed. Settlers on the frontier of Kansas and Nebraska, that this year are locating just in front where the last year's wave of migration expended itself, by next year find that the new wave has swept over and beyond them, and now rolls on thirty or forty miles ahead. In a year or so more, they will find themselves so far in the rear that they are no longer able to tell how far and to what point the front line has advanced.

In that time they will, however, find that the condition of their community is improving; and that surrounding circumstances are more favorable. In fact they find that prosperity is dawning upon them. Five or six years more and they find themselves surrounded by all the comforts and amenities of long established and consolidated communities.

Immigration is rapidly filling up Colorado, but there is no onward wave there at present, rising higher and higher, and rolling farther West every year, much less a reflex wave coming back on the Plains. The gold and silver regions, the coves and parks of the mountains, and the plains immediately along their base, are the objective points first attracting immigrants, for reasons that in all ages have swayed and determined the migrations of mankind.

In migrating, man's physical wants are always the paramount considerations that govern him. His first and absolute necessities everywhere are food and raiment. Hence he is impelled to select the locality where these are to be found; or where the means for procuring them can be obtained. He may safely undertake to cultivate the soil if he have a reserve to draw upon, until the soil has time to remunerate him for the capital and toil expended upon it. After that it will supply his bare necessities. But luxuries, and even comforts, must remain in abeyance, not only until he has a surplus of productions, but a market for that surplus. Agricultural products are too bulky to bear the expense of transportation over long distances; therefore in remote and isolated communities the demand for them is limited to supplying the deficiency in the community itself. The outside trader or merchant shuns such communities, not because his wares are not wanted or needed there, but because he cannot make available for his purposes what he has to take in exchange for them.

But if the precious metals are discovered anywhere, it matters not what long journeys they have to make, what deserts to be passed, what mountain precipices to be scaled, what dangers to be encountered, and what hardships to be endured, the merchant and trader are there almost as soon as the miner. He is not only there with the bare necessities, but with the luxuries and comforts of civilized life, for all to indulge in who can afford the means. The pioneer to Colorado therefore knows the shortest way for him to provide for the wants and comforts of himself and family, is to delve into these mountains and bring up the precious metals.

But the mountains are not a total barren waste of rocks and precipices; for large areas are covered with the luscious buffalo grass; and the dells and coves are decked with the living green of the wild timothy and blue grass. The settlers bring in domestic animals; milk and butter and cheese dairies spring up to supply the wants of the mining towns and camps. And such butter as is made here! Ah! the dwellers in the trough of the Mississippi Valley, can have no conception what a luxury sweet, delicious and aromatic butter is.

The mountain dells are also well adapted to the growth of oats, hay and garden vegetables, especially turnips and cabbage, which grow to an enormous size. All these find ready sale and at highly remunerative prices in the mining camps, as has been stated more particularly elsewhere. I was told by old mountaineers that there was more money in a good hay or vegetable ranche, than in any *placer* in the mountains. This certainly has been the case, as many of these ranchemen have realized comfortable fortunes by their business; but the extension of railroads into the mountains will interfere with their large profits by bringing them in competition with the ranchemen on the Plains.

The Plains along the base of the mountains are selected by settlers for special, as well as for general reasons. They are admirably adapted for raising all kinds of stock to supply the wants of the mountain settlements. They are extremely fertile, and as we have seen, unequaled for raising the cerials, either as to quantity and quality. Land near the mountains, besides its contiguity to the only real market that ever will be there, is more desirable and valuable than land more remote. They are not only nearer to an abundance of water, and, therefore, easily and cheaply irrigated, but the climate is far milder and more equable than farther off, down on the Plains. From 10 to 15 miles along the base of the mountains, stock, nine years out of ten, have no need either of shelter or provender during the winter, making their own living and thriving on the dried buffalo grass, the natural hay of the Plains.

Lower down on the Plains, in proportion as you recede from the mountains, the snow falls deeper, lies longer on the ground, and the cold is severer. Stock has not only to be housed but provender provided to feed with during the time that the Plains are covered with snow. There are exceptional seasons when this is not absolutely necessary, but generally it would be disastrous not to be provided to meet such contingencies.

The reasons are therefore very plain why immigration flows into the mountains, or spreads settlements only along their base. When railroads, as they will before many years, once penetrate and pierce through these mountains, as they are metaliferous through their entire breadth, settlements will rapidly extend farther West, until the remaining gap is closed, and the westward tide of migration that has flowed from time immemorial will cease forever. A reflex wave recoiling from the mountains and rolling eastward, has yet scarcely commenced. It never will have much impetus, and will move slowly and cautiously. The obstacles to settlement on the Plains east of the Platte are truly formidable. The most serious are the want of living streams, for Stock and irrigation in summer; and the severity and long continuance of the winters. To remedy the first evil, it is said that the Kansas Pacific Railroad Company, who own millions of acres on these Plains, has it in contemplation to carry the waters of the South Platte from the mouth of the canyon where they debouch upon the Plains, in a canal eastward to the head springs of the Smoky Hill. This is entirely feasible, but whether it can be done compatible with the rights and interests of settlers on the Platte below, is a serious question.

This is a remote and almost unknown region. Though considerable has been written and published about it of a general character, yet nothing specific enough to enable anyone to form a definite idea of its capabilities, natural resources, soil and climate. Ample reasons therefore exist for giving these minute details. It is performing a good service to those contemplating settling here, to furnish them with reliable facts as to the inducements held out here to immigrants, and what are the influences here determining locations of settlements. In order that they may be enabled to select their location judiciously, I have endeavored to furnish them with a survey of the whole field in advance. My sole object is to benefit those going into the territory whether for pleasure, recreation, health or settlement. I have no object in view, and no interests to subserve except those of truth. As far as the modes of settlement are concerned, truth does not permit me to speak very flatteringly of the colonies established here. How could I, when it is notorious that great dissatisfaction exists in nearly all of them. Charges of mismanagement, corruption, selfishness, with crimination and re-crimination are rife in nearly all of them. I have not assumed to judge who, if any one, is in fault; prefering the more charitable course, to attribute their internal condition to the inherent viciousness of the system which is not adapted to the condition of things here. However, the manager of one of these colonies has taken offence at my remarks as applied to his colony; and in one of the leading papers in the territory charged that favorable reports could be had of all itinerant scribblers, if they would take charge of them, give them free lunch and plenty of whisky; adding, that to do the latter would be difficult, since there was not a place in town where it was sold. I now publish this as an important fact and one which I could not have discovered in a year's exploration; my investigations not tending in that direction. I think it however entirely reliable, for other "itinerant scribblers" have been there since, and state it to be a fact, but in compensation, for its absence, medicine for curing snake bites is plenty, and answers just as well.

I now repeat the advice to all desiring to go to Colorado for settlement, go alone, be your own colony, free to go where you please and to exercise your own judgment when you get there, so that you may select the location best adapted to your purpose or pursuit. If you go with a colony, you cannot do this. You have to locate where it locates, spend your money in providing shelter for yourself and family; and when that is done find your exchequer exhausted, and without remunerative employment to keep the ravenous wolf of hunger from your door Away from the mountains, your colony is at a disadvantage in getting a market for its products, or of transporting them where there is a market. Besides the colony affording no great diversity in pursuits its productions will be small and chiefly of one kind glutting the little market there is. But, in the vicinity of the mines, or in the towns whence the miners draw their supplies, there is a demand for all kinds of fabrics and productions. Tillers of the soil are wanted as well as miners, metallurgists, machinists, experts in the different operations and treatment to which the ores in process of reduction must be subjected. Here artificers in wood, in stone, iron, brass, clay, hides, leather, wool and lint are all in demand, to carry on the industrial machinery. Like elsewhere, some localities are better than others for particular pursuits. All that is necessary is that the adventurer is free to select, from all the localities offering, the one best calculated for the success of his particular business. This is my advice, and I believe it to be the surest and safest that can be given. It is, however, optional with each immigrant to follow it, or not, as his judgment may determine when he gets there. But let him go untrammelled.

CHAPTER XIV.

Animal life depends upon plant life; and plant life upon the presence of a proper plant food in the soil. Plants, like animals of different genera, feed upon different kinds of food. Some subsist entirely upon mineral matter, some require both mineral and vegetable food; and another class, the epiphytes, depend entirely upon decomposed vegetable matter. The first class will thrive anywhere, under favorable conditions, where mineral substances alone are present. Not only so, but they have the faculty of decomposing crude mineral matter containing their food, if it be not free. The most primative forms of plants belong to this class.

The higher order of plants, in so far as they depend on mineral food, must have it free in the soil, because they have not the ability to decompose rocks. Neither have they the faculty of decomposing vegetable and animal matter; therefore this part of their food must also be free in the soil, already decomposed, stored up and subject to their draft in such quantities as they may need to perform their function in Nature's economy.

Of epiphytes and other parasitic plants, it is not necessary to speak here, since we have no purpose of writing a general treatise upon plants, and the variety of their food, but only of making some brief remarks upon favorable conditions, for abundantly growing those absolutely essential to man. These may be termed the omnivorous class, since they can flourish only where there are abundant stores of decomposed matter, mineral, animal and vegetable, laid up for them. A little reflection reveals the fact that they comprise grasses, grains, fruits, etc.; in fact all plants that serve for food to animals, and which man has to produce to sustain his herds, his flocks and himself.

It is evident that every crop he produces, makes a draft upon the different kind of plant food stored up in the soil. If he removes the crop from the field on which it grew, he impoverishes the soil to the extent of the draft made by the crop upon its stores; and lessens its ability to meet subsequent demands upon it. This reveals a necessity imposed upon man, to make restitution in some way of the amount withdrawn, and to keep up ample deposites in bank, or his drafts will come back dishonored.

To keep a sufficient surplus on deposite, and of the right kind of funds, are serious questions which have vexed man ever since he became a waster of stores in other respects than in terra-culture. Plants do not relish indifferently all minerals, but each kind of plant affects particular minerals, and must have a full supply to meet its wants, or it will fail to accomplish the task assigned to it, or expected of it. Some plants demand salicates, others carbonates, while others must have phosphates and others again sulphates. The problem therefore is a complicated one which demands a solution from the farmer, even when viewed only from the mineral standpoint; while it is no less complicated while viewed from the standpoint of vegetable and animal manures. Worse than all is the fact, that whatever may be claimed for Agricultural Chemistry, it is entirely unable to aid him to determine, whether all the elements of fertility are present in the soil, and in the exact proportions necessary to satisfy the demands of his various crops.

I do not subscribe to the doctrine that soil leaches except the surplus of saturation; for Nature is all harmony. There is the most cordial relations and amenity between her ordinate and co-ordinate departments, between organic and inorganic substances, and between dead and living matter, for Nature has ordained them to be inter-dependent. The soil as the harbinger of the plant, most kindly prepares the way in laying up stores for it, and by an inexorable law holds them till the plant, the only proper claimant, appears. Therefore wherever there is a point where there is a surplus of plant food accumulating over and above what can be stored away, whether mineral or vegetable, it becomes the radiant point from which the elements of fertility depart to be distributed. Since water is the most efficient agent in effecting this distribution, therefore the radiant point should be the summit and sides of a watershed, the sources and fountains of brooks and rivers.

Applying these general principles to Colorado, (but they apply with equal force to all the States that lie on or flank the Andean Chain), we see at a glance what an immense advantage terra-culturalists there have over those in the trough of the Valley of the Mississippi, or on the Altantic Slope. The granite, gneiss, feldspar, quarts, metamorphic and igneous rocks of the mountain chain, contain silica, lime, magnesia, soda, and potash; the ores they carry are either sulphurets or carbonates; and many springs are living fountains of soda-water, carbonate, chlorate and sulphate. The mountains also are deposites of immense beds of vegetable and animal mold, the accumulated stores of myriads of years elapsed since plants grew on and animals roamed over them. The soil and subsoil are super-saturated with these fertilizing ingredients; and therefore they are ready to yield up at all times their surplus to living water running down the mountain slopes after rains, or from melting snows.

The waters flowing from these mountains to the plains below, are therefore strongly impregnated with all the ingredients of plant food, ready to deposite them there if man so direct; but if not, to carry them forward to the sea. If anyone doubts the fertilizing properties of waters flowing from any highlands, let him tell us the secret of the exuberant fertility of the alluvial deposites along all rivers and streams from the centre of continents to the seas. Let him tell us whence are derived the fertilizing qualities of muck, so much valued in the mountain districts of the Eastern States. Let us know why it is that the valley of the Nile has produced without artificial manuring, annual crops from time immemorial, and is to-day as productive as it was in the days of Joseph.

From the fourteenth to the sixteenth century, during which Spain attained the highest summit of her power, glory and prosperity; when her soil was the granary of the world; when her plains sustained a denser population than ever before or since; she constructed those immense dams whose remains are still found across her mountain gorges, making reservoirs to receive and retain the waters of the winter rains and snows to be used in summer for irrigating her arid plains.

The ability of Asia to sustain a population numbering nearly to a thousand million, and for thousands of years, is owing to the application she has made of her waters whose sources are on the loftiest mountains of the Globe. Irrigation is the magic wand by which she transformed arid wastes into fruitful fields, and made "the desert blossom like the rose." Where the system has been kept up, as in China and India, there has been neither deterioration in products nor decrease in population. But in Persia and in the valley of the Euphrates, where the system has measurably fallen into desuetude, there have been degradation of soil and climate, failure of agricultural products, and depopulation as a necessary consequence of destitution and starvation. Irrigation, though practiced in the East from time immemorial, was not introduced into Europe until Rome reached the summit of her power and greatness. By its introduction into Italy, a writer of the highest authority for accuracy says, "Large unproductive districts were made to yield sustenance for hundreds of thousands of animals, and for millions of men."

The Spaniards brought the system to Mexico and all Spanish America, whence it spread along the Andean Cordilleras both north and south with the Spanish settlements, being thus introduced into Sonora, California and New Mexico.

Since the advent of the Americans in California, New Mexico, and Colorado, and of the Mormons in Utah, it has been practiced by them with the most satisfactory results. At first they adopted it from what seemed to them a necessity, as a substitute, and a poor one at that, for rain; but experience has taught them better and demonstrated to them that rain is no substitute for irrigation. They find, as in the case of the irrigated valleys of China, of the valleys of the Ganges and of the Nile, that irrigated lands never grow old and become worn out. The plant food dissolved and held in suspension by the water, perpetually renews the soil keeping it fresh and vigorous. Nor in California, Utah and Colorado is this solution of the problem demonstrated, but also in the Eastern States. There are meadows in the valley of the Connecticut which are irrigated from that river, which have not had a particle of manure applied to them for twenty years, yet which annually yield four tons of hay to the acre, which is more than double the quantity that can be produced on land not irrigable with all the artificial manure that can be put on it.

The products of plant life are vegetable tissue, starch, gum, mucus, sugar, etc. All these are composed principally of three elements; namely, Hydrogen oxygen, and carbon. The other elements are silica, alumina, lime, soda, potash, etc. Hydrogen and oxygen are principally supplied by the roots, they being the constituent elements of water. Humus (that is, decayed vegetable and animal matter,) consists largely of carbon, and in combination with nitrogen forms ammonia. Therefore carbon is also taken up largely from the soil by the roots. But the leaves have also the faculty of taking in carbon from the atmosphere by decomposing carbonic acid. It is only the mineral substances that are exclusively taken up from the soil; and their quantity can be ascertained by burning any vegetable matter, and weighing the ashes. It will be found that they are but a small fraction of the whole weight of the body consumed; yet they form, (if the expression is permissible,) the skeleton of the plant. In the mysterious operations of plant life by which are elaborated the products of vegetation, they also perform important functions in breaking up old and forming new combinations. Each of the mineral salts, has a distinct function; hence the necessity of its presence in the soil when its services are demanded.

It has been ascertained by observation that on an average, crops require not less than seventeen inches of rainfall during the season of growth. If less than that falls, they suffer from drought and fail in proportion to the deficiency. But rains generally fall faster than the soil can absorb the water: consequently much water is wasted by flowing off to brooks and creeks. Not only wasted, but worse; the water takes along with it a large portion of soil containing its richest ingredients. A heavy rain therefore often has a more impoverishing effect on the soil than two crops.

In irrigating we will suppose that fifteen inches of water is sufficient to meet the demand of the crop. This will give 407,271 gallons of water to the acre. The time that the water is used for irrigation, is the time of floods from the melting snow. It is therefore the time that they are the richest in mineral, vegetable and animal matter. I was unable to obtain any analyses of waters made at any time, much less at particular seasons, for the purpose of ascertaining the amount of plant food they hold in suspension; consequently cannot state with precision the amount held in solution. But as the water used in irrigation is utilized when richest in these ingredients, I will assume that each gallon contains twenty grains. This gives 8,145,420 grains or more than 1,162 pounds of the quintessence of manure, which the water will convey to, and deposit in the soil per acre. This is more than the most exhaustive crop demands or can utilize.

Scientists have long sought, but in vain, for ingredients whose combination should constitute a perfect manure, not only to replace deficient elements in the soil, but to keep it in perennial fertility. They have failed to find them, and consequently to solve the problem, and ever must fail, until they can tell, not only the quantity of a missing factor, but the exponents of each factor that enters into the solution.

Nature who is wiser than Man, but who offers to him her wisdom as a free gift, has solved this problem completely for him, and in the simplest manner. She has piled up on every continent her cloud constraining mountains, compelling them to leave on their summits their stores of rain and sleet and snow. These mountains from their composition are the radiant points whence the elements of plant life take their departure, and spread themselves over the continents. They are therefore Nature's compost heaps from which she fertilizes the Earth.

CHAPTER XV.

Middle Park is the gem of the Rocky Mountains. The variety, singularity, wildness, grandeur and sublimity of its scenery; the beauty of its grassy and flower-enameled glades, presenting, as they do, such a marked contrast in color to the sombre appearance of the evergreens on the surrounding hills and mountains; the sheen of its crystal and sparkling waters that thread it as with silver bands; the solitude of its forests; the tranquility of its landscape, the fascinating beauty of its clear and calm mountain lakes, that mirror-like not only reflect the deep blue overhanging sky, but the surrounding forests and ice clad peaks, and the enjoyment of all these enhanced by being seen through an atmosphere so translucent as apparently to annihilate distance; will forever make Middle Park attractive to all lovers of Nature. While the purity of its air, the coolness, salubrity and invigorating influence of its climate, will make it the Mecca of invalids seeking the boon of renewed vigor and restored health, or when these are out of the question, temporary amelioration and relief from physical infirmities. It is as yet, only the central point of attraction to Coloradians, bent on enjoying a few weeks of recreation and pleasure in Summer. But to the outside world, it is almost as complete a *terra incognita* as though it were in the moon. During a portion of the year it is still the hunting ground of the Utes, who yet claim it, for the Indian title has not been extinguished; and they look with no friendly eye upon the encroachments of the palefaced ranchemen, gradually extending down the valleys of the Blue and Grand.

The valley of the Blue is separated from that of Grand

River by a mountain chain running through the Park, from Gray's Peak in a northwest direction, and terminating near the junction of the two rivers. The Blue river valley is, therefore shaped like a ham, with the hock end resting on Grand River. In the upper part of it, is the town of Breckenridge, the county seat of Summit county. This portion of the valley is very rich in the precious metals. All the mountain streams are auriferous, and the most extensive *placers* in the Territory are here. Gold Run, Galena, American, Georgia, Humbug, French, Gibson, Corkscrew, Negro, Illinois, Hoosier, etc., gulches, and Stilson's and Delaware flats, are all famous *placers*, and yield now about $500,000 annually, and are said to be capable of yielding double that annually a long and indefinite time to come. The mountains are full of gold lodes but are not worked, and will not be whilst *placer* mining continues to yield so richly as now In fact *placer* miners are opposed to lode mining. On the head streams of Snake River, a tributary of the Blue are, two mining districts, Montezuma and Peru. The latter is at the south base of Gray's Peak. Montezuma is a few miles further southwest, at the foot of Glazier Mountain, on a branch of the Snake. It is about 15 miles southwest, as the crow flies, from Georgetown, but by the wagon road through the chain, near the base of Gray's Peak, it is 20 or more. From South Park, these districts are reached through Tarryall Pass. Montezuma has a silver reduction works; and at St. John's, a half a mile distant, the Boston Mining Association have reduction works, sawmill, etc. The girdle of snow clad mountains that environ Middle Park, is the culminating point of the Rocky Mountain chain. The Snowy Range, as this towering mountain escarpment is appropriately called, since it rises from 3,000 to 5,000 feet above the line of perpetual snow, here flexes or doubles upon itself. Commencing on the north wall of Grand River Canyon, it runs first north some thirty miles, thence a few points south of east, to Long's

Peak. Thence south by way of James' and Gray's Peaks to a point some fifteen miles south of the latter; thence southwest to Mount Lincoln; thence west some 25 miles; and thence north to the south wall of Grand River canyon. Its flexure thus forms a huge fold like that of a gigantic anaconda. Within this fold lies Middle Park, some eighty miles long from north to south, and forty wide from east to west. It belongs to the Pacific side of the Continent, since its waters flow west, and its springs are far the most distant tributaries of that ocean. Here at the culminating point of the American continent, at the apex and most easternly trend of the Great Cordilleras, and amidst eternal snow and ice, they commence their long journey to the sea. At first taking their course due west, they flow for hundreds of miles through the craggiest, roughest and wildest mountain district in the world. Then they enter the four hundred mile canyon of the Colorado of the West, the chasm of which is from 3,000 to 5,000 feet deep. Emerging thence, they hold on their way through sandy deserts for hundreds of miles more, till they reach the Gulf of California; and finally reach the Pacific Ocean, near Mazatlan, in Mexico, south of the Tropic of Cancer.

The elevation of the Park above the sea, is from 7,000 to 8,000 feet. The wall of porphyritic rocks constituting the Snowy Range, rises from 3,000 to 5,000 feet above the Park; and huge tower like peaks from 3,000 to 5,000 feet above this snowy wall. The highest of these peaks is Mount Lincoln, on the south. The next in altitude is Long's Peak, on the northeast, 14,350 feet high. Intermediate between these two, both in height and position, are Gray's and James' Peaks. Long's Peak and the range adjacent to it, as seen from Middle Park, have a rugged, sharply cockscombed, or deeply serrated appearance, characteristic of all mountain chains composed of eruptive rocks.

The north branch of the Grand, heads in the angle of

the Snowy Range at the southwest base of Long's Peak; and the south branch near the summit of Berthoud's Pass, north of Gray's Peak. They unite near the centre of the eastern-half of the Park. The course of the river is nearly due west; and it receives the Blue just before it enters the canyon by which it makes its exit through the wall of the western mountain. Blue River heads near the base of Mount Lincoln, and flows nearly due north for fifty miles along the base of Blue River Mountains till it meets Grand River. Near its mouth it is about 90 yards and Grand River about 160 yards wide. Both rivers have strong and swift currents.

The surface of the park is generally rough and hilly; even rising to mountains of 1,200 and 1,500 feet in altitude on that range jutting out from Gray's Peak to the junction of the two rivers. In fact it is composed of a series of parks. Both Grand and Blue rivers have many broad savannas hedged round by mountains; and on all their affluents there are glades of greater or less extent enclosed by precipitous hills and mountain peaks. The higher hills, as well as the base of the Snowy Range up to the "timber line," are heavily covered with pine, spruce and other evergreens, besides quaking-asp (*Populus tremuloides*). Some of the lower portions are covered with a dense growth of sage brush, a tough aromatic plant which attains a hight of from two to three feet, and is not found anywhere east of the Snowy Range. Grasses, such as wild timothy (*Phleum Alpinum*), two species of blue-grass, (*Poa serotina* and *P. Andina*), red top, wild oats and the lucious buffalo grass are so abundant and luxuriant that neither horses nor cattle require any other food summer or winter. Elk, black-tail deer and mountain sheep resort to this Park during the winter, seeking its rich pastures and on account of its comparatively mild climate and greater exemption from snows than the surrounding mountains. Though the snow falls to the enormous depth of from 12 to 15 feet in a season; yet it is a well observed fact that the Pacific Slope, however remote from the ocean, has a milder climate than on the Atlantic or Eastern Slope. In summer the climate is cool, pleasant and extremely exhilerating. Though scarcely a week passes without some frost; yet, strange as it may seem, flowers bloom throughout the season, and straw-berries ripen even to the hight of 11,000 feet above the sea, and in close proximity to the eternal snows.

Gold and silver have not yet been found in paying quantities, except on the Blue as already stated; consequently but little has been done towards the settlement of the northern portion of the Park. The latest prospecting, however, indicates the presence of the precious metals in rich and paying quantities on the sources of Grand River. Quite a number of cattle ranches however already exist on the Grand and its tributaries, and are extending down the valley of the Blue towards the junction. Wheat has not been tried, but oats, potatoes, turnips and cabbage find here a congenial climate and yield enormous crops. When the narrow guage railroads now projected from both Denver and Boulder to Salt Lake are completed, * this Park will become one of the most desirable portions of the territory, not only for grazing purposes, but for the manufacturing of lumber from its large and heavy forests of pine and spruce.

Near the head of Grand River, amongst the side mountains of the Snowy Range lies Grand Lake, about two miles long, and of unknown depth, since a sounding line 500 feet in length has failed to reach bottom. The mountains forming its sides rise abruptly from the waters' edge; Grand River forming both its outlet and inlet. Up through the canyon through wich the river comes tumbling down, are several smaller lakes; and still higher up is

*The one from Denver, to run by way of South Park through Hoosier Pass and down the valley of the Blue; and the one from Boulder, through the Snowy Range and down the valley of the Grand, thence by the Grand River Canyon through the middle basin of the Colorado of the West into Salt Lake Valley.

Estes' Park, a miniature glade on the verge of the "timber line" where Mountain Jim has a cattle ranche.

The streams and lakes are filled with fish, mostly trout. Deer, elk, mountain sheep, hares and grouse are plenty in the Park, and the coyote and grizzly bear in the forests and mountains. When Fremont was here in 1844 the Park was filled with buffalo, but they have all left these parts now. Beaver are also plenty on all the streams and mountain brooks. On one stream there are at least fifty dams within a mile, and a regular Venice-like beaver city.

There are many coal beds in Middle Park; in fact the only true carboniferous coal in Colorado is found here; which will be of immense value should the mineral depositos prove as rich as it is now anticipated they will. Fossil-wood is found in all the tertiary deposites which cover four-fifths of the Park. The petrifactions of fossil palm trees are recognized by their endogenous structure, but the most of the fossil trees were exogens. A species of magnolia has been found and identified as belonging to a sub-tropical species.

South Africa has the largest and richest diamond fields in the world. Middle Park has no diamonds, but it has the richest known deposites of the inferior precious stones. There are thousands of acres of agate patches, and fields of jasper, amethyst, opals, emeralds, chalcedony and silicified wood; in fact there are enough of these to supply the world for ages. Many of the agates are what are popularly known as moss agates, from having those dendritic forms resembling petrified moss. These forms however originate, as has already been stated, from crystallization of manganese under the reaction of oxide of iron.

The epoch in which the great changes of climate were effected, and of the upheaval of this *mesa* to its present altitude, was one when terrible energy manifested itself on a tremendous scale. It has forever left the impress of its character on the turreted battlements of peaks above peaks, mountains on mountains and hills on hills, and on the deeply rifted canyon walls of its flowing streams. The whole topography of the Park is an almost unvaried series of igneous rocks forming immense cones and dikes of basalt and lava.

On the banks of Grand River near the centre of the Park, are yet numerous hot sulphur springs. Mr. Charles Dabney, of Boulder, gave me a piece of sulphur foam, which he gathered from the basin of one of these springs. It weighs about twelve ounces. He described the spring as a stream of hot water of the capacity of twenty-five "miner's inches," issuing from a fissure in an over-hanging rock. The orifice is about fifteen feet above the basin into which the water pours. The whole surface of the basin is covered with this incrusted sulphur foam to the depth of four and five inches. Immediately below the hot spring there is Grand Canyon, three miles long, where the river cuts its way through an upheaved ridge of massive feldspathic granite between walls from 1,200 to 1,500 feet high.

On Troublesome Creek there are monumental stones similar to those on the Divide, east of Pike's Peak. They are the remains of sandstone that have otherwise succumbed to the erosions of the elements operating upon them for unknown thousands of years. They are said to be extremely picturesque, fantastic and weird, surpassing even those on Monumental Creek flowing from the Divide south of Denver into the Arkansas.

Near Troublesome Creek is a rectangular mural hill, or rather mass of light colored rock two hundred feet high. The sides are nearly perpendicular, and have been so fashioned by the erosions of the elements as to resemble a huge castle. There are towers, battlements, abutments and gateways, so that when seen by moonlight or in the gray dawn of morning the effect is most charming and impressive, and the illusion is complete of an old massive castle, such as are seen upon the Rhine.

There are several passes over the Snowy Range into the Park. Hoosier Pass at the source of the Blue, near the base of Mount Lincoln, leading into South Park, was estimated by Fremont, who passed over it in July, 1844, on his return from California, to be 11,200 above the sea. His estimate was deduced from the boiling point of water, having broken his barometer late in the previous year on the Columbia. Berthoud's Pass, about five miles north of Gray's Peak, at the head springs of Clear Creek, as determined by Prof. Hayden, in 1869, is 11,816 feet above the ocean level. Boulder Pass, some ten miles further north, at the head of the South Boulder, also affords easy access to the Park. I cannot ascertain that its altitude has ever been determined. Its altitude probably does not vary much from that of Berthoud's. It is rather singular that on the summit of all these passes, the springs which send their waters in opposite directions and to different oceans, are in close proximity, only a few feet, or at most, a few yards, apart. From Georgetown, there is a good wagon road over the Range at the south base of Gray's Peak to the silver mines on the head waters of the Blue, and from the same place, through Berthoud's Pass, the head waters of the Grand are reached.

There are four of these parks in Colorado; namely, North, Middle, South and San Luis. To which might, with propriety, be added a fifth; namely, the upper basin of the Arkansas, which has all the requisites of a park as the word is here understood. Of North Park, in which the North Fork of the Platte rises, it is not necessary to speak. It is yet beyond the pale of civilization and not visited by tourists. The easy accessibility from the Plains has secured to South Park an early settlement, and makes it a favorite resort of tourists, though its scenery is said not to be of the first order. As it has been often described by tourists who visited it, it would be presumption in me to attempt a description who have not seen it.

The following are the estimated areas of the three northernmost Parks:

	ACRES.
North Park	1,600,000
Middle Park	1,900,000
South Park	1,400,000

West of South Park, and separated from it by the Buffalo Peaks, lies the Upper Basin, or Park of the Arkansas, which heads at the western base of Mount Lincoln. In it are Oro City, Dayton and Granite, all of which were at one time flourishing mining towns, but now are somewhat dilapidated; not because gold is not there, but because it takes labor, skill, and perseverance to obtain it. Prosperity, however, must sooner or later return to them, because not only are the *placers* rich, but the lodes in the mountains give bright promise of the future when capital, skill and science will be directed to their development.

Dayton, situated on Twin Lakes, is the most charming village in the mountains. The Twin Lakes are the largest lakes in Colorado, and are unsurpassed for beauty in the world. They were the scene of a sad accident while we were in the mountains. Young Copp, of St. Louis, whom a few days before we had seen at Denver, full of life, spirits and expectation, was drowned here by the upsetting of a boat.

Chapters could be written in describing this lovely, charming, picturesque and delightful valley, and its matchless scenery, without exhausting the subject. Every tourist should make it a point to visit it, for no one ever regrets having gone there.

South of the Upper Basin of the Arkansas, and beyond a range of snowy peaks, lies San Luis Park, the most southern, the largest and the least elevated of the series. It contains about 12,000,000 acres of arable land, and its altitude above the level of the sea is about 6,500 feet. It is generally said that San Luis Park lies in the basin of the Rio Grande del Norte, though a portion of it really is a continental basin. It is separated from the Taos Valley by the Sierra Blanca (White Mountains) running on its southern border nearly due east and west. They are the grandest, most imposing and picturesque range in Southern Colorado. Southeast of the Park, in the second range of mountains, the Spanish Peaks raise their towering heads above the clouds. The mountains that wall in San Luis Park on the east, from the Sierra Blanca north to Poncho Pass, are of eruptive rocks, and grand in aspect and vast in proportions. The north wall is of metamorphic rocks and rises above the line of perpetual snow. To the west are the Sierra San Juan (pronounced San Whawn). The Rio Grande rises in Los Animas (the Spirits') Park, flows at first east to centre of San Luis Park, and then turns south. The northern portion, a continental basin, is San Luis Park proper. This northern portion is about 60 miles long and 15 to 20 miles wide. In the centre of it is Saguacho Lake twenty-four miles long and ten wide, at its widest part. It looks like a vast thicket of "grease wood," (*Sarcobatus vermicularis*). It has no outlet. It seems to be a vast swamp or bog, and has some 15 or 16 large streams flowing into it. It is said that in the interior of this bog, small lakes exist, the largest of which is three miles in length. The waters of these lakes, and of the bog itself, are said to have an ebb and flow with the regularity of the tide. I will not vouch for the truth of this, but it comes to me from so many credible sources as to entitle it to mention here. If it is true, it is a remarkable phenomenon, worthy of scientific investigation. As its elevation is so great above the level of the sea, it cannot be a tidal wave, yet there must be a uniform physical cause in operation to produce it. Assuming it to be true, I would suggest atmospheric pressure as the probable cause of it. From the nature of the facts existing here, we can very readily infer the laws operating to produce the phenomenon in question. The facts are, fifteen or sixteen, large, besides many small streams, discharge their waters into this bog, yet like the sea it does not become full. The water therefore must sink, since its volume is too great to disappear by evaporation. Now supposing there is an air tight cavity, or a series of air tight cavities filled with air connected with the cavity by which the water slowly discharges, and these air cavities lower than the surface of the lake; then what would be the effect of atmospheric pressure in such case? From well established physical laws, there would be low water in the lake under a high barometer, and high water under a low barometer. I use a fountain inkstand, and can always tell whether the barometer is rising or falling. If rising, I have constantly to push down the India rubber air-chamber to keep up a supply of ink. But when the barometer is falling, I have constantly to raise the air-chamber to keep the ink from overflowing. Precisely the same thing would happen to this Lake, if our supposition of subterranean air-chambers be correct.

Now as we know that there are two normal maxima of atmospheric pressure, and the same number of minima in a day, and also the hours of their uniform occurrence, therefore the ebb and flow of these waters, if our explanation be correct, must be synchronous with these maxima and minima each to each. The major flow, or highest water would therefore be between 3 and 5 o'clock in the afternoon, and the minor high water between 3 and 5 o'clock in the morning. The major and lowest ebb would be at about 10 o'clock in the morning, and the minor low water at about 10 o'clock at night. The hours of these maxima and minima would shift like those of barometric pressure with the altitude of the sun during the seasons. Observations would soon settle the questions whether there are such ebbs and flows as reported; and if so whether the periodicity of the phenomenon corresponds in point of time with atmospheric pressure, as shown by the barometer, which it must, if the explanation here offered be the true one.

What makes both the facts and explanation more probable is, that it is not the only instance in which a similar phenomenon has been observed. Every one must have noticed, or if not, must be a poor observer of what is going on around him, that dried up springs in long droughts just preceding a change to rainy weather, often send forth large volumes of water, so as not only to swell the brooks, but to send living streams through dry ravines. What is the explanation of this fact? Simply that since every rainstorm is preceded by a low barometer, therefore the air contained in closed cavities of rocks, when the external pressure of the atmosphere is removed, expands, displaces and drives out a volume of water equal to its own increase of volume by expansion.

The streams falling into this lake, are perennial, and are filled with mountain trout; and the pasturage in their valleys is so rich that the Mexicans call them "*los vegas,*" the meadows.

Altitude, latitude and moreover being surrounded and hemmed in on all sides by lofty mountains, jointly have a modifying effect upon the climate of San Luis Park. It is exhilarating and bracing, yet mild and equable. No extremes of either heat or cold are experienced the year round. All the cereals, excepting corn, yield abundant harvests; and as a stock-raising country, it is not surpassed in the world.

It is a singular fact that on the Plains, near the Mountains at La Porte and Boulder, though one and a half to two degrees farther north, and nearly of the same elevation, the wheat harvest is from five to six weeks earlier than in San Luis Park. Prof. Hayden, in 1869, found them in the midst of harvest at Boulder on August 5th, while on the 21st of September they had not yet finished it in San Luis Park. Above Santa Fe and in the Taos Valley, though lower than Boulder, he found, the same year, the harvest fully four weeks later. Here is a problem for physicists to solve, from as yet unknown factors. San Luis Park contains about 12,000,000 acres of arable land. My early and esteemed friend, Ex-Governor Gilpin, owns, or did own, a little over one-sixth of it, or about 2,250,000 acres, acquired by purchasing Spanish and Mexican concessions. Being down at his residence in the Park, whither I did not go, I did not see him while in Colorado. Rumor said, (and it is so published in the *Colorado Gazetteer*, of 1871) that he had disposed of a part of his interest to some English capitalists, for $2,500,000. He was then engaged in settling colonists on his estate, but I learned nothing of the principles embodied in his colonial scheme.

While these pages were going through the press, I met him on his way to the Eastern cities. I learned from him that the narrow gauge railroad building from Denver to Santa Fe, and already completed beyond the mouth of the canyon of the Arkansas, will be completed to San Luis Park by November, 1872; and that there are yet millions of acres of vacant public land in the Park subject to settlement either by homestead pre-emption, or entry, and that there is an abundance of water for irrigation. As I am under a promise to pay him a visit when next I go to Colorado, I may hereafter more specifically describe this Park. In the meanwhile let no one who visits Colorado with a view of settlement in agricultural pursuits, especially stock-raising, fail to examine the adaptation and capability of this Park for his purposes. There is no lack of precious metals in the surrounding mountains, but they have as yet received no development.

These parks are indentations or bowls formed by the upheaval of igneous matter which has formed rims around the enclosed, elevated table-lands or *mesas*, as the Spaniards say. These plateaux are not only the culminating point of the Rocky Mountain chain, but the apex of the Continent. Each is an independent watershed, having its own system of springs and fountains. They do not commingle their collected tribute with those of any other, but they send their waters in opposite directions to the four cardinal points of the compass and to different oceans. The Indian name for these parks signified "cow-lodges" or "bull-pens" on account of the immense herds of buffaloes with which they abounded. The Canadian French trappers, the first intruders into these mountain recesses, for the same reason called them "*parcs*," which in French signifies an enclosed pasture. The buffalo which then constituted the greater part of the animals in these enclosed pastures, have now disappeared; and the elk, deer, mountain sheep and antelopes, are rapidly diminishing in numbers. Not many years therefore will elapse before the name of park will be a misnomer. The name is also applied, all through the mountains, to little openings or glades on the borders of mountain streams, which is a total perversion of the term. In our language the term park, is exclusively applied to an enclosure for holding wild animals of the chase. When the buffalo roamed here and filled these mountain glades enclosed and shut in by mountain walls, the term was both appropriate and descriptive, and we might add poetical. But the onward march of civilization, in this as in many other cases, is sweeping into oblivion the facts that made names pertinent, thus leaving coming generations to wonder that there ever could have been such misapplications of names.

These park regions in many respects resemble Switzerland and the Alps; and the resemblance would be complete if glaciers existed in them. Those who have been to Italy as well as to these mountains, say that the most impressive view of the Alps from the Italian side, is from the banks of the Po, above Milan, across the plains of Lombardy; and that the view of the Rocky Mountains from the Plains, say twenty miles east of Denver, has much similarity to it but is the more imposing of the two. Here you have in one view, the towering masses of Long's and

Pike's Peak as *termini* of a cocks-combed irregular snowy curtain, 145 miles long connecting them, which in length and massiveness has no analogue any where in the Alps. The great Plains stretching up and lying against the mountain wall, has also vaster proportions than the plains of Lombardy: while the immense mountain wall in sight, 250 miles in length, stretching North and South in the western horizon, is a view without a parallel along the base of the Alps.

The mountains of the western rim of Middle Park, sometimes called the Blue River Mountains, have so impressed travelers with their similarity to the Alps as seen from Southern Germany, that they never fail to recognize their resemblance to the Helvetian Mountains, and have proposed that name for the range.

These bowl, or saucer shaped table-lands, collect the waters from all points of the compass that issue from underneath the perpetual snows and ice of their mountain rim. The causes that formed these larger basins, formed also many smaller ones between lower hills or mountains. These minor basins in many instances are reservoirs where the water collects, forming numerous lakes of greater or less extent. Though in size they will not compare with the lakes of Switzerland; yet the torrents of ice water by which they are fed, dashing through chasms and over rocky precipices form many cascades, which for beauty and the wild scenery surrounding them, are unsurpassed by the cascades of the Alps. The cocks-combed serrature of the encircling Snowy Range is not surpassed by any view of the Snowy Alps.

Before closing let us take a brief review of the attractions and inducements held out not by these parks alone, but by the whole mountain system of this region, to those seeking health, relaxation, or pleasure. We take for granted, that the enfeebled invalid, the care-worn man of business, the overtasked artizan, the enervated student, and the curious pleasure seeker, need more than mere relaxation and inane recreation. They want something to break up the routine of thought to which their daily pursuits necessarily, in a measure restrict them; and to open up new and wider channels for the flow of the mind. With relaxation from their treadmill drudgery, they want recreation to elevate their tastes and sentiments, and to enlarge their range of thought. In a word they want recreations as diverse as their tastes and as their mental capacities. Variety, grandeur and sublimity of scenery, are all essential elements of recreation and enjoyment, but they do not meet every requisite. They suffice to those of a romantic turn of mind for subjects of revery and day-dreaming; and to the poet for inspiring themes for verse. To all admirers of Nature's handiwork they afford the most pleasurable emotions and the highest order of enjoyment. In other words they speak to the poetic element which is the common patrimony of the human race, and awaken that exaltation of mind which is the effect of inspiration. But the *real* is also as important and as irrepressible an element of human nature as the *ideal*. Man desires not alone to feel, but to think; not only to imagine, but he wants to know. The fountains of knowledge must therefore be as free and flow as copiously as the fountains to induce feeling and inspiration, or he fails in the attainment of the highest enjoyment as an intellectual being.

There is no region of the globe where these requirements are more completely met, than in these matchless mountains. In juxtaposition with the wildest and grandest scenery in the world, is every geologic formation, and every mineral and metal known to science. Here if anywhere is the plain and legible record of the mysterious processes by which the inhabitable globe has been elaborated. Here is a lithological record, which contains the history and describes the character of each epoch that supervened in the Past, and engraven in stone are the grotesque and unique forms of vegetables and animals that appeared with, lived through, and perished, with the epoch that gave them birth. Here is impressed in indelible characters upon the stern features of these mountains the omnipotent energy of the Physical Forces as they manifested themselves in the earlier history of the globe. What an immense field for exploration is here opened. Geology, lithology, metallurgy, paleontology, meteorology, botany, in fact every branch of Physical Science finds here copious stores of materials, not only for their study but for their enlargement. To those of scientific tastes, and to men of science, no part of the globe offers richer stores, holds out stronger inducements and affords greater opportunities for collecting specimens for their particular branches; nor more agreeable pastime and diversion than to turn over the pages of this immense and new volume, and studying the histories it embodies.

CHAPTER XVI.

All the pleasures and enjoyments of traveling flow from the gratification of the eye. When beautiful, wonderful and sublime objects are presented to the eye the attributes of those objects powerfully affect the sensibility, giving rise spontaneously to exalted and pleasurable emotions, that may carry the mind to the highest pitch of enthusiasm. But while a view of many objects afford pleasure to the highest degree, but few of them inspire enthusiasm. Then again we are differently affected by the same object according to the standpoint from which we regard it. For instance, our point of observation may be the top of a high building, the point of a pinnacle, the top of a tower, or the summit of a mountain. The pleasurable emotions that arise in this case, spring from the extended view and the number and variety of the objects seen. All of these objects when taken singly, may be incapable of inspiring any emotion whatever, yet when taken in by a single glance, afford the highest kind of pleasure. It is the *view* that affects us rather than the form and character of the multiplicity of objects that compose it. A *view* however is incapable of awakening enthusiasm in its highest sense. We generally call views beautiful, grand, and even magnificent, but never sublime.

Again, our standpoint may be at the head of a lane, in the opening of a row of trees, or we may look down lengthwise between the two sides of a mountain gorge, and we may call the vista beautiful or charming, but never magnificent, much less sublime. The emotions excited by fine vistas, though highly pleasurable, are not even of so exalted a character as those arising from a grand and magnificent view.

Finally, our standpoint may be, in front of a splendid building, at the bottom of Niagara, in the abyss of a mountain chasm, or at the foot of a precipitous, craggy, cliff overhung by toppling rocks, and crowned by mountain pines; then in looking up, we are smitten with wonder, awe and astonishment. We had seen the same objects at a distance; they then were component parts of our views and vistas, and as such merely objects that filled up points in the more or less extended space in sight. We hardly regarded even their forms, much less their attributes. But now we are regarding them singly. We then only saw enough of them to perceive they were trees, houses, cliffs, cascades, precipices or mountains, but we now see that they are extraordinary trees, houses, cliffs, precipices, etc. Then we saw no attributes except such only as enabled us to classify them; now we see nothing but attributes. We now see they have beauty, symmetry, harmony, vastness, grandeur in all grades up to the highest degree of sublimity. These fix the gaze and rivet the attention; a glow darts through our veins, the imagination is set on fire and enthusiasm is awakened; and then if under the influence of their inspiration we attempt to give utterance to our feelings we call the *sight* beautiful, grand, magnificent, sublime.

To meet fully the demands of the traveler the country visited must possess objects and scenery that will afford all of these three sources of pleasurable emotions; namely, beautiful and charming *vistas*, grand and magnificent *views*, and grand, stupendous, magnificent and sublime *sights*.

Of late years traveling has degenerated almost exclusively into sight-seeing of the lowest order. Our citizens visit the large towns and cities of our own and of foreign lands, which have more fame for being dens of iniquity and infamy, than for affording sublime and inspiring sights. The rich, large, munificent and splendid cities of continental Europe especially, seem to have particular attraction to those having the desire and the means to see the World; by which they understand the manners, customs, habits and vices even of man. As for sublime sights, they believe they have seen, everything worth seeing, when they have looked at, although they may not have taste enough to admire, the most famous specimens of architecture in the world.

The ancients had seven wonders: 1st. The statue of the Sun, at Rhodes; 2d. The Mausoleum of the King of Caria; 3d. The statue of Jupiter, by Phidias; 4th. The Temple of Diana, at Ephesus; 5th. The walls and hanging gardens of Babylon; 6th. The Pyramids of Egypt; and, 7th. The Palace of Cyrus, the younger; these were what they called the seven wonders of the World, and, as is seen, every one of them was the work of human hands.

It is, therefore, an ancient idea, that the great, the grand, the beautiful and sublime, must be sought in the works of Man. Which are the greater and more sublime, the works of Nature or the works of Man, is not even admissible as a question; for it has been truly said, "Man made the city, but God made the country." In the cities, Man has built St. Pauls and St. Peters, the Louvre, the Tuillieries Sans Souci, arches, columns and domes; but Nature built Niagara, the Alps and the Andes, the cliff, the gorge and the abyssimal chasm. Of Man's works we have less in this country than there is elsewhere, but of Nature's more. Not only more, but of a higher order, and of a unique type. They have only to be known to be appreciated; not only by us, but by the World.

Were I called upon to designate the country having the most beautiful and the greatest variety of scenery, and in its greatest perfection all the elements of grandeur, magnificence and sublimity, I would unhesitatingly name Colorado.

Lately it has become fashionable for tourists to visit the White Mountains, and ascend to the top of Mount Washington; and when they return, they tell us they have been above the clouds. Why, any of the towns of Colorado, on the Plains along the flank of the Rocky Mountains, are as high above the sea as the top of Mount Washington; while those on the mountains are from three to four thousand feet higher. As for sights, go to the bottom of one of those awful chasms that seam the great Cordilleras in all directions, and look up the side of the cleft mountain that lifts its rocky escarpment to the clouds. How utterly insignificant is anything man has done, or can do, when compared with this cyclopean work of Nature!

Everywhere, in threading the labyrinthine mazes of the mountain canyons, these overhanging, cloudcapped and oftentimes beetling cliffs are met with. But foremost amongst these stands Boulder Canyon, unequaled either in these remarkable mountains or in the world, for the variety, grandeur and sublimity of its scenery. Its only possible rival is the Yosemite Valley of California. But the Yosemite is a spectacle of a different order. It is a valley quiet in all its aspects; the very embodiment of tranquility, if we except the Bridal Veil and the cascade of the main source of the Merced, pouring themselves into the head of the valley from under the everlasting snows and ice of the Sierra Nevada. But the Merced itself flows through the valley so gently that it scarcely shows a ripple upon its tranquil bosom. It even forms a calm lake in the centre, which is scarcely ever ruffled by a passing breeze. This lake is hedged in on all sides by lofty spruce, and the whole enclosed by a loftier wall of smooth weather-worn rocks. On this wall, said to be from 3,000 to 4,000 feet in height, rise high, huge and bald battlements of giganitc rocks, named respectively, the Half Dome, the Dome, the Three Brothers, etc. All these have been eroded by the elements until they appear as though the waves of the sea had rolled over them for myriads of years and effaced every angular vestige. The Half Dome, however, appears as if, at a more recent period, one half of it had dropped in the abyss below, and consequently on that side has a sharp angle. The Three Brothers are a beetling cliff from which jut three immense rocks, looking as though three huge hexagonal crystals were superimposed one above the other, with their points directed horizontally towards the valley. Though the Yosemite has an exhuberant growth of spruce within it, yet the mountain wall and the country surrounding it are entirely bare. No sign of vegetation is to be seen on it; and therefore its smoothness, combined with the utter sterility surrounding it, give it an exceeding tame and commonplace appearance. In fact the whole environment of the valley looks as though desolation had swept over the region and had blasted and annihilated all vegetal life, except what is enclosed in this secluded little dell, two miles long, and half a mile wide. The surroundings therefore have a dreariness and monotony that are absolutely painful, and the valley, or more properly dell, taken as a whole, fails to affect and impress the senses vividly.

Not so, however, with Boulder Canyon. Its walls are as steep and high as those of the Yosemite, yet they are not bleak, bare, smooth and sterile, but for fifteen miles are fearfully wild, rough, bold, angular and grand, with their sides clothed, and their summits crowned with evergreen shrubs and trees. Its waters are not a calm lake nor an unruffled stream, but a milk-white, dashing, roaring mountain river, rushing through a rocky gorge often having a descent exceeding five hundred feet to the mile. In density of thicket and number of trees at any one point, it cannot be compared with the Yosemite, but in size it can, for it has trees four feet in diameter and upwards of two hundred feet high. The Falls of the North Boulder cannot be compared with the Bridal Veil, but the whole river is a continuous cascade which immensely enhances the wildness of the scenery and stamps its impress on the mind. The Yosemite and the Canyon are therefore spectacles of entirely different orders. As already stated, one is the impersonation of repose and tranquility, the other, that of restlessness and intense activity. These two orders must impress the mind with different feelings and emotions. Inspiration always comes from without. We drink in the very spirit of the objects we behold and contemplate. If it be a quiet scene, however beautiful and grand it may be, the spirit that pervades it will instantly evoke is counterpart in our own bosoms. If it be wild, violent and turbulent as well as grand, beautiful and sublime, our emotions will be of the same order.

For exciting intensity of feeling, wild and turbulent passions and overwhelming emotions, Boulder canyon must have an incontestible superiority over the Yosemite Valley.

To give relaxation to the mind and variety to the eye, beautiful and charming vistas are essential. It has been asserted that the Rocky Mountains, unlike the Alps, do not afford them. I must contest this assertion. If there is a more beautiful vista than that to be seen in Boulder canyon, near the narrows, where you look out from under a canopy of immense spruce trees, and up the gorge, down which rolls a foaming torrent, enclosed by perpendicular walls, and see at about a hundred rods distant a transverse mountain many thousand feet high, forming an apparent *cul de sac*, then I have not heard of it, nor seen it described. Then again there are the many mountain lakes, sometimes nearly encircled by perpendicular or overhanging precipices, at others surrounded by a forest of picturesque, tall and tapering fir trees. If a look through dense groves of tall evergreens and across, or up the lake walled in by a rocky escarpment, a thousand feet high, or hedged around by an evergreen forest, is not a charming vista, then I do not understand what is meant by that term. Again you can take your stand at the head of a narrow vale. The mountains that form its sides are fir-clad, steep, rugged and impassible, confining the view to a single point down the dell. It widens out somewhat as it descends, but curves round to the right or left and is finally cut off from view by the mountain wall on that side. But as it curves, you see mountain after mountain terminating on it endwise, like huge folds of a garment, until finally over the vanishing point dominates a stately, majestic cone, rising many hundred feet above the surrounding peaks. Surely if this is not a lovely vista of unsurpassed beauty, then tell me what constitutes such. Now such scenes as here described, are constantly to be met with by those who ramble over these mountains, or while threading and exploring their interminable gorges and chasms. He who cannot discover them, or enjoy them without borrowed enthusiasm, had better remain at home, for he will call by traveling very little knowledge, either useful or pleasurable to himself, or that will tend to enlighten the world.

The trouble however is not the absence of vistas, but that some person of taste, genius and imagination, and an enthusiastic admiration of Nature, has not preceded these befogged tourists, and discovered and described them. Had there been, then it would be fashionable to follow in his footsteps, going wherever he went, and admiring, too, whatever he admired; for if they did not, it would be evident that these bell-weather-led tourists were people without any taste.

As for views, the most captions admit that they are not only numerous, but grand, varied, and many of them magnificent. There is scarcely an elevated point on the plains or mountains, from which a splendid view cannot be obtained. This is my experience, as will be seen by the perusal of these pages, yet I ascended none of the highest peaks, found only in the Snowy Range. I found the peaks near the edge of the Plains give the most varied and therefore most charming views. It appears to you as though the cone on which you stand were a mere high hill on a vast table-land constituting the mountain, while around you rise similar pine-clad peaks northward and

13

southward as far as the eye can reach, and westward also, until they culminate in the bald Snowy Range. Eastward, almost at your feet, lies the Plain, drained by the South Platte and its affluents. Beyond the Platte is the Denver Pacific railroad to Cheyenne, upon which are seen trains going in opposite directions; and beyond that to the boundary of the horizon, a hundred or more miles of the mythical "Great American Desert" are in sight. The eye follows with pleasure the Platte and its affluents, by the silvery sheen of their waters, marked out also by a straggling row of cottonwood. The basin of the Platte is diversified by towns, villages, hamlets, farms and ranches. On the uncultivated Plain, thousands of cattle are seen grazing. The irrigating canals are even visible, stretching out through the characteristic bluish gray of the Plains, to the wheat and cornfields that fleck and diversify it with patches of deep green. Such a view there is near Golden City, which I have already described, and such views there are in the vicinity of Boulder, and I presume anywhere on the high peaks along the Plains. Between the Middle and North Boulder, some two miles below Castle Rock, there is a high peak, which Mr. Barnabas Smith, one of my *compagnons de voyage* ascended, which he thinks must have been the Mount of Temptation, so beautiful, grand, rich and extensive is the view from it. At least, he thinks that if the Devil owned and could show a good title to all that can be seen from it, it would be a tempting bait to mammon-loving souls, if offered as a bounty for enlistment in his service. It is too far interior to see the settlements immediately along the foot of the mountain, but Denver, Valmont, Erie, Burlington, Longmont, Evans and Greeley, are all in sight, while the course of the Platte, from above Denver to far below Greeley is seen glittering in the sun, and marked out by the line of cottonwood trees. Beyond it are the great Plains, unbroken, except by the railroad near the river margin, on which are seen the passing trains. Between the foot of the mountains and the Platte, the plain is seamed as if by silver threads, by the two Boulders, Left Hand Creek, St. Vrain Fork, Big and Little Thompson and the Cache-a-la-Poudre, all mountain torrents, draining the Cordilleras east of the Snowy Range; and their margins lined by villages, farms and ranches to their junction with the Platte.

Immediately north, and at a distance of about two miles, rises Sugar Loaf Mountain to nearly a thousand feet higher than this point. Farther north and west, at a distance of some 25 miles, is the Rabbit Ears, a double peaked cone; and to the northwest, at the distance of thirty miles, is Long's Peak, rising to an altitude of 14,300 feet, and covered with perpetual snow. West lie the unbroken but serrated Snowy Range. The view from Sugar Loaf is still more extended, and that from Long's Peak is said to be inconceivably grand.

The vicinity of the Boulder and Sugar Loaf Mountain would be very attractive to tourists, if there were a hotel there. The waters of the two Boulders, Four Mills and Left hand creeks are filled with mountain trout, and in the heavily timbered district around about are mountain grouse, blacktailed deer, elk, mountain sheep, and occasionally a cinnamon bear. Old grizzly, it is said, has left these parts in disgust.

James' Peak in the Snowy Range at the Boulder Pass into Middle Park, and Gray's Peak further south in the same range and west of Georgetown, are well known points and much affected by tourists for the fine views from their summits. Farther to the southwest and on the northern line of the South Park, stands the Titan of the Cordilleras, Mount Lincoln, said to be over 17000 feet above the sea. Being more remote and in a less frequented part of the mountains it is not so well known and appreciated as it deserves to be. However, from the difficulty of ascending it without a guide, and the March-like cold and wind always on its summit, prevailing even in mid Summer, it will never become so popular as other peaks.

The whole of Mount Lincoln is auriferous and argentiferous, and many rich lodes both of gold and silver are worked on its sides. From the base a road has been constructed a mile and a half long up to the edge of the timber line for hauling quartz, which is obtained from a lode nearly 12000 feet above the sea. Several thousand feet above this is a rich silver lode, the ore of which is packed on jackasses and carried down to the end of the road. From the end of the road several trails can be followed; some steeper, more rugged and difficult than others. Hence the necessity of a guide, or of being accompanied by some one familiar with the mountain. One the more difficult, but shorter, is up through a valley extending from the "timber line" to an abrupt precipice. This valley is from an eighth to a half a mile wide, has a stream of ice water flowing down it, and has several ponds or small lakes in it. From where the valley terminates it is two miles to the summit with an incline of forty five degrees covered with loose pebbles, shells and rocks which make the footing very difficult and insecure. However by laborious effort and persevering climbing with frequent pauses to rest, necessitated by the rarity of the atmosphere at this great altitude, the summit is finally reached. The more popular route however is to ascend a ridge running East from the summit of the mountain. By this route, the ascent can be made to within 800 feet of the top on horseback; then leaving the horses at an immense snow bank, the remainder of the ascent can be made on foot up a steep acclivity. But having attained the summit the view is inexpressively magnificent. You have left the world and its din behind, and ascended far above all signs of life, either animal or vegetable. On every side, but far below you, are bleak, dreary, sullen, stern and icy peaks. Colorado is spread out at your feet, South Park sixty miles long and thirty wide, with its undulating hills, green meadows, glittering lakes and silver streams, is a mere speck on the vast panorama. You look over Long's Peak north almost into Dakota; to the west stretching towards the golden shores of the Pacific, you look over the plains of Utah, South over the Spanish Peaks into New Mexico. To the Southeast over Pike's Peak, into the valley of the Arkansas; and eastward beyond the Cordilleras upwards of a hundred miles away, rise the bluish gray sea of the boundless Plains.

The sources of Blue river in Middle Park which falls into Grand River, an affluent of the Colorado of the West; and those of the Arkansas westward in a deep mountain canyon, are all in sight. The lake, frozen the year round, from which issues the northern branch of the South Platte more than 13000 feet above the sea, seems so near though several miles away, that it appears as if a stone might be thrown into it from this summit. Though far outside of the usual route of travel, good accommodations and excellent fare can be had at the village of Montgomery at the northern base of the mountain.

The numerous mountain lakes well stocked with speckled trout, are interesting objects to visit, both for the unsurpassing beauty of their scenery, and for the sport they afford to the disciples of Sir Isaac Walton.

Golden Lake, in Boulder county, Green Lake, west of Georgetown, and the Chicago Lakes, in Clear Creek county, all lie in convenient distances on the usual route of travel and are easily accessible. In fact, in every part of the Mountains and in the great Parks, these lakes are found.

When satiated with mountain scenery, let the tourist descend to the elevated plateau that runs out eastward into the Plains from Pike's Peak, for nearly one hundred miles. It is well covered with pine, mostly the *Pinus ponderosa*, and is called the "Divide," since it separates the waters flowing north into the Platte from those flowing south into the Arkansas. It has many springs and from its sides issue Plum Creek, Running Water, Cherry, Kiowa,

Bijou, Coyote and other creeks that flow into the Platte; and Big Sandy, Monument, Fontaine qui buille, Camp and other creeks flow into the Arkansas. In fact, the Smoky Hill, Solomon, Salina and even the Republican forks of the Kaw, have their sources in its eastern flank. It is the Paradise of ranch-men and farmers; and is already comparatively thickly settled. It is an Arcadia of beauty and tranquility which will enchant the admirer of a rural landscape, while its geological formation has a peculiar interest to the scientist as well as to the curiosity seeker. Those, so called, monuments abound in more or less frequency through its whole extent from the foot of the mountains to its most eastern flank on the Plains. But they are especially abundant in certain localities. Monument Creek, has been appropriately named so for the number of these eroded stones standing in its basin, especially at one point. This is one of the most curious and singular spectacles that can be found in the world. It consists of yellowish, white sandstones, composed of *strata* differing considerably in hardness. Under the erosive action of the elements, the softer *strata* have disintegrated more rapidly than the harder. Consequently these shafts or columns exhibit every variety of phantastic forms. At some points worn very slender, at others leaving large protuberances; it requires but little aid from the imagination to see, or to fancy you see, in some immense folds of drapery hanging from what may be taken as the shoulder of a gigantic statue; and in others the bare chest, or the outstretched arm of an Indian brave. In fact, there is no limit to likenesses or supposed likenesses the fancy may conceive and the imagination form, while looking at this singular spectacle. For instance: a towering triangular one about thirty feet high, has been imagined to resemble Washington; and as the top of it, having withstood the action of the elements better than the softer *strata* below, gives it a number of angular projections not unlike a three-cocked hat, the resemblance is conceived to be complete; and as it is also surrounded by a group of lesser columns, these have been imagined to represent his staff. Hence the whole group is fancied to represent General Washington holding a council of war, and it has been named so accordingly. Another has been imagined to represent an Indian chief with his arm extended, and his blanket falling in folds from his shoulder; and another as an Indian maiden. Though there are many spots where these singular columns are found alone and in groups, yet on account of the number found at this one point, in the midst of a large grove of pine trees, it has been called Monument Park.

Near Colorado City, on the Creek, named by the French traders, *Fontaine qui Buille* (that is the Boiling Fountain, because it rises in four effervescent soda springs whose constant bubbling give the water the appearance of boiling violently), there are what are called the Gardens of the Gods. The larger, called the First Garden of the Gods, is an enclosed area of six or seven miles long and from a few rods to a quarter of a mile wide. The enclosing rock is composed of various strata, but its predominant one is red sedimentary sandstone of a brick color. The entrance has a gate-like appearance of perpendicular rocks two hundred feet high, and the wall generally is from 200 to 275 feet high, having an inclination of a few degrees from the perpendicular, but at places actually leaning over from five to ten degrees. As at the proper season this little dell is a continuous, glaring and gaudy floral plot, all the richly colored wild flowers indigenous to this region being found in it, it has been very appropriately named the Garden of the Gods.

About for miles northwest of Colorado City is the second Garden of the Gods, through which flows Camp Creek. Its gateway is through a passage cut by the creek at right angles to the ridge. In this enclosure there is said to be a fine echo.

This must suffice for the present, not because the subject

is exhausted but because if we entered into a complete detail of all the sublime and wonderful scenery of this mountain region this narrative would be drawn out to an almost interminable length. I have shown enough to make it incontestible that Colorado possesses in the highest degree, every requisite to meet the demands of the tourist, and is deserving of their attention, before thinking of going abroad

CHAPTER XVII.

Colorado in its early history was the theatre of stirring scenes, such as marked the early settlement of but few incipient States; and which are not excelled, if equaled, in thrilling interest by those of any Territory in the Union. Originally included within the geographical limits of Kansas, yet so wild and remote that it was visited only by a few daring trappers and traders. Its nominal inclusion within the jurisdiction of Kansas was regarded as a mere empty form; for it was not supposed that the Territorial government of Kansas could exercise any show of authority in this remote region; or that even the General Government would find it possible, if necessary, to do more than to keep the roving tribes of savages somewhat in check, and to restrict them to desirable limits.

But when the "Pike's Peak fever" broke out, gold hunters, and, consequently gamblers, desperadoes and almost every kind of desperate adventurers flocked to this supposed Eldorado: the former to seek gold; and the latter to look for chances to plunder with impunity; in many instances they being fugitives from justice in the States.

The miners spread themselves in lone camps for hundreds of miles along the eastern flank of these mountains; temporarily to prospect and search for the precious metals, and to make permanent homes here if their labors should prove successful. In the latter case mining villages soon sprung up, which became *nuclei* for concentrating and distributing supplies; and consequently also the points for exchanging "dust" by the fearless prospectors, who pushed their explorations and search for gold into the most remote untrodden wilds, and gloomy recesses of the mountains. These villages soon were found to be infested with gamblers, cut-throats and other desperadoes, so that neither life nor property was safe. Lawlessness became so rife that even murder did not seek the obscurity of the night to perform and hide his deeds. Crime in all its hideous forms stalked abroad at noonday, bold and defiant. There was no government to restrain it, much less to punish it. The law-abiding, industrious miner had either to flee the region, or to take the means of protection into his own hands. By men who had single-handed encountered and vanquished the grizzly bear, and defied and kept at bay the wily, blood-thirsty savage, the idea of yielding ground to sneaking, cowardly thieves and assassins, could not be entertained, and therefore they determined to expel them from the country. Amongst the miners were many, good, true, brave and resolute men, equal to any emergency that could arise. These soon devised and perfected an organization for mutual protection. They constituted themselves the guardians both of the public peace and safety, by devising, enacting and executing such rules and laws as the emergency required. These laws were enforced most rigorously through the "People's Courts." Life was demanded for life, and the murderer had short shrift and summary punishment; other offences and criminals were as summarily dealt with; and in a short time there was such a hegira of scoundrels from the mountains as was never witnessed anywhere before, nor since. Lawlessness and crime had not only relaxed their grasp upon the community, but let go their hold, and terror-stricken were fleeing from the presence of the avenger. Since then, now more than eleven years, the country has been free from violence, and life and property as secure as anywhere, except as endangered by savage raids. The prominent actors in these stirring times, now the most prominent citizens in their respective counties, are yet to be found everywhere, and you can hear the thrilling narratives of these bloody scenes from their own lips.

It was a stormy and gloomy time when, in 1861, Col. William Gilpin, the newly appointed and first Governor, arrived to organize the Territorial Government. More than one-half of the area of the cismontane portion of the Union was in open rebellion against the Federal authority. As a large portion of the population here was from the Southern States, a division of sentiment based upon the sectional line had taken place from the earliest period of the controversy. When the war broke out, the gathering tempest soon marshalled and concentrated its forces in this distant land, and the storm was about to burst in all its fury when the Governor arrived. Delay would have been dangerous, so he took prompt measures to organize the territorial government at once. It was a sad sight in a weak and defenseless community, remote from succor and surrounded by savage foes, to see such fierce and irreconcilable dissentions. True, brave and tried men who had stood firm as a rock, braving danger in all its forms, and acting together in case of necessity, like a solid phalanx not only against the wily and murderous savage, but the no less cruel and barbarous white outlaws and desperadoes, now had become divided into hostile factions and ready to engage in a conflict in which victory was not so much the object, as extermination. One party was ready to dare and do anything that the infant colony might be offered up a sacrifice to the Moloch of Slavery, while the other was just as determined and resolute to sacrifice all their worldly possessions and life itself if necessary, to maintain this rich and beautiful land sacred to human freedom and liberty. Collision was only prevented by the prompt, energetic and decisive measures taken by the new Governor, being himself one of the oldest residents of the mountains, and who, they all knew, was a daring, fearless, brave and resolute man. The crisis therefore passed without any serious disturbance; and the better and bravest portion of the southern party either acquiesced in the established order of things as determined by the majority, or instead of making it a neighborhood warfare, took up the braver and more manly course, of returning to their respective States and entering the regular service of the Confederates. Not so however with that part of them who belonged to what in the States were styled the "home sneaks," men too cowardly to fight, but malicious and brutal enough, in the dark or under cover, to act the neighborhood assassin, these latter went to New Mexico and Texas to organize military and marauding expeditions against the defenseless colony thinly scattered over these mountains or along their flanks on the Plains. But worse than all, some of these malignants went into the country of the wild Indians and excited them to hostilities, and thus brought upon this infant colony the merciless butcheries of a savage warfare.

To thwart the machinations of these malevolent discontents, Governor Gilpin organized three regiments of volunteers, which did efficient service both at home against the Indians and in New Mexico in repelling and defeating the Texas military expedition. However the savages encouraged by bad white men, and emboldened by the apparent tardiness or impotency of the General Government to punish their crimes, continued making their murderous forays upon the mining camps of the mountains, or the agricultural settlements on the Plains; and committed the most shocking and revolting atrocities, during the entire war and for two years after, when they were summarily chastised both by the General Government and by citizens of the Territory. Under such a state of things it is no wonder that the exasperation was great, and that when the hour and opportunity for taking vengeance had arrived, it was executed summarily and relentlessly.

My object is not here to give a narrative of these Indian atrocities, marked by the merciless butcheries of defenseless woman and children, the desolation of homes and the extinguishment of entire families and settlements, these must be left to the historian and the romancer, but to give an insight into the causes and extent of these troubles, which at least palliate if they do not justify the signal and decisive acts by which they were avenged, after having been endured for seven long years. Go wherever you will at night either on the mountains to the camp-fires of the miner and prospector, or to the hamlet on the Plains, and you will there find plenty of actors in these stirring and tragic times, who will relate harrowing tales that warm to wrath, or chill the blood by their horrors, all founded on facts, of the atrocities of the fiendish Utes, Apaches, Navajos and Espinosas. The tears will roll down over their weatherbeaten faces, while they mournfully tell you of a noble, brave and beloved friend who in the dead of night with all his family perish under the fiendish onslought of the prowling savage. Another will tell you of a dear, generous noble friend, an old trapper, explorer and miner who fell unknown where into an ambush of the wily foe then lurking and swarming over the mountains and perished where his bones may yet be found unburied. Then he will recount the stories of his many adventures, brave exploits and manly virtues concluding with a sigh, "ah, poor, poor fellow, it is a long time ago since he went over the range."

Ask them what they know about the "Chivington," or as it is more generally known in the States, the "Sand Creek massacre," and the answer is: "I know all about it, for I was there. That has been stigmatized as a massacre and we have been ajudged as murderers by those who know nothing of the facts about our wrongs, nor of the outrage that led to it. We did our duty then, if ever, to ourselves, to humanity, our country to our God. You have been told in the States, these were peaceable and friendly Indians. Peaceable and friendly indeed! Why there was not a mining camp in the mountains, nor a town on the Plains where there were not daily brought the bodies of our friends and neighbors and sometimes the bodies of whole families, all gashed, scalped and chopped to pieces; murdered in cold blood by these fiends, and our own homes pillaged, burnt and left desolate. We were impelled to take the remedy into our own hands, because the military officers were fond of the quaker method of dealing with the savages and refused us protection, while they seemed always ready to accord it to our murderers. Why, these Indians had just made one of the most murderous and destructive forays into our settlements and were returning heavily laden with plunder to the friendly protection of Fort Lyon, when we undertook that long winter march and surprised them almost under the guns of the Fort, and—Ah, well, they gave us no trouble after that! Now that you may know what kind of friendly Indians they were, we will tell you what we found and captured in their camp: Sugar, coffee, dry goods, whole boxes of boots and shoes, clothing, greenbacks and bills of lading showing that these were the plunder obtained from some trains which had been captured, and those in charge murdered, a short time before on the Platte; but worse than that we found female clothing all bloody, a partially worn lady's shoe, which evidently had been filled with blood, and the scalps of white women and children dangling at their sides or decorating the shields of their braves!" I asked if there had not excesses been committed on the occasion; that I had read that they had fired upon and killed the squaws after the men had either been killed or had fled? "That's true," was the answer. "But after the *braves* were killed or had *fled* the squaws took up the fight with the fierceness of grizzly she-bears when fighting for their cubs. Now if our object had been to rid ourselves of old Grizzly, and he had quit the field, being too cowardly to fight, would we have been deterred from our purpose because the she-bear stood her ground? Certainly not; nor would we in a fight with any other wild beasts, for these Indians' blood-thirstyness are worse than wild beasts! But we only fought them as long as they fought us. Why, what else could we do? If we had run away from the squaws, or shown that we would not fight squaws, why they would have fought us with squaws ever after."

Now I do not pretend to judge who was in the right and who in the wrong in that unhappy affair. But this much is evident, there are two sides to that as well as to every other question. One side has told its story long ago, and if these men have been wronged and injustice done them, it is time that their version of the affair be heard. If we persist in prejudging the case against them, they can at least put their protest upon record, and bravely tell us to "*strike* but *hear*."

Whatever may be the true explanation of the affair, of one thing I am certain, that malicious revenge and wanton cruelty is foreign to the nature of every one, (and there were a good many of them,) that I met in the territory, who participated in it. They are quiet, peaceable and inoffensive men, enjoying the universal confidence and respect of their neighbors. Col. Chivington, the leader of the expedition, I did not meet, because I did not visit the immediate portion of the territory where he resides; but I understood he is a leading and influential citizen of his section, highly respected and loved by the people who have known him best and longest.

Afterwards, in 1866, Kanihache, a Ute chief, murdered and plundered defenseless settlers and immigrants in the vicinity of Trinidad, in Las Animas county, in the south-eastern corner of the Territory. Emigrants to New Mexico and many defenseless settlers were pounced upon, murdered, their property plundered or burnt and their cattle and horses driven away. At first so little resistance was offered, that the savages become bolder, and followed their own inclinations to murder and plunder with impunity. They even threatened to depopulate the entire region. Finally, Col. Anderson with a troop of cavalry from Fort Stevens, was sent to adjust the matter. In a conference with the chiefs, the Colonel at first used the Quaker argument of moral suasion; asking them to desist and to state their grievances and he would have them removed, and justice done in the matter. But they not only declined positively to state their grievances, but defied him to punish them. Whereupon he used the sabre and Sharpe rifle argument, gave them a terrible thrashing, killing most of their braves and driving the balance out of the country over the mountains. This affair and that at Sand Creek taught these savages that prowling over the territory, murdering its defenceless inhabitants and stealing stock was no longer a pleasant pastime, but a dangerous exploit, and they have not much fondness for that kind of sport since.

At these camp-fires you hear not only these stories of Indian wars and butcheries related, but also the exploits of the principle characters that took part in them.

As might be expected Kit Carson is the hero of a great many of these camp-fire tales. The Bents, St. Vrain, Bill Williams, the Autobeas, Roubideaux, in fact all the old mountainers, are central figures around which many tales of adventures and exploits are grounded. Carson was from Missouri; and so I believe was the noble hearted and brave Bill Williams, long the terror of the wily Red skin thieves and assassins. He was finally ambushed and killed by them, in 1860, near the "Dead Camp of Fremont," so called because of the disaster that befel the party of this brave explorer in 1849 on the San Juan Mountains.

The Bents, St. Vrain and Roubideaux are from St. Louis. All this heroic band spent the vigor and prime of their lives in the danger and excitement of the border as trappers, traders and Indian fighters, and became the heroes of many exploits that will carry their names down to posterity. Being married to Mexican wives they finally settled in the southern part of the Territory on ranches, and are leading a quiet and civil life. None ever went back to the States to live except Roubideaux who founded the city of St. Joseph, where he died a short time ago at an advanced age. Col. St. Vrain lives at Toas, and of the "Autobeas," that is, Tom and Charley Tobin, Tom, lives on the Trenchera and Charley in the Valley of the Huerfano, on ranches, extensively engaged in stock-raising.

But the most conspicuous figure in this heroic group is Col. Pfeifer. Whenever not on the war path, "Old Pfeifer," as he is called, (his age however is not yet forty-five,) makes his home at Fort Garland, in San Louis Park, and Conejos. He is a grave silent man, and loves to wander alone amid the scenes of his exploits, and the graves of his comrades. He came to the Far West in 1847, when but a mere boy fresh from the military school of Stockholm, Sweden, of which country he is a native, though of German descent. He soon became conspicuous for his coolness and daring, and early gained the distinction of a good and brave Indian fighter. In the whole series of long wars with the Camanches, Apaches, Utes and Navajos, he bore a distinguished part. He was Lieutenant Colonel under General Kit Carson during the Navajo wars of 1863, 4, 5 and 6, which resulted in the surrender to a small volunteer force of 11,000 of the supercilious marauders who called the Mexicans their herders; and which resulted in the forced removal of their tribe from the San Juan country to the Basque Rodondo Military Reservation. Many daring exploits and wild stories are related of him; all of which are more or less actual occurrences. He without exception is the bravest, most reckless and daring man in the country. At Santa Fe, on one occasion he wrapped a *serape* around his head, and went into a store on fire, and brought out two kegs of powder already charred and blazing. At another time, with a knife in his right hand, he killed a grizzly bear that was chewing his left arm. Single handed he fought two Capote Indians, all the parties being armed with camp knives, and

14

killed them both though badly wounded himself. In a fight with the Apaches at his ranche, at the Ojo del Muerte (that is, the Spring of the Dead), his wife and children were brutally massacred and he besides helpless from wounds in both of his legs, had his body so riddled with balls and so cut into gashes that there was scarcely room for a fresh cut or another bullet hole. He however survived, but ever since has been unhappy. Since then his only pleasure has been revenge. It was a sad day for the Apaches when they killed Old Pfeifer's family. He now often takes lone trips into their country; is often absent for months, and for a few days after his return seems pleased and satisfied. In a few weeks he is off again with his horse and trusty rifle. He is always accompanied in the Apache country by half a dozen of wolves. Once he said to a friend, "they like me, because they are fond of dead Indian and I feed them well." Kind hearted and gentle as he is said to be in social life, his thirst for revenge almost makes him the personification of Murder, as described in the "Masque of Anarchy:"

> "I met Murder on the way,
> He had a mask like Castlereagh,
> Very smooth he looked yet grim,
> Seven blood-hounds followed him;
> All were fat; and well they might
> Be in admirable plight·
> For one by one, and two by two,
> He tossed them human hearts to chew
> Which from his wide cloak he drew."

The main incident in this narrative reminds me of a romance based upon the legends of the early settlements of Kentucky, written about forty years ago. If I remember correctly it was entitled "Jibbenayinosah, or Nick of the Woods." The author was Dr Bird, a popular romance writer of that day. The hero, "Nick of the Woods," was a Quaker. The Indians having murdered his family, and he being alone in the world, took no other pleasure than in seeking and taking revenge for the irreparable wrongs he had suffered. If the romance is to be believed, his thirst for vengeance must have been inordinate if it was not satiated by the number of his foes he sent to the "happy hunting grounds."

The stirring and thrilling events between advancing civilization and retreating barbarism, are of so recent occurrence that they have not passed into legends and traditions, but live in the memory and recollection of the present generation. Here yet linger the most conspicuous actors in them, who can relate them and vouch for their truth, because like the Roman narrator they can say: "All which I saw, and part of which I was." Other events, however, have left their record here, which perhaps never will be deciphered. So long ago, indeed, have they occurred that even tradition has forgotten, if it ever knew, by what race of men they were enacted or at what period they occurred. In the southwestern portion of the Territory, many ruins of indubitably Aztec towns are found Tradition says, that when Cortez invaded Mexico, and laid siege to its capital, the noble but unfortunate Montezuma called to his aid all the worshippers of the Sun; and that the faithful obeying the summons of their monarch, abandoned these their cities, and rushed to the rescue to fight the battles of their God and country. They went forth to battle, but never returned; for the Aztec army melted away before the powerful invader, like snow before the face of their Sun God.

There too are those enigmatical ruins of the "Seven cities of Cibola," or rather seven human hives; buildings scattered over the Plains containing from 600 to 900 rooms each, and rising in terraced stories to the height of four stories. In front extends a semi-circular court yard containing from three to five acres, surrounded by a stone wall. The hive closes by a straight line the semi-circle, so that the building and wall represent the letter U if closed and filled to half its height. What people built these? What were their modes of life, manners and customs? History and tradition here stand mute, affording no clue to unravel the threads of the inexplicable mystery. The architectural remains of Aztec, Tescucan and other semi-civilized Indians of Mexico, Central and South America, though differing entirely both in design and execution from that of the Old World, has no semblance whatever to that of these Seven Cities. They must, therefore, be the remains not only of a distinct race, but of a distinct and different order of civilization. Of what race were they, and what became of them? Were they an offshoot representing a more advanced stage of civilization of the Mound Builders, who, in the central part of our Continent, vanished before the rude hunter tribes, leaving no memorial of their existence except those mysterious mounds in the Valley of the Mississippi?

I would not advise novel writing, and far less their reading; but if such inane literature as modern novels is to continue to be the almost exclusive staple of reading and consequently the mental *pabulum* of both young and old, then I say the legends of Colorado will be found a rich placer for treasures of a new sort. The change will also be for the better; for writers and readers will in degree leave the region of the fabulous and to that extent will enter the domain of actual life. The romancer will then give us a *few* facts instead of *all* fiction, and at least a tithe of an idea that will be of some service in life, instead of nothing, or rather worse than nothing as now.

What intemperance is doing to Man physically, modern novels are doing to him intellectually, and it is a debateable question, which is the sadder sight, a man in physical, or in mental ruin.

Besides the exploits of the Indian fighters, there are the thrilling adventures of the old trappers, a race now almost extinct in the mountains; a few having died, while the many have fallen victims to the untameable ferocity of the savages. A few of them still linger here, not as trappers but as sedate ranchmen surrounded by their herds of sheep and cattle and droves of horses. To succeed in their hazardous adventures, some of these had ingratiated themselves with the chief of some powerful tribe; had been admitted as a member into it; learned its language, adopted its habits and customs, and been initiated into its religious mysteries. Yet all this was no avail, for it depended only on what mood the Indian was in whether life was safe. Many of these after a residence of thirty years amongst the Indians have been butchered in cold blood without a cause. Fremont found a Sioux chief and two or three braves, down on the Republican Fork, nearly perished and surrounded by Pawnees, by whom they had been defeated. He supplied their wants, protected them and took them in safety to their home in the mountains. In less than two days after they left his camp, they murdered in cold blood an old trapper who had lived amongst them thirty-five years and had been adopted into their tribe. Such is the nature of the noble Red man of our morbid sentimentalists!

I have learned from these men, that the Indians have their nursery tales as well as we, and that they have traditions and legends of giants in older times who performed feats of strength and deeds of valor equal to that of the Greek Hercules.

Legends of Indian exploits long anterior to the advent of the white man are also numerous. There is scarcely a brook, canyon or peak, of which some Indian tale is not related, derived from the Indians themselves by the daring trappers who were domiciled amongst them. One of these only I will relate. While at Boulder, I expressed my admiration of the picturesque and singularly turretted mountain peak, just south of the canyon, but which I regret is so poorly represented in our engraving as not to show the turrets at all; the most picturesque and striking feature of the mountain, and I expressed a regret that some stirring Indian tale of heroic deeds or tragic occurrence was not associated with it, to spread its name and fame abroad over every land. There is, was the reply. The Indians say that a thousand moons before they ever saw a white man's face, and when millions of buffalo grazed upon the Plains watered by the South Platte, a party of Utes from their look-out on the mountains had spied what they supposed to be a small band of Arapahoes on the Plains. They immediately went down and attacked them; but the Arapahoes were stronger than they suspected and not only repulsed their assailants but pursued them so closely to the mountains that the Utes sought safety upon that peak. Here they defied their pursuers and kept them at bay. The latter tried to take the heights by storm; but their enemies rolled down huge stones upon them and drove them back every time they attempted it. They therefore beleagured them and starved the whole party to death. It is said that ever since, the Utes have a superstitious dread of that pinnacled mountain.

If the tales of a wild hunter's life should be more desirable staple for a romance, there is no lack of them also, whether of those who long since "have gone over the Divide," or of those who are "still on the Range." The recital of these will melt the heart into pity, or freeze the blood with horror. While we were in the territory a miner came over the Snowy Range, from Middle Park, with the news that "Mountain Jim"—a character whom they all knew, had a terrible fight with a grizzly bear in the Park, and was almost "chawed up" before he succeeded in killing the bear with a knife. He said that Jim had his right eyebrow bitten off, his left arm litterally chawed up, his ribs, and one of his thigh bones laid bare by his ferocious assailant; and though victorious in the fight, he would have perished had not some prospectors and tourists discovered him and kindly taken care of him. Since then I have received a private letter from Central, from which the following is an extract:

"I saw Mountain Jim, in town last Thursday, who was

so terribly mangled by a bear in Middle Park about the time you were here. His left arm is yet in a sling, and is entirely powerless. His right eye is still bandaged, the scars on his face show how terribly it was lacerated; and he walks with difficulty. He is on his way to Estes' Park where he has a ranche and considerable stock. He says he has heard that tourists are riding and driving through his ranche and leaving the gates open, and that his cattle are scattering. He has a man with him to collect his cattle and take care of them. With a moist eye he speaks with gratitude of those who befriended him in his late misfortune, both gentlemen and ladies. "Why," says he, "I did not know I had so many friends before. They took care of me as though I were a prince."

Colorado previous to the advent of the white man was the battle-field where all the neighboring tribes were constantly contending for supremacy; and where the victors of the fight to-day, were beaten and driven out by the victors of to-morrow. The mountain streams whose issues swell the Platte and the Arkansas, water a plain covered with luscious grasses, and hence the natural pasture land of the buffalo, who in millions roamed over it and occupied it the whole year. The possession of the Plains of Colorado, was therefore the possession of the immense herds of buffalo that cover it. Narrowed down, it was a question of food and raiment, for the primitive savages of this region clothed themselves in buffalo robes. In these conflicts the hostile parties taxed their utmost resources, both physically and mentally, to overcome, expel and if necessary to extirpate their adversaries. Art, stratagem and cunning were the weapons employed, wielded by boldness, bravery, resolution, recklessness and desperation. Tragic events of blood and cruelty were enacted, that fiends might imitate but could not excel. No tribe, however, attained at any time more than a temporary possession of the coveted land. Such was the position of things when the white man, a new claimant, appeared upon the stage.

The old tragedies with aggravated horrors were now revived; because here was the common enemy of the red man. Coalitions and confederations of the formerly hostile tribes were made not only to check his advance, but to expel him from the country; but the contest was unequal this time. Neither physically nor mentally is the savage able to cope with the civilized man. As the rising day drives back the shades of night, so the wild Indian flees towards the setting sun from the irresistible advance of the civilized and enlightened man. The untutored savage may return to the attack, and make renewed efforts to avoid his fate, but he is doomed. He may even be inspired to desperation by despair, but brute force cannot contend successfully against intellectual power. The ordinance of Nature has so ordained it. History does not record an instance where barbarous and civilized and enlightened nations have dwelt side by side in amity and friendship. The contrasts are too great and the antagonism too irreconcilable between civilization and barbarism, so that collisions are inevitable. Civilization may not seek, yea, may do all that is possible to avoid such collisions, but they will be forced upon it by barbarism. When it comes to blows, victory in the end must perch on the banner that is the representative of the highest intellectual culture. Not only is this true between civilized and barbarous nations, but it is likewise necessarily true between nations of relatively different degrees of civilization. All the recent great wars bear evidence to the truth of this assertion; conspicuously amongst which may be named the late war between France and Germany. The Frenchman who wrote from the prison camp in the German lines, these memorable words, "their common soldiers know more than our officers" stated both the cause and the philosophy of the result.

Our Indian troubles are to be deplored, but in the very

nature of things they are unavoidable. Philanthropists with laudable efforts, are endeavoring to avoid them, but they have mistaken the means. Moral suasion used with the Indian, and homilies read to the whites will never do it. The first step to save the Indian race from extinction is to teach it fear and the art of behaving itself. But how is this to be effected? By moral suasion? The Indian knows nothing and cares less about moral influences. All the moral suasion to do him any good is that which is inspired by fear. Since he does not know that it is his duty to behave himself, let him know that he *must do it;* and that if he does not do it, that sure and swift punishment will overtake him for his crimes. Bring him under the wholesome restraint of fear, and hold him there while you cultivate his moral nature. That accomplished, you may extend his lesson to civilization in general, and teach him the duty, yea, the absolute necessity of supplying his own wants by physical labor. Then intellectual training and social elevation will naturally follow.

No doubt in many of our border troubles, the baser class of whites are the first aggressors, and deserve not only censure but severe punishment. But it is a squeamish sentamentalism in every instance, and upon all occasions, to lay the fault at the door of the whites. The honorable, high minded, noble red man has no existence in Nature. He is not a real, but an ideal character. And worse than that, the ideal is the worst possible caricature of the reality, as all ought to know who have ever come in contact with the original. In judging of the conduct of remote settlements towards the Indian, we ought to think of him as he is, not as we imagine him to be; and not justify him while we mete out indiscriminate censure against our own race. Especially ought we to be chary in our judgment when we find whole communities affected by his mis-conduct, rising as one man and expelling him from the land.

I have had ample opportunities upon the Indian frontier for observation and forming an unbiased opinion on the causes of the disturbed relations between the whites and Indians. I lived eleven years, (eight in Alabama and three in Iowa) in the immediate vicinity of large bodies of Indians in daily contact and intercourse with the whites, free to come into the settlements and to go whither they pleased and when they pleased. It is true the Chickasaws and Chocktaws of the South were in a rudimentary civilization of a very low grade; but so were not the Sauks and Foxes of Iowa, and these moreover had only some six years before been severely punished in the Black Hawk War; yet in all that time, in neither locality was there any collision between the two races, nor even a cause for any. There was a most cordial feeling of good will, trust and confidence between the parties; the whites regarded them as a weak and helpless people, and therefore entitled to kindness, generosity and protection. Any one who would have injured a simple minded Indian, would have incurred as much odium as if he had struck a woman, or maltreated a child. Thus even upon the rude frontier, the innate impulse of the strong to protect the weak and defenseless, manifests itself as strongly and signally as it ever does anywhere. When I therefore hear the frontier settlers accused as lawless aggressors, exercising wanton cruelty and perpetrating merciless and fiendish butcheries on peaceable and unoffending Indians, I cannot believe it; because it is contrary to all experience and observation. It is an impossibility in the very nature of things. Frontier men are daring; men of decision, energy, vim and pluck; but they are neither outlaws nor savages. They are, in fact, the very kind of men in which the manly and heroic virtues, of which protection to the weak and defenceless is one, shine the brightest. Cowards could be guilty of such wanton cruelties, but brave men never.

It is, however, undeniable that violence and bloodshed mark the extension and stain the progress of settlements now as they did in the days of the Pilgrims. How can they be accounted for? Very easily. Sharpers trading with them shamefully swindle them. Outlaws who no longer find it safe to ply their robberies and thefts amongst whites, plunder and oftentimes murder them. These are about the only offences that are chargeable to the whites; and for which there is a remedy, if the Indian could only understand that the guilty alone must be held responsible for their crimes. The intrusion of the whites upon the Public Domain to which the Indian title has not been extinguished, is a source of irritation, but no crime. It is against the ordinance of Nature that myriads of square miles of rich and arable lands should be doomed to barrenness, and lie vacant merely to furnish a hunting ground to a few vagabond savages. The white man so regards it, and conceives he is obeying the commands and executing the decrees of the Creator when he enters upon and occupies it. As these intrusions cannot be prevented, and should not if they could, the Government should take early steps to prevent occasions for these conflicts by extinguishing the Indian title.

On the other hand the causes of Indian wars originate with the Indians themselves. Their native ferocity, which springs from regarding all men not belonging to their tribe as deadly enemies; their moral obtuseness which prevents them from discriminating between *meum* and *tuum* until taught by fear; their inveterate Bourbonism which never forgets anything, nor learns anything, and which impels them, however frequently vanquished, to renew perpetually the conflict with the Inevitable; these are the true sources from which nearly, if not quite, all our Indian troubles spring, as the history of American settlement everywhere shows. They are the causes in operation now in Texas, New Mexico, Arizona, Colorado, Montana and all the States and Territories on the Plains, the Mountains and on the Pacific Coast; and to lay the entire blame upon the whites, is both gratuitous and disingenuous, when the conflict, aggravated by a long series of wrongs, outrages and barbarities, does come, we must make some allowances for the exasperation of feeling manifested, and the almost inappeasable resentments these outrages have provoked. We may regret the extent and severity of the chastisement inflicted; but until human nature, as it always has been and ever will be, is changed, it never can be otherwise. There is no remedy, except that the savage man must learn the severe lesson which the civilized man has even yet so imperfectly learned by sad but wholesome experience, that "they that sow the wind must reap the whirlwind."

CHAPTER XVIII.

Any sketch of Colorado and her natural resources is imperfect that does not include her mines and mining industry. Disastrous as may have been enterprizes undertaken to develop her mines of gold and silver, and sad as may have been the experience of those that have risked their money in that enterprise; yet the fact remains undeniable that her mountains are rich in the precious metals; and that immense and inexhaustible stores of gold and silver only abide the time when capital will furnish the means, labor the skill, and Science the knowledge to treat the ores successfully and make them surrender their rich treasures.

However rich we deem her mineral resources, it is undeniable that at present the character of her mines is under a cloud, and stocks in them at a heavy discount. By some the mines are regarded as humbugs, by others as deficient in richness; and by others, who admit their richness, as worthless because of the refractoriness of their ores.

There are causes for all this diversity of opinion; but they are so numerous that an attempt at their enumeration were futile. The great and controlling cause was and is, not the low grade of the ores, but their character. The ores are richer than the ores of California and Nevada, as their analyses show; but their character is such that under the stamp-mill (the processes that in California and Nevada save from 85 to 95 per cent. of the gold or silver in the ore), they will not yield on an average more than 30 per cent. of the precious metals, contained in them. In many cases, ores that by smelting will yield from $200 to $300 per ton, yield nothing under the stamp-mill. In California the ores contain the metals free, or else are carbonates; in Colorado they are sulphurets. Where the metal is free, or where its composition is that of a carbonate, it is submissive to the influence of mercury and forms an amalgam with it; but when it is a sulphuret, it is indifferent to the influence of mercury, and hence cannot be saved by what is called the amalgamation process. Now the stamp-mill process is the simplest and least expensive process of treating ores known. With it the treatment does not cost on an average more than five dollars per ton. Hence it is *par excellence* the process for treating ores of low grade. This is the secret why the Comstock mine, in Nevada, has been so profitable and enriched all concerned in mining it, and treating its ores. Though, as already stated, its ores have not averaged more than twenty-five dollars per ton, (a quality of ore that would be worthless in Colorado), yet as it was all "mill ore," three-fifths of its yield was profit. I have been assured, by a gentleman who had an interest in a claim on it and formerly was engaged in working it, that the cost of mining and mill treatment of that ore in no case exceeded ten dollars per ton. There are 22 claims on the Comstock lode; the bullion product of all these claims is over $200,000,000. Up to the year 1869, from official tables, I learn that it was $137,382,000.

It was very natural that the earlier miners in Colorado, who were familiar with the successful modes of treating the California and Nevada ores, should form high expectations of the products of the richer lodes of Colorado; and that they should be sadly disappointed at the results obtained in working them. Nay, that they should be struck with consternation and dismay at the results. What was the more inexplicable to them, and added to their astonishment, was that while the disintegrated quartz on the surface lasted, the results were satisfactory, and as good as could be expected from ores of so low grade. But when the pyrites and sulphurets* were reached at greater depths, the metallurgists, who knew nothing except what experience had taught them in the *arastras* and stamp-mills of California, became nonplussed. Here was something they had not dreamed of in their philosophy. The more they thought about it, the darker and more incomprehensible it became; and finally they had to confess that they were at their wits' end. The, to them, unknown character of the ores, was the first and the most serious cause of failure in lode mining in Colorado. To be sure they were not a new kind of ore; for they constituted almost exclusively the kind known from time immemorial; and successful methods of reducing them were equally well known to metallurgists; but both were new to the stamp-mill men of California and Colorado.

The earlier investments were generally made in good faith, both by the miners and by capitalists. That they were so, it is sufficient to state, that men who had acquired a competency by saving their hard earnings amid dangers and privations, in the earlier days of California mining, invested their all in lodes and stamp-mills in the mountains of Colorado. Many capitalists who had been successful in mining enterprises in California, also eagerly invested in lodes that were richer than those of California, as shown by analyses made by competent metallurgists. These men knew nothing, either by experience, or by theory, of the character of ores, and of their method of treatment. The natural assumption was that they were of the same character as those of California, and hence of course would yield up their treasures by the same process. Consequently, the inference was that the same kind of machinery had to be provided for, and the same methods to be pursued here as there. When, therefore, both failed to produce the desired result, the presidents or agents of

---

* The distinction between pyrites and sulphurets is merely nominal. Pyrites are sulphurets of iron, whereas combinations of sulphur and other metals are called *sulphurets* and not *pyrites*. Pyrites, however, may have besides iron, the sulphurets of other metals.

mining companies thought the fault lay in the incompetency of the foreman of the stamp-mill. He was discharged and another employed, but with no better success. Still the opinion was that if an expert could be obtained, the results would be satisfactory, so he was also discharged; but matters grew from bad to worse, until a consternation and panic ensued amongst the stockholders. There were no dividends declaring; yea worse, things had come to that point that the concern did not begin to pay running expenses. This prepared the way for the supervention of the most disastrous fate that ever fell upon any undertaking.

In the great extremity of the stockholders, light broke forth in a dark place. This, however, was a false light; being no more or less than a new process, a pretended genius claimed to have discovered; and claimed that the "refractory ores" yielded ready obedience to it. *Claimed*, did I say? No, that was not the word. Claimed would have left the matter in doubt until it were proven by experiment. No, it was not *claimed* that the new process would do certain things, but it was boldly asserted that it *did* do them; and to prove it, the testimony of easy good natured and complaisant newspaper reporters and a few credulous and ignorant spectators, was adduced, certifying to the statement that they were present at an experiment conducted by the interested party, and saw everything performed satisfactorily as claimed by the patent. Hope revived in the desponding hearts of the stockholders, and they believed, because "the wish was father to the thought," that the intricate problem of making refractory ores tractable had received a final solution. Prudence would have suggested, that before the costly machinery be procured, that the matter be examined by a competent committee of disinterested experts, and that a trial experiment to verify both the theory and process be made by themselves, or under their supervision. But incredulity was laughed to scorn under the joy and excitement of the moment; and the manipulations and statements of interested parties were received and accepted as true without question or any apparent misgiving as to their correctness. Then commenced that disastrous new process mania, lasting for three years, from 1864 to 1867, by which millions of capital were sunk, the character of the mines damaged, and the fair fame of the territory aspersed and almost ruined.

When the stamp-mills failed in working pyrites and sulphurets known to be rich, then the conclusion became general that the ores must be roasted; that is, the sulphur burnt out of them and the baser metals calcined, before the gold and silver could be amalgamated. Immediately there appeared any number of processes for desulphurization of the ores with expensive machinery. Of these desulphurizing processes many were disastrous, some sheer humbugs, and even the best partial failures. While other new processes too numerous to mention were all miserable failures without any redeeming qualities. They were not based upon either scientific or metallurgic principles; and even if they had been, were so expensive that they could not be economically applied. The only valuable legacy these processes left, was a large amount of wholesome experience, and some more or less useful second-hand machinery which now is utilized for more rational purposes.

Upon whose shoulders the blame of these failures should fall, it is hard to determine. One thing is certain, the fault was not and is not in the mines. Perhaps the blame is about equally divided between operators and jobbers, between so-called scientific men, without practical experience and often blest with only a modicum of common sense, and blundering practical men without science; honest men without capacity, and smart men without honesty. That the disaster was wide spread and ruinous, there is painful evidence everywhere. Crumbling walls and tottering chimneys of "played out," reduction works. Pon-

15

derous, broken, and rusted machinery and curious shaped furnaces, whose fires have been extinguished for years, meet the eye everywhere and chill the hearts of capitalists anxious to invest in the rich mines of these mountains. The fact that mining has survived these terrible trials and disasters is proof of its inherent vitality in Colorado, and a pledge of its future prosperity.

For the four years, commencing with 1860, the statistics show that over $30,000,000 of gold was shipped from Colorado, while it is well known that immense sums were carried away by individuals. In other words, the yield of gold by the mines of Colorado was upwards of $7,500,000 annually. But as soon as the experiments with the new processes commenced, the quantity began to diminish, reaching its minimum in 1867 when it was less than $1,800,000. The new processes had now run their career and were generally abandoned as worthless, or if not worthless, too expensive for economical application. Men now returned to the stamp-mills and although these generally wasted from one-half to two-thirds of the precious metals and all of the copper and lead, yet they afforded a living profit. The old and tried processes of Germany of dressing and smelting the ores, improved by American ingenuity, were gradually introduced. Since then the production of the mines has gradually increased from year to year. In 1870 it reached about $5,000,000 as the shipments show, and the present year (1871) it will nearly, if not quite, reach $6,000,000.

Though chlorination and smelting are perfect as metallurgical processes, yet they are too expensive to be economically applied to a large class of ores. The uninitiated have no means of telling what the average cost is of treating a ton of ore by these combined processes. But as the owners of reduction works charged miners from $30 to $35 per ton, the cost can certainly not be more than $25, and may be less than $15.

However, the stamp-mill and the amalgamation process.

are the only means yet known cheap enough to treat ores of a low grade, since the actual cost in no case exceeds $5 per ton. With ores containing the precious metals free, that is, uncombined with sulphurets of other metals, they will save from 80 to 90 per cent. of the metal. But with pyrites, and sulphurets, and especially when the particles are indefinitely small, the mill will not save more than from 30 to 50 per cent. Unless the expenses for reducing ores by chlorination and smelting are much less than interested parties would induce us to believe, the great problem of the future is to find a cheap process that will leave the precious metals in a condition to form an amalgam with quicksilver after the pyrites have been calcined.

It is yet a mooted question whether the gold contained in pyrites is so in a mere mechanical mixture, or in chemical combination. The weight of authority and experiment is in favor of the hypothesis of mechanical admixture. However the gold of Colorado is generally alloyed with small quantities of silver and copper. The gold obtained by pulverization of pyrites mixed with copper, zinc-blend and lead, is not of a bright yellow color and metalic lustre, but has a grayish brown tint. It is what is called "rusty gold," and is indifferent to the action of quicksilver, it therefore will not amalgamate. From this fact the stamp-mill process fails to save it. It has not yet been determined what is the cause or nature of this coating. In the refining crucible this "rusty gold" gives a regulus of 99 per cent. However mechanical rubbing in pans, roasting, or chemical treatment, removes this rusty film and leaves the gold in an amalgamable condition. Also when copper sulphurets combined with other metals are desulphurized the gold cannot be extracted by amalgamation, because it has this same film rendering it indifferent to the action of quicksilver.

When the great problem is solved of treating, upon a large and economical scale, pyrites and sulphurets so that the contained gold and silver is left in an amalgamable condition, then the stamp-mill, as it is the cheapest and simplest of all known appliances, will supersede all other methods of reducing such ores as are found in the hither-side of the Rocky Mountains, from New Mexico to Montana. The fortunate individual who will succeed in accomplishing this feat, will reap the richest harvest yet gathered in the field of discovery, while at the same time he will confer untold blessings and incalculable wealth not only upon the great mountain region of the West, but upon the World.

But it is evident that as the case now stands, private economy comes in conflict with political economy. The object of the individual is accomplished when he succeeds in extracting the precious metals in paying quantities at the least possible expense, regardless of how much he wastes.

It has been already stated that on an average, stamp-mills working pyrites, and sulphurets, do not save more than one-half, some say one-third, of the precious metals contained in the ores, while they waste all the copper and lead. But the interests of society demand that there should be no waste. The common yield of one cord, (about seven tons,) of average gold ore at the stamp-mill is from $120 to $130. Say the average yield is a medium between these, that is $125 per cord. According to the highest estimate this is only one-half of the assay value of the ore. Deduct $25 for mill fees and there remains the net yield of $100 from seven tons of ore worth $250. Suppose now that the cost of the combined processes of chlorination and smelting is $15 per ton or $105 for seven tons; and that only 90 per cent. of the metal is extracted, which is $225. Subtracting the cost of reduction from this sum we have a net yield of $120. The difference of profit therefore would be 20 per cent. to the owner of the ore; besides which the production has been largely increased and many more persons have been furnished with employment. The estimated yield of bullion of the mines of Colorado for the present year (1871) is $6,000,000. Deducting from this for the proceeds of gulch mining and smelting works $2,000,000, and the product of the stamp-mills for the current year is $4,000,000. According to the foregoing estimate this is only one-half of the bullion contained in the ores treated by them. The actual value of the ore worked by them would, therefore, be $8,000,000. By the combined chlorination and smelting process upon the supposition that they saved only 90 per cent. this ore would have produced $7,200,000. The additional gain of the owners, therefore would be $800,000, and to the public $3,200,000. Such an increase of bullion alone would not only enrich Colorado but would affect the business and prosperity of the whole country. Besides this the copper and lead saved would be worth a million of dollars more.

That mining operations in Colorado can be made highly remunerative there can be no question. The success of the reduction works of Stewart, and of Huepeden & Co., at Georgetown, and especially of Prof. Hill's smelting works, at Black Hawk, places this beyond controversy. The Caribou Company have now completed, at Middle Boulder, the most extensive and complete works in the Mountains. They cost about $150,000, and I have been informed that since they have been in operation they have shipped from 8,000 to 8,500 ounces of bullion per week.

However, to make mining successful and the investment safe, men must go into it as they do into any other legitimate business. There is a great deal of capital in the country seeking profitable investment, but those who have the control of it, have spent all their lives in other pursuits, and have never had their attention drawn to mining; especially mining of the precious metals. They have besides had their fears excited by the losses their friends have sustained who had ventured into such enterprises. Capital generally is timid when controlled by those who have accumulated it. Within the field of enterprise wherein they have gathered it, they can make a calculation of results with almost unfailing accuracy; but in new fields of enterprise they can neither make a calculation, nor feel or see their way through it. In fact every kind of business has so little margin for profits, that it requires the closest sailing to the wind to keep within the margin, and make a successful voyage. Moreover the margin being small the operation must be on a large scale to make the profits an object. Hence the many shipwrecks that befall even the most wary. Besides the uncertainty of prosperous circumstances, is the fluctuation in prices of the commodity on which the transaction is based. The price depends upon the supply and demand. The latter may be two-fold the ordinary and extraordinary demand. The prospect of an extraordinary demand may put up the price, yet aften all the demand may be only an ordinary one. In such cases more or less losses must be sustained, and these may be often ruinous. Of late years also the commercial centres have become theatres of operations which are no better than gambling. Thousands by these means become shipwrecked both in capital and character. It is generally the most unscrupulous that win. But there is one consolation, the victor of to-day becomes the victim of to-morrow. It is therefore a serious question for capitalists to consider whether they cannot invest ther capital in other enterprises than those which are constantly drawn into, and engulfed in the vortex of speculation and whether such investments would not be safer and the profits surer.

In the kind of new enterprises, mining deserves the most serious consideration, but let it be done with a view of *business* and not of *speculation*. Gold and silver are the measures of value the world over, by which the prices of all other commodities are measured; therefore there can be no fluctuation in *their* value. The only questions to be determined are, how much can be produced? and what will be the cost of production? Both of these questions can be accurately determined by dispassionate investigation and calculation. In fact this is the course now pursued by all who mean business.

While in the Mountains, I met English capitalists, accompanied by a professional geologist and metallurgist, and by an expert miner. They would not look at a prospect; but when a developed lode was offered, the geologist examined carefully the country rock, the size of the crevice and its material, and made a series of qualitative and quantitative analyses; while the miner determined accurately the cost of mining. The supply of ore and the cost of reduction were then calculated from known *data;* and if the result showed a fair margin for profits, negotiations were opened for purchasing the mine. With such precautions as these no one need make a misadventure. This is the only way that investments should be made, whether the object in view be mining and reduction combined, or only reduction. Mr. Wm. Cope, an English capitalist whom I saw in the Mountains, after his return to England sent a written proposition to the "Central Register" saying that his company, the British and Colorado Mining Bureau of London, "stood ready at once to erect smelting works on a large and comprehensive scale, for the treatment of all descriptions of ores, whether gold or silver, to invest $1,000,000 in the works and for the buying of ores, provided that mine owners will give sufficient guarantee that said works shall always be fully supplied with all the ore they can possibly use," and promised to revisit Colorado the present year (1872) to see what inducements mine owners would hold out for such investment.

Mr. H. B. Grose, an English metallurgist who has spent nearly four years in the mines of the Mountains, in a communication, dated London, Oct. 4, 1871, and published in the London Mining Journal, says: " The country (Colorado) is a good one for mining, and parties interested in *bona fide* mines under practical management have no need to fear loosing their money; for I am fully convinced that there is not a richer country in the world for minerals than Colorado is, and especially for gold and silver. I have been through all the mines that are yet opened up, and have taken every means to ascertain their value, cost of working, &c.; and after allowing for all extra expenses, I find the average yield of the lodes to be greater in value than in any other country, and with proper management would leave greater profits. There is no doubt the mines of Colorado have been badly managed; in fact there is not a mine that I have seen, worked in a proper manner; neither is there a mine with the sole management in the hands of a practical man. It was quite a surprise to me to see how some of them are worked, and the waste of money incurred."

Mr. Grose since then has returned to the Mountains, and did good service in exposing the tin swindle at Ogden, Utah.

Having sufficiently established the fact that the mines of Colorado are rich, and under proper management must be productive. It may perhaps be pertinent briefly to show the causes why so much capital has been irretrievably swamped in operations looking to their development.

In many cases failure was a foregone conclusion, which without a miracle could not have resulted otherwise. The management of the enterprize was entrusted to utterly incompetent, or if competent, to reckless men, whose extravagance made success an impossibility. Not even ordinary prudence, foresight and judgment were exercised in selecting the sight for reduction works. Expensive works were erected, where the company owned the only lode in the vicinity, and that a mere prospect. At other places the prospects in the vicinity for mines were plenty but not a single mine developed; so that neither the nature and character of the ore, nor the capacity of the district to furnish a supply of it were known. Besides, worse still, the owners of prospects had not the means of opening them up, or if they had, they had not the inclination to do so. This is yet a serious obstacle in the way of making reduction works successful.

The defect is in the law, which allows a man to find and hold any number of prospects with a mere nominal amount of work on each. To homestead a piece of land it requires improvement of it and residence on it for five years; but for obtaining a patent for a lode it requires only the sinking of a shaft ten feet deep; whereas it should require its development by an expenditure of not less than $500. This, or something like it, I believe is a provision in the new law relating to mining now pending before Congress.

As the case now stands no guarantee of a supply of ore can be given; and consequently no assurance that the works will not have to stand idle. Summer, the best season for operating reduction works, is also the bewitching season for prospecting which the miner cannot resist. He therefore leaves and for months explores the mountain sides, the deep gorges, the canyon walls or the towering peaks. for new lodes.

In early days this evil necessarily was much greater than now; and consequently the first adventurers in mining and reducing enterprises suffered more from it than they would now. But it is as yet a serious drawback, and retards a rapid development of the mines. It was a fruitful source of failure then, and it has entailed many evils on the mining interests which are still felt and will be felt for sometime to come. Besides creating a prejudice against the mines, it has reacted against the miners; for shrewd capitalists that have since gone there and erected works, taking into consideration the uncertainty of a supply of ore, make it pay while they do run, both for the time they run, and may be idle; and hence pay very low rates for ores. Assure them of a constant supply the year round; and they will advance their prices for ores thirty per cent.

So far I have only spoken of legitimate transactions in

the Past and Present; but there have been many transactions, (and unless people are careful, there will be many more hereafter,) that were neither legitimate nor honest. It is necessary to speak of these also, to make the causes apparent of that widespread disaster and consequently deep mistrust in the mines and mining in the mountain territories.

Upon the discovery of gold and silver here, those who had made profitable investments in California were not backward in venturing capital here; because their knowledge and experience in mines justified them in doing so. Insensibly others, who had no such experience, were drawn into like investments; and the buying and selling of mines and mining stock became a speculation. This soon ran wild, because the purchaser did not know, or if he did, did not care to make the distinction between a prospect and a mine. The mountain men were not slow to perceive that a good prospect was equally as saleable and brought as much money as a good mine; and they were not backward in profiting by it. As it answered all their purposes, if they could show a well defined metal vein in a crevice, so they devoted themselves to the task of finding these. But the fact that undeveloped mining property found a ready sale, and often commanded exorbitant prices, in the end proved to be the most serious blow that it was possible to strike at the character of the mines and at the prosperity of the mining interest of the mountain territories. Such sales begat intemperate speculation, and speculation begat a rage for finding prospects. The quickening influence of speculation converted nearly the whole mountain population into prospectors; and their efforts would have supplied prospects for reasonable speculation prolonged indefinitely. But speculation was soon intensified into a mania, which like all such transactions, by the operation of an inexorable law, collapsed and left widespread disaster in its train. It is necessary here to produce as testimony the most shameful record of those times, showing how the thing was done.

A swarm of unprincipled speculators made their appearance in the Mountains, whose only object was to enrich themselves at all hazards, and by any means however foul and disreputable, and then flee with their plunder from the country. They had confederates in New York and other eastern cities who were coworkers with them. These at first were ready to buy all prospects that were in market, and while their supply of money lasted, which was not long, they did so. But what then? Where there was a purpose and a will, there was a way. Ink was cheap, the pen nimble, lithograph stone docile, and paper patient; therefore one could be made to say, and the other to show anything calculated to strike the excited fancy of men laboring under a delusion. Fraudulent mining companies were gotten up, stocks issued, engravings made of the company's Reduction Works and of the surrounding mountain scenery, lithographed plats of the property, showing the location of the lodes; fraudulent certificates of pretended assays of the ores, signed and sworn to by fictitious metallurgists before fictitious officers attested under seal, &c., and with these the Eastern cities were flooded. Millions were thus paid for what was not worth even a chance in that most worthless of all things, a "Gift Enterprize."

But who is responsible for this state of things; and where lies the fault that disaster and ruin ensued from such transactions? Surely not in the mines, for they were only the *occasion* for, not the *cause* of them. It has been said, in music there would be no *flats* if there were no *sharps*. Whether true or not in music, many from sad experience can testify that it is true in some other things. Men possessed of some money which they did not earn, and the value of which they, therefore, do not know, of sanguine temperament, little or no experience, and dazzled with the prospect of becoming millionaires with a single season's operations, are very liable to become *flats* if *sharps* are about. It needs no labored argument with the facts set forth, that this is what was the matter with these transactions for which the existence of gold and silver in the Mountains gave the occasion. They were mere "tricks upon strangers."

Before closing we must address one word of caution and advice to those who will undertake a mining enterprize. You must do it upon strict business principles. Buy no property whatever until either by personal inspection, or by examination of a competent and honest expert, you have satisfied yourself of its character and ascertained its true nature and value. Never invest your capital in any company whose main object is to pay fat salaries to one or more favorites; and who, in order that they may not be put to any inconveniences, will have the ore brought clear across the continent to be treated at home. The failure of such a company is a foregone conclusion. The ores must be smelted in the mountains, and as near to the mines as facilities can be had. Labor is about as cheap there as anywhere and fuel much cheaper. At Boulder city, for instance, coal is delivered at $2.85 per ton. The "*matte*" may be transported elsewhere for separation and refinement, but that only so long as Express Companies and Railroads charge the enormous rates they now do for transporting bullion. The refining can be done there now as cheaply as anywhere, so there is even no economy in having smelting works in the Mountains and refining works at Omaha, St. Louis, Chicago, Newark or New York.

When the works are completed, put the technical operations in charge of a scientific expert, and the business management in the hands of a man of tact and capacity, who will supervise the whole by constant attention, and the greatest possible vigilance. The success of Prof. Hill is mainly due to the fact that he gives his entire time and attention to the business management of the works while the technical operations are entrusted to a skillful German metallurgist.

The present is a favorable time for investment. The country has not yet recovered from the recoil and revulsion caused by the earlier failures. People are cautious as they should be; and when you mention Colorado mines they are as suspicious as the mice in the fable, that a cat may be concealed in the bottom of the meal tub. A year or so longer, and people will have recovered confidence, when everything of value will be bought up for the purpose of legitimate business. Reduction works also will have been erected at all favorable points, so that rich mines now almost without value, being in the vicinity of such works, will be so much enhanced in value that the same favorable opportunities for investment will not exist.

CHAPTER XIX.

The time had now arrived for us to turn our faces homeward, and it was with deep regret that we yielded to the inexorable necessity. After a sound and refreshing sleep, such as can only be enjoyed in its full fruition in Colorado, on the 17th of June, I was up as usual with the dawn and out for a walk to enjoy for the last time the life inspiring breath of the morning air; to view once again the sublime and gorgeous scenery of Nature's greatest and best effort, and to feel once more the emotions of enthusiastic admiration and inspiration which alone such grandeur, sublimity, yet unadorned simplicity can enkindle.

Both here and at Golden, whenever awake during the night, it was a most pleasurable sensation to be soothed and lulled to sleep again by the ever-murmuring waters as they flowed down the plain. Consequently, I seemed to be in fellowship with them, and felt a strong desire to hold communion with them whenever opportunity offered. I was therefore irresistibly drawn to their side, and on to the bridge over them, ready to muse and lose myself in day dreams. Oh, how sweet it were to spend life here, where everything speaks with such irresistible eloquence, yet soothingly and feelingly, to the eye, the heart, the mind and the imagination! There the everlasting mountains spring up at a single bound four thousand feet, to kiss the blushing, pure and smiling skies. Grand, awful and sublime are they, with a history that human pen will never record, a mystery that the human mind will never unravel, and involving laws that human reason will never unfold and explain. Yet they are as beneficent as their presence is great, majestic and imperious. From the icy fountains under their stern and snow-covered crests issue these pure, limpid waters, to gladden the valleys, refresh the parched plain, clothing the land with verdure, and filling hill and dale with joyous life.

> From them, ye supercilious, proud,
> Learn the great lesson which ye so much need,
> That to be truly great is to be good,
> Benevolent, beneficent and kind,
> And scatter blessings all around the land.

Ah! surely this is a place for the poet to catch new inspiration and pour forth songs on themes never attempted in verse, and where the moralist can draw ennobling lessons of instruction, and enforce them by the great sanction of Nature.

Listlessly and with a heavy heart I left the bridge and sauntered down the margin of the stream, then down the lane bordered by meadows and wheat-fields, through which runs the Denver road. I felt oppressed with an indefinable sadness which I could not shake off, for in my ears seemed to be ever ringing the words, "Once more, but never again." I was at last arrested by the thrilling notes of a skylark on the fence before me. Whilst listening with wrapt attention to his song, I could not refrain from repeating the following stanzas from Shelley's address to a skylark:

> "What objects are the fountains
>   Of thy happy strain?
> What fields, or waves, or mountains?
>   What shapes of sky, or plain?
> What love of thine own kind?   What ignorance of pain?"

> "Teach me half the gladness
>   That thy brain must know,
> Such harmonious madness
>   From my lips would flow
> The world would listen then, as I am listening now."

But even his cheerful, joyous and ringing notes could not break the gloomy spell that had settled on my feelings. I therefore returned to the hotel to prepare for the homeward journey.

After breakfast, everything being ready, our kind Boulder friends came in troops to bid us a final farewell. The drive of twelve miles down the plain, through which flows the Boulder, by Valmont, and through the village of the same name nestled at its feet, to the then terminus of the railroad at Erie, was delightful and pleasant. The sky was perfectly transparent and of that deep azure blue of which tourists in Italy speak so enthusiastically. But in the East, as usual, over the plain hung a grayish, purplish haze. I do not know how common this haze is, but every day I was out on the Plains fifteen or twenty miles from the mountains, while in Colorado and Wyoming, I encountered it. It is a meteorologic fact which should be investigated, as it is a precursor of, and synchronous with, electric disturbances to the eastward of it. Its density also indicates the intensity of the electric disturbance. From the mountains I had noticed for several days that the haze was more than usually dense and lurid. I then predicted great electric disturbances to the eastward, and got laughed at for being so weatherwise. Yet on those very days tornadoes were raging from Galveston to Nebraska and eastward to Louisiana and Ohio. It was on one of those days, namely, the 16th of June, that the town of Eldorado, in Kansas, was totally destroyed by a tornado. That night, as we left Denver, there was a brilliant aurora, which even the dense haze could not hide, seen as far east as Ohio; and the following night, the 18th, a most brilliant aurora was seen over the whole of the northern part of the continent, I therefore renewed my predictions, not only of storms but of earthquakes. The storms extended from Central Kansas to New York, and the earthquake occurred in New Jersey and Brooklyn on the 19th, and one at Lima on same date. It is well known that in California they dread an earthquake whenever a lurid haze spreads over the sky; and the recent terrible hurricane in the West Indies and the coast of Florida, accompanied by an earthquake, was synchronous with a lurid haze that spread from Western Nebraska to Central Ohio and south into Mississippi, and with a most brilliant fiery red aurora. The record of physical phenomena occurring all over the globe, which I am keeping, shows the unvarying contemporaneousness of earthquakes, cyclones and other electrical disturbances, with auroras, lurid haziness and sunspots as far as I am able to obtain the latter. In Europe, as my record also shows, these electric disturbances are often preceded by the phenomenon of mirage.

Returning now to our drive to Erie: When we had ascended the terraced plateau some four miles east of Valmont looking eastward, I saw distinctly an image, though faint, of the mountains behind us reflected in the haze. It soon vanished, and I saw it no more. I called Mr. Ephraim Pound's attention to it, (who was kindly taking us in his carriage to Erie.) I remarked, " I suppose we must call that mirage, though to do so knocks all the philosophy of the wiseacres into a 'cocked hat.'" They have only one explanation to give of this phenomenon, and that is, that it is caused by the refraction of light through superimposed strata of atmosphere of different densities; but this is not the *refraction* but *reflection* of light.

"This mirage," said he, " is a wonderful thing. I have seen it, not faint as it is now, but as clear and distinct as if it came from a looking-glass. One day I was driving along listlessly, almost in a half dreamy state, when suddenly I raised my eyes, and my first impression was that somehow my horse had turned around and was going home again. But looking behind I saw that he was all right. I then knew it was mirage, but more distinct than I had ever seen it before. I then saw that it came as though from a looking-glass more elevated than my position; for I could see objects reflected that I could not see from the point where I was. There was White Rock and Valmont just as you see them now, and there was the Boulder flowing down through the plain as distinct as though I stood over it, and Boulder City and the mouth of the canyon, too, which you see are hidden behind Valmont. It was the most wonderful sight I ever saw." Fremont, in his journal, mentions the same phenomenon. Seeing, what he supposed, some horsemen opposite in a fog-bank, he sent one of his men to meet them, to ascertain who they were, why they were apparently trying to head him off, and what object they had in view. As his messenger departed, he saw one of the strange party do the same; and discovered it was his own party mirrored back by the haze.

We had now arrived at Erie, and had but ten minutes to spare. We therefore took cordial leave of our friends, Messrs. Pound, Corson and Captain Austin, who had taken us to the depot, and who wished us a pleasant and safe journey, which we reciprocated by wishing them long life and continual prosperity.

Once on board the cars, attached to a freight train taking coal to Denver, we were soon on our way. We will state here that we were indebted to the liberality and generosity of Col. S. W. Fisher, the General Superintendent of this railroad, the Boulder Valley, as well as of the Kansas Pacific, Denver Pacific and Colorado Central railroads, not only for free passes but for other favors while in the Territory, for which we tender him the most cordial thanks of our whole party.

As soon as the cars got under way, I took my seat at the window to take a long and farewell look at the glorious old mountains now fast receding from view. A spell came over me, and I ventured for once upon the dangerous hight of verse, to indite them a long and lasting farewell.

FAREWELL TO THE ROCKY MOUNTAINS.

Farewell, ye icy Crests; ye fir clad Peaks;
Ye Chasms deep; and foaming Torrents wild;
Ye stern old Mountains, with your flow'ry dells
And valleys green, and pouring cascades, white
As your own snow-clad brows; a long farewell!
   Ye are a gorgeous temple, such as ne'er
By mortal hands was reared, nor extasy nor dreams
E'er built in cities of enchanted land.
I gazed upon your wonders, and I garnered
Stores to fill the mind, and feed the loftiest thought;
And fire and inspiration drew from out
Your scenes; whilst health I drank from your pure balmy air.
I cannot choose but gaze upon you now;
A glamour and a fascination sit
Upon your brows, and dwell within
Your deep abysms. A music, while I gaze
Soft, entrancing, sweet as if it came
From tongues angelic, falls upon my ear
And I'm again amidst your pathless wilds;
Amid your hills, and vales, and glens, and chasms
I hear the Æolian strains of winds at play
Amid the lofty tops of mountain pines
And firs. Anon, I'm in the canyon wild
And gaze upon its weird, gigantic forms;
The sound of rushing waters, and the roar
Of cataracts leaping with impetuous bound
From mid air to the yawning gulf below
Fall on my ears; and I'm entranced again.
   Hail! All hail, ye Mountains! and ye Hills
Ye Valleys, Glens, and Precipices steep!
All hail, ye everlasting Snows, pure and white
Unblemished, unpolluted; though of Earth,
Unsoiled, where all else festering reeks
With foul polution and corruption dire.
Hail Boulder, mighty magic canyon hail!
Thy raving, foaming waters rolling down
Through rocky gorge, now dark, now glist'ning in
The sun, swift down the precipice they leap
In cascades wild, with roaring, stunning sound;
Thy battlements of rocks, now bare and smooth,
Then rugged wild and threat'ning, high aloft
Upon their craggy sides, a giant brood

Of firs and pines they bear, which overarch
Thy deep abyss. The blue o'erhanging sky
Looks down and smiles upon thy beauty wild.
Swift sailing clouds their fleeting shadows throw
In thy abyss, and then the charming scene
Is bathed in twilight gloom. And high o'erhead
The golden eagle soars in circles wide,
And shrieks in triumph his hoarse thrilling notes;—
The exulting shout of Liberty. While
I gazed on thee and thine, I was entranced,
And saw things strange, and wonderful, sublime
Beyond all utterance. My thoughts afire
All wild on wandering wings soared upward far
Above this mocking unsubstantial world
Of shadows, to realms empyreal, where
Nor change, nor death, nor phantasy have place.

  Ye great and glorious Mountains, hold the keys
T'unlock the secret chambers of the heart;
Ye have the power to change the fickle soul
And harmonize its music with the spheres.
Earth has no greater joy to me than this:
To flee the world and its corroding cares,
And dwell amidst your rugged scenes, and fields
Of ice and snow; to hear the soothing hum
Of flowing waters, and a requiem sung
By odorous winds; to hear the eagle's shrill wild shriek;
To listen to the thund'ring cataract's roar;
To see in wild confusion, rocks on rocks,
And cliffs on cliff that scale the low'ring cloud;
To lay the ear upon your breast and feel
The throbbings of your mighty heart, and hear
Entranced the gushing forth of Nature's sweet
And glorious harmony, until I feel
My soul enlarged, enraptured, transported,
Exalted far above the sordid cares,
Gross pleasures, and blind passions of the age;—
Ah this is real, noble life indeed!

  The transient spell that on my dreaming mind
Had fallen and kindly ta'en me back
To thoughts and scenes so wild and glorious
Is broken now; and from afar I look
Upon your snowy fields, and jagged peaks
All clothed in sombre blue.
                Ere drops the veil

That must forever hide from me, your all
Imposing grandeur, and majestic mien,
Say, cannot ye unseal those silent lips
That keep the secrets, which from eldest Time
Frail man has tried, in vain, to wrest from you
And yours; and which with expectation wild
The world on tiptoe e'er has stood to hear?
Thus far to me your bosom ye've unveiled,
And with a voice melodiously sweet,
And mien all eloquent, me have ye taught
To understand the weighty import of
The lesson great, ye were designed to teach
To my benighted race, of grandeur, power,
Wisdom, purity, and Omnipotence.
Will not ye, whose resounding echoes make
So many-tongued the thunder's awful peal,
Make me your confidant and whisper now
Though in the lowest, gentlest breath, the word
That gives the clew by which to tread the maze
Whose intricacy has, till now, perplexed
Confounded and embarrassed, and defied
The purest, nob'est, highest efforts of the mind;
And solves the laws and causes of your birth?

Ye prattling tell-tale Waters whose glib tongue
The palsying frost doth strive in vain to hush,
To me will ye not now divulge the strange
And thrilling secrets of these mountains old,
By telling how they rose above the sea
And plain? Will ye impart the wonderful
Mysterious argument to fill the blank,—
The abysmal blank, up on the scroll
That men call history; how living things
Arose and flourished; then in Ocean waves
O'erwhelmed, how long they lay in darkness and
In ruin; how amid the earthquake's shock
When reeled the world and stars were blotted out,
And darkness prime had filled again the deep
Abyss, their forms arose above the sea,
For aye preserved in stones as fossils strange?
How long they've lain as now they lie upon
The mountain side, or deep beneath the plain?
Ah, yes, enumerate the cycles long
Of loveliness, of ruin, which have swept
The earth by turns; how oft the Earth so lovely, green,

And filled with life exuberant, became
The bottom of the sea, by deluge whelmed
And drowned for myriad years, then rose again
To light, put on her wonted vesture green,
And populous became again; how in
The realms of Space, new suns came forth and blazed
Awhile, and then extinguished quite became
In darkness, deep, impenetrable, stark.
Ah, tell how oft Destruction fierce and fell,
Revival lovely, mild and calm, in turn,
Have stepped upon the stage, and there have played
Their magic parts, ere Man, the glory and
The shame of Earth, first trode the scene to act
His tragic, comic, or imposing part.

Ye heaven-pointing Peaks, and pearly Floods
That teach to Man so much; will ye not now
Unfold the thrilling and transporting story
Of all ye saw, and part of which ye were
In all the great illimitable Past?

What! Silent still! Not one small voice comes forth,
The echo of the myriad years, to tell
The wond'ring world the mystery of your birth!
Ye will not for a moment lift the veil
Implacable that hides the unrecorded Past;
Nor deign to tell the strange events that since
Your birth have come and gone! Ye are to all
Entreaty deaf and resolute and dumb,
And sacred keep the secrets of your charge.
The poet's vision, reason's grasp, and proud
Philosophy, in vain, have tried to wring
From you the trust, and to the vulgar gaze
Unfold your wondrous lore; and failing have gone mad.

Ah, while I gaze, a vision bright flits by
A glimpse it gives so fearful, grand, sublime
Of that dread night which gave ye birth, that while
The spell is still upon me I'll portray,
If fitting words fail not, your natal hour.

'Twas a tempestuous night; the lamps of Heaven
Were blotted out; commotion red had seized
This trembling sphere: wild whirlwinds racked the Earth,
The air, the sky. The flashing lightning cleft
Th'abyss of darkness shrouding Heaven and Earth:
'Twas then in earthquake's couch, while Ocean seethed,
The sickened Earth yawned wide, and gave ye birth.

Ye wonderful, sublime, majestic, grand
And beauteous Mountains. The tempest then grew calm;
The storm's dark clouds flew swift as leaves before
Th'autumnal blast; the gentle Moon looked forth;
And silvery stars beamed bright and calm
In the etherial space. Anon the pure
And golden dawn broke forth; and Orient Sun
Before his throne drove back the ebon spirit of
That fearful night; and when green Earth awoke,
She found a cloudless sky. Mild zephyrs blew
To fan and cool your glowing, infant brows:
And there ye stood as now ye stand, glorious,
Resplendent, great, magnificent and calm,
Sublime, immutable, majestic,
And proud, a mystery unfathomably deep,
The ever-during wonder of my puny race.

When I in contemplation wrapped behold
The instability of Man, his works;—all that
He is, and what he's wrought; how rapidly
New nations, tribes and peoples have, in turn,
Arisen like the bubbles on a stream
And danced, and glittered for awhile, then burst,
Dissolved and disappeared from Earth;—effaced
For aye, and vanished into airy nought;
Ah, well may I a frail ephem'ral child
Of clay then weep, to see the pride and power
And evanescent glory of my race,
Fade like a morning mist, and lost to sight.
Yea, from all memory lost.
                    Relentless Time
Has ever fed upon his off-spring; spared
Nor young, nor old, nor beautiful, nor brave.
We call him cruel, but alike he treats
Proud Man, the crawling worm, the mountains high,
And continents and seas; e'en the bright orbs
That roll in glory through celestial space;—
All are engulfed and swallowed up by him.
I weep, but sweet it is to shed such tears,
For thus the heart o'erburdened finds relief,
And throws its sorrows off. But ye ne'er weep
Nor know of sorrow, feel no grief nor care;
For ye seem ever-during as the Sun;
Nor Time writes on your brows the boding lines
Indelible of coming change and growing age.
Storms beat upon your naked breast, and then

The lightning glares upon your brows; the hoarse
And bellowing thunder shakes your sides;
But azure calm returns, and finds no wound
Upon your breast, nor scar upon your brow.
Day follows night, and Night the dying day;
The seasons come and go; and fleeting years
Pass and return, yet on your adamantine front
Though stern and old, Decay nor Death will set
Their withering seal, nor leave a trace or mark
Upon your brow; but warmth, a radiance mild
Unfading beauty, and the vigorous glow
Of an immortal youth, sit high enthroned
As erst:—the pledge secure of endless years.

  Ye Mountains, rugged, strong, unchanging, grand,
With beauty wild and terrible, your dark
And deep, mysterious chasms, o'erhung
By toppling rocks, and your cold icy peaks
That glitter like a distant star; ye seem
Eternal; think ye the poignant words "NO MORE"
Do not apply to you; reesrved for such
As me and mine? Yet in the future age
To you will come, as comes to all beneath
The stars, destructive change. Rent, hurled and whelmed
In ocean waters deep, the rolling wave
Will be the mound that marks your grave. Alas,
Who then will come to weep and shed the bitter
Tear above your tomb, save I from far,
From bright abodes where the Eternal are?

  'Tis thus we part, but part to meet again,
Both now and then. A tenant for awhile
Of this terrestrial sphere, though I may roam
Afar, I still behold your shadows weird;
And though to eyes your wondrous forms no longer speak
With burning words and eloquence so fierce
That set my soul afire; yet in my heart
I hear amongst your pines the soughing wind;
I gaze upon your silvery lakes, your cliffs
And rocky ramparts, icy peaks, fir-clad
Escarpments, gorges deep and roaring waterfalls,
And rushing, surging streams in rocky beds;
And as I gaze melodious voices fill
Mine ears, a glowing thrill darts through my veins,
Mine eyes dilate, my heart with rapture swells,
With wonted fire my soul's imbued again,
And holds communion with the Great Unseen.

We soon ran into the gray haze which shut out the mountains, as well as cut off everything from view on the Plains, and we saw them no more. The sun had a lurid glare; and a perfect gale of hot wind blew from the South. Several jackass rabbits loping away, a few antelopes scudding off over the Plains, and the killing of a calf belonging to herders who had not precaution to clear the track of their stock in time, were the only incidents that diversified the trip to Denver, where we arrived at three o'clock. Rummaging through the contents of a news depot, we found some stray copies of different dates of the *Democrat* and *Republican*, which together posted us both as to news at home and the world abroad that occurred while we were buried in the recesses of the mountains. With these we whiled away the time until half-past nine, when the eastward-bound train left. We were soon ensconced in the comfortable berths of Pullman's palace sleeping cars, and oblivious to everything passing around us. But on we sped in charge of the fiery steed, and day met us at Kit Carson, near the eastern limits of Colorado.

CHAPTER XX.

At Kit Carson there had been rains within a few days, and vegetation looked fresh and thrifty. At Arapahoe (pronounced Ah-rap-a-ho) thirty-five miles east, it had rained heavily, as the buffalo wallows on the Plains and excavations along the railroad were yet filled to overflowing with water. At Pond Creek, at an elevation of over 4000 feet, the industrial agent, R. S. Elliott, of the Kansas Pacific railroad, has one of his experimental stations, at which were sown wheat, rye, barley and corn, all of which looked remarkably vigorous and thrifty. The barley and rye were just coloring and would be ripe in ten days. There was also a nursery of various species of deciduous trees grown from seed the present season, which were very flourishing, and the brilliant green of their leaves contrasted beautifully with the black moist soil on which they stood.

At Wallace, a meal station, where we took breakfast, we met Mr. Elliott, who expressed himself sanguine of the triumphant success of his experiment. So far as we could judge there appeared nothing to prevent the realization of his fondest hopes, namely: That of abolishing the "Great American Desert."

Off again, we successively passed Sheridan, Gopher, Monument, Carlyle, Grinnell, Buffalo, Coyote, Park's Fort, Ogallah, etc., all stations from ten to fifteen miles apart, consisting generally only of the station house and tenements of the railroad employes. These mostly are of those subterranean dwellings already mentioned, or cabins, though occasionally there are a few neat and comfortable cottages. The whole horizon otherwise encloses an expanse of treeless, shrubless plain, covered with the short, velvety buffalo grass. The only thing that gives variety is the old buffalo trails, leading straight as the flight of an arrow north and south over the Plains, which can be followed with the eye, as far as sight can reach, by the deeper color and richer green of the buffalo grass. At short intervals we passed prairie dog villages, and, as we had nothing else to do, we watched, for amusement, their antics when alarmed by the approaching train. The first thing was for each member of the family to run home on the approach of the train, then take a peep for an instant, when up would fly heels and tails, and they were out of sight. The old one of every hillock, whom we took to be the *paterfamilias*, generally faced about when he got to the hole, and set himself up straight to look at and study the monster that creates such alarm and consternation in the village whenever he passes. When sitting up straight, in color, size and position he looks like a ten-pin set on top of the hillock.

Well, since there is so much uniformity and sameness in the landscape of these Plains, the variety of objects is limited and their discussion soon exhausted. For want of something else, let us while away time by talking of this our unjustly stigmatised little friend, the Prairie Dog. A welcome friend he always is, for he relieves us of *ennui*, and breaks up the wearisomeness and dull monotony of these wide expansive and treeless Plains. For this reason he possesses, aside from his novelty, a permanent and abiding interest to all traversing this part of the Continent. He was discovered by Lewis and Clarke, in their ever memorable expedition across the Continent to the Pacific, in 1804, '05 and '06, and described for the first time in their Journal. They called him the Prairie Dog, not because he is any way, even remotely, allied to the dog, or resembles him in nature and habits, but simply because he sounds his alarm note, "chip-ip-ip," so rapidly and shrilly as to have some resemblance to the yelping of a pup. But then, everybody talks of the barking of a squirrel, yet nobody thinks it a sufficient reason for calling it a dog. Why then should the one be libelled, by being called a dog, for yelping, and not the other for barking? Each yelp he gives, when he sounds the alarm of danger, is accompanied by a twitching of the tail, similar to a squirrel when barking.

Well, if we are not to call him the Prairie Dog, what are we to call him? Sure enough, what? A question well and pointedly put. Unfortunately he has been many times christened, but the names have not stuck well, except the vulgar one given him by his discoverers.

The Indians called him *Wishtonwish;* and he is so called in the description given of him in the Journal of Pike's Expedition to the Mountains in 1806. Guthrie, in 1815, proposed to call him *Arctomys Ludovicianus.* Literally, Arctomys means *Bearmouse,* or Bear-rat. It is the generic name given to the Marmot family; one species of which, the *Arctomys Monax* is familiarly known as the wood-chuck or ground-hog. Ludovicianus comes from *Ludovicus,* the Latin for Lewis. The name proposed by Guthrie, therefore, when translated would be, Lewis' Marmot. The name is not only inappropriate, for the Prairie Dog is not a marmot, but the name, Lewis' Marmot, was already appropriated to another animal and a true marmot, the *Arctomys Lewisii.* Prof. Say, who accompanied Col. Long's Expedition to the Rocky Mountains, in 1820, describes him under the name proposed by Prof. Guthrie.

Audubon proposed to call him *Spermophilus Ludovicianus,* because it seemed to him that he was nearer allied to the spermophiles than to the marmot. He is, however, less lithe and less active than the spermophiles, and not so short and clumsy as the marmot. In fact, in form and habits, he is intermediate between the two. Warden proposed to call him *Arctomys Missouriensis.* Others have proposed the generic name *Sciurus,* that is, squirrel, for him. Ah! but look at his tail! Yes, look at it. *Scia*, a shadow, and *oura*, a tail. Do you call him with that stumpy, scraggling haired vertebral appendage, an animal that can sleep in the shadow of his tail? Bah! Sciurus indeed! Why all Squirreldom feels insulted by the proposition! But recent zoologists have called him *Cynomys Ludovicianus*. Cynomys literally means Dog-mouse, or Dog-rat. Hence it seems that scientific men are not in accord as to what he actually is, nor as to what he shall be named, except the specific name of his first describer, Lewis.

The common names proposed for him have not shared a much better fate than the scientific, always excepting that given him by Lewis. Those who have not fancied the latter, have proposed to call him the Prairie Marmot Squirrel. The French Canadians, trapping in the Mountains, call him "*Le petit chien*," the little dog. But, notwithstanding, the obvious impropriety of the term first applied to him, he is now generally called and known by it; namely, the Prairie Dog; and he will bear it till his race becomes extinct, by the extension of settlements over the vast Plains of which he is now the only denizen that has a fixed habitation.

He is found spread over the Plains, eastward of the the Rocky Mountains, for five hundred miles, and from the Missouri to south of the Red River in Western Texas. They are always found in communities; sometimes numbering hundreds of families living together. Their habitations are called "dog-towns," or "prairie dog villages." It is said the burrows are connected by subterranean galleries. Old rangers of the Plains, amongst other strange stories, say the towns are intersected by streets, and that the streets are kept scrupulously neat and clean. These streets must be underground, as above ground I but rarely saw even evidences of a regular beaten path.

The female has ten *mammae*, from whence it is inferable that they are very prolific.

Any one of them seeing the approach of danger, immediately scampers off to his burrow uttering that peculiar cry which has been fancifully compared to the yelping of a puppy. At the first cry of danger from the outskirts of the town, the whole community takes it up, every one making for his own hole. A thousand guinea fowls, alarmed by a hawk, could not make more racket than the denizens of a dog-town on such an occasion. Arrived at home, without stopping to see whether the danger is real or imaginary, all plunge into their holes by a kind of ludicrous summersault, excepting some old quidnunc who has an aversion of being humbugged and then laughed at for being so easily sold after all his pretentions to superior wisdom. Having arrived at his hole, he sits himself up perpendicularly on his hind legs, and takes a cool survey of the vicinage to satisfy himself whether there was any cause for all this commotion, or whether it was a mere hoax played off by some wag of the village. I have, on many occasions, seen them rise on their hind feet to have the better view. If there is real danger, he *caches* in a twinkle; but if the alarm was false, he runs to a neighbor, apparently exchanges a few words with him, and then runs back to his own burrow, giving a shrill whistle. Soon a head is seen cautiously peering out of each burrow, and when satisfied that there either was no danger, or that it is over, they venture out and set up a chipping until the whole village joins in the concert. That concluded they attend to pleasure or business as though nothing had happened.

The young colored man who had charge of our sleeping car, and who, by the way, was a model for politeness and honesty, and most sedulous in his attentions to our welfare and comfort, seemed to have taken a great interest in these little fellows, and to have studied their character and habits well. Besides he was well posted in all the stories told of them by the old rangers of the Plains.

He told me many curious anecdotes about them, which

cannot be repeated here without becoming tedious. Whilst staying at Ellis one day the idea struck him of going out on the Plains and seeing the dogs at home, and ascertaining what kind of a life they led.

Creeping as near to a village as possible without being discovered by them, or of alarming them, from his favorable position he could overlook the entire plot of the town, and such a frolicsome, wild and madcap set of fellows, he had never seen before. The younger ones were romping, rolling, tumbling and playing like so many kittens, whilst the older ones were running about saluting each other and chatting in the greatest glee. Every one was constantly on the move, except a big old fellow who sat very stiff and stately on the hillock around his burrow, never moving. Evidently he was the "big dog" of the town, perhaps, its Mayor, and could not unbend his dignity enough to take part in the sports and amusements of the village. Every dog in the town would run up to him and have a short chat with him and then scamper away; but he felt too much the cares of State, or his own importance to relax one moment from his gravity.

From observing their habits and studying their character, the young man has become fully persuaded that to avoid disorder, each village is a municipality consisting of a regularly organized government; and that this grave old chap is at the head of it. He also averred that in some villages he had observed that the Jackass Rabbit was the Potentate. He reasoned in this way; that if the race of big dogs through dissipation became degenerate or extinct, then if the village had no dog large enough to fill the bill, they elected a Jackass Rabbit; because the first qualification for chief of a dog-town is, altitudinal dimensions, so that they will have to look up to him. If that is so, there should be no hesitation to admit that they are a wise race. Man, himself, could go and learn lessons of wisdom in politics from them; for the Human race have in no case, excepting that of Saul, selected their head man for qualifications that would constrain them to look up to him, either physically, morally or intellectually. However, in one respect they copy remotely the precedent set by the Prairie Dog; they generally take the animal, *minus* the rabbit.

I saw, myself, a Jackass Rabbit, of the largest size, sitting on the highest hillock of the town looking as grave and dignified as any Lord Mayor, and surrounded by the dogs, but whether he was lord paramount and was there officially to receive us and tender us the hospitalities of the town I cannot say, as we very unceremoniously passed by without stopping to ascertain. But there he was sitting up straight and immovable, although the train passed within fifty yards of him.

The young man said, when a dog-town is governed by a rabbit, they show as much respect and deference to him as *if he were a dog*. Just as we do, said I, to our Jack.

This called forth another argument from the young man, to this effect: "I see you don't believe it; yet you believe that a beehive is governed by a queen. Now from what you have seen, to which would you assign the greater intelligence, to the bee or to the Prairie Dog? As you must to the latter; which then is the greater strain on human credulity, to believe that law reigns in the beehive or in the dog-town?" Continuing, he said, "I tell you these little fellows are almost human. You can't find an old ranger of the Plains that will kill one of them, unless forced to it by hunger, though their meat is tender, juicy and delicious. The tenderness and affection they show to each other, has touched the feelings of these exteriorly rough and seemingly hardened men. You kill or maim one, and instantly the tenants of the burrows sally forth, regardless of danger, and carry him home. The old rangers say that this shows more than human affection, and that they will not, except in case of necessity, be instrumental in striking down with death the loved ones of such a household and fill it with sorrow and grief."

I believe Lockey mentions a general belief that the elephant is a religious being in his native forests; and that it is their custom once a month, on the night of the full moon, to assemble on the banks of a river in South Africa for general worship. The Prairie Dog has a similar custom. On a summer evening, they have either vespers or else prayers after their fashion; and on the night of the full moon these services are continued far into the night and with unusual clamor.

It has not been settled what office the burrowing owl holds in the municipality. Some think it is that of scavenger or doctor; and others say it is that of fool-catcher, ridding the community of pestiferous members. Some again are satisfied his sole occupation is that of snake-killer. If the latter, then he, like our street cleaner, is evidently very remiss in his duty. All, however, are agreed that the rattle-snake is an unwelcome intruder, a loafer who insinuates himself where he is not wanted, a regular nuisance that has to be tolerated or worse would ensue.

The following are the dimensions of the full grown Prairie Dog:

From the tip of the nose to the root of the tail 13 inches; length of vertebrae of tail 2 5-8 inches; length of tail to tips of hair 3 1-8 inches; width between the eyes 1 1-2 inches.

As the body of our Western fox-squirrel is but 12 inches; and that of the Eastern 14 inches, it will be seen, that the Prairie Dog is intermediate in size. His color resembles that of the fox-squirrel, but is more clayish-yellow. On the Plains and North, on the Upper Missouri, he hibernates. According to Lieut. Abert, on the frontier of Texas he does not go into winter quarters.

After the Prairie Dog, the novelty of the snow fence attracts attention. The snow fence is placed north or northwest of a deep cut some fifty yards distant. Imagine a plank fence some seven feet high, with a support inclined at an angle of forty-five degrees, and you will have a tolerably correct idea of the appearance of the snow fence. The wind in striking it "becomes demoralized" and drops its burthen of snow, instead of carrying it forward and, as with *malice prepense*, blocking up the road in the cut.

The buffalo trails of former years also present novel features. They lead over the Plains northward as far as sight can penetrate, perfectly straight. The first impression is that a furrow had been made by the plow; and as the young grass in them is of a more vigorous growth than that on the Plains, they appear like a narrow band of deep green stretched over the prairie.

We saw a number of jackass rabbits and a few antelopes, which fled at our approach. A short distance east of Ogallah there was an immense patch of the beautiful *Gaillardia picta*, the first we had seen on our return. It was a real treat to look at their large purple blooms, fringed with yellow, and it was a relief to the eye to see something else than the greenish gray buffalo grass and dull gray Patagonian plaintain.

A mile west of Ellis there was a large area of prairie freshly broken. A stream of some size from the north here empties into the Smoky Hill Fork. Ellis is 303 miles west of the State line, that is 581 miles west of St. Louis.

We here entered into a sirocco that blew a perfect gale from the south. It was so hot that on your hands and cheeks it produced a sensation like that of a sunbeam, and the brass, iron and wood of the seats felt hot to the touch. Our conductor told us that they blow on an average once, and sometimes twice a week, from the middle of June to the first of September; that they were from ten to fifty miles wide; and were invariably the precursor of a storm either there or further down on the Plains. In January, February and during the early part of March, similar cold blasts, called by the railroad men, "Nebraska zephyrs," sweep south. As my informant said, "they are keen enough to shave off the hair of a buffalo."

A few miles east of Hayes we came upon ten buffalo. They first started off in a trot, but as we neared them, up went their tails and down their heads and they galloped away as far as we saw them with a speed truly surprising. The conductor remarked, we will probably soon see a large drove. Before we lost sight of the first we came upon twelve more, who also fled at our approach But a large drove of hundreds soon came in sight; in fact, the Plains as far as we could see were covered with them. The nearest being about two-thirds of a mile off, they kept grazing and paid no attention to us.

At Fossil, and some distance both east and west, there is a valuable white limestone for building purposes. It is so soft when "green" as to be more easily cut into blocks than wood; yet when thoroughly dry it becomes so hard and firm that it is said it will bear the weight of the largest structures.

At Wilson's creek, 1586 feet above tide and 522 miles west of St. Louis, the winter wheat sown late in November at the experimental station was nearly ripe. The stand was excellent, hight fine and heads large and well filled, with no signs of rust on the blade. Its yield per acre must fully equal the average of wheat in Missouri and Illinois. The rye was unusually good and fully ripe. Corn and sorghum were dark green and very thrifty; vegetables, such as peas, beans, potatoes, tomatoes, melons, etc., very promising. The nursery seedlings of deciduous trees looked so vigorous and thrifty that there can be no doubt that timber can be grown on the Plains. It was yet too soon to judge whether evergreens, such as pines and spruce, would succeed, though so far they appear to do well. The European larch had also been planted for trial, but like the evergreens, it takes a whole season to determine whether it will succeed.

In the vicinity of Wilson's some immigrants, who had

pushed west thus far in advance of the settlements, had broken up some considerable prairie. At Ellsworth the advancing wave of settlement rolling westward meets you. Here is a snug little village of perhaps seventy houses, and considerable land in cultivation. In all directions, on the Plains, the cabins of those making homesteads or pre-emption claims could be seen, generally surrounded by a new breaking of the prairie sod. The soil is black and very friable, and judging from the growing crops, fertile and productive. I cannot conceive how there can be a lovelier rustic landscape than this must become, when entirely subdued and under cultivation.

At Brookville, twenty-three miles east of Ellsworth, we met and exchanged civilities with Messrs. Adolphus Meier, C. S. Greeley, and Wm. M. McPherson, officers of the road, on a tour of inspection. Brookville, just 200 miles west of the State line, (483 miles from St. Louis,) is a flourishing town for its age. Its elevation is 1250 feet above tide-water, and is situated on a rolling grassy and rich prairie, which is fast settling up. The machine shops of the Kansas Pacific railroad are located here, which have given an impulse to its growth and settlement.

It was quite dark when we left Salina, where we stopped for supper. Before retiring, and while our berths were preparing, I went on the rear platform of the sleeping car. I observed that there was a dark bank of clouds lying along the whole western horizon, in which there was an incessant play of vivid lightning. I recalled the prediction of our conductor as forecast from the sirocco. This phenomenon ought to be observed and investigated by the signal office, as it may involve and unfold an important law of meteorology.

It will be observed from the distances made that the rate of the trains on this road is only twenty miles an hour. Yet, on the return trip, I found we had to stop once an hour, and oftener, to cool the car boxes by pouring water on them to prevent them from taking fire. In a conversation with those having charge of the train, they told me the difficulty to a great extent was owing to the meteorologic condition of the weather; and that they were much more troubled with heated boxes before, during and after these siroccos than at any other time; and that they could almost unerringly foretel a sirocco, by observing the temperature of their boxes. If this is so, it will suggest the existence of a new physical law, in the transformation of the cosmical forces, a law more than suspected from other physical facts.

The storm overtook us at Manhattan and it poured down till near daylight. We found water standing everywhere, when day met us at Lenape, 22 miles beyond the State line. The creeks were booming, and the culverts at many points of the road were overtaxed and the water threatening to break over the road. On the Missouri Pacific, beyond Pleasant Hill, we found a break, which however had nearly been repaired when we got there, and the Blue near by was up to within a few inches of the bridge; and many cornfields were under water.

The rain had extended to some ten miles below Jefferson City, when all traces of it vanished, though a violent wind-storm swept over all Eastern Missouri and Illinois. Around Sedalia, and especially west of it, is a landscape whose conformation and natural features at once remind you of the lovely plains of Kansas. But there is this difference; every foot of this plain is under cultivation, while in Kansas they are yet practically in a state of nature. I could, therefore, not refrain from recalling the emotions of admiration and enthusiasm I felt on first beholding the wide expanse and beauty of the undulating plains in Kansas. In his course around the earth, the sun does not look upon a lovlier scene than they. Yet here I could see what mighty changes time and art will effect in them. On every knoll stands the ample mansion of the farmer, surrounded by shade trees, orchard and vineyards. Here are hedges stretching far away over the plain enclosing fields of wheat, rye and barley filled with shocks or already garnered: and there the dark green corn, the meadow and the oat field cover the vast plain as far as the eye can reach; and then yonder again are pastures filled with herds and flocks, a pastoral scene that would tax the powers of a Homer or Virgil to describe.

Before another score of years are numbered with the past, this picture will have been reproduced on a more western landscape, on the more ample plains of Kansas, improved and embellished by intelligent industry, judicious care and refined taste, in proportion to the vastness of the theater on which it is done.

After having spent days and weeks upon the treeless and even shrubless plains of Kansas and Colorado, it was quite an agreeable change and a welcome relief on entering Missouri to see again the hills and valleys covered with forests, fields bordered by growing timber, and the expansive cultivated plain interspersed with pleasant groves.

At 8 o'clock P. M., June 19th, we arrived at home, just forty-six hours from Denver, distance 923 miles.

ERRATA.

Page 34, second line, for "*the two best,*" read "*to the best.*"
Page 37, fourteenth line, for "*mainly*" read "*namely.*"
Page 124, seventh line from bottom, for "*bistoria*" read "*bistorta.*"
Page 207, first line, for "*Indian' blood-thirstyness*" read *Indians in blood-thirstiness.*"
Page 203, fifteenth line from the bottom, for "*grounded*" read "*grouped.*"

Several minor typographical errors in mis-spelling escaped notice until too late for correction. As the intelligent reader can correct them, it is not necessary to note them.

INDEX.

CHAPTER I.

Leaving St. Louis 6.—Arrival at Kansas City 9.—Anecdote 9.—Reception at Atchison 11.—Trip to Waterville 14.—Surroundings of same 15.—General character of landscape 15.—Summary of general features of landscape, character and quality of soil and sanitary condition of country passed over 17

CHAPTER II.

Leavenworth as seen from Military Reservation 20.—Railroad bridge across the Missouri 21.—Leavenworth as a commercial City 23.—Trip to Lawrence 24.—Arrival at Lawrence 26.—History of Eldridge House 26. et seq.

CHAPTER III.

Trip southward 29.—Ottawa 30.—Flora on route 32.—Eli Thayer 33.—Coal 33.—Lands 34.—Return to Lawrence 35.—Early settlers and character of the people of Kansas 36. et seq.

CHAPTER IV.

Leaving for the Mountains 37.—Observations on wheat crop 40.—New Flora 41.—River system of Kansas 42.—First Prairie dog village 44.—Experimental stations of Kansas Pacific R. R. 45.—Water supply 49.—Horned frog and buffalo calf at Fossil 50.—Insensate slaughter of buffaloes 50.—Building stone 51.—Buffalo grass 51.—Antelopes and buffaloes 52.—Coyote 53.—Night closes on the Plains 54.

CHAPTER V.

Return of day 55.—First glimpse of the mountains 56.—Arrival at Denver 57.—Early settlement of why 58.—Off for Golden 61.—Description of 61.—Pulpit Rock or Castle Butte 63.—Flora found at Golden 64.

CHAPTER VI.

Morning view from Castle Butte 67.—Chimney given 69.—Flora in same 70.—Ascension of dominating peak 71.—View from same 72.—Exhilarating effect of an attenuated atmosphere 75.—Causes of same 76.

CHAPTER VII.

Return to Denver 75.—Route down the Valley of the Platte 78.—Landscape around Evans and Greeley 79.—Union colony at Greeley 80.—Plains between Greeley and Cheyenne 82.—Fantastic forms of erodid rocks 83.—Cheyenne 83.—Grazing in Wyoming 84.—Return to Denver and excursion around vicinity 85.—Colorado strawberries 85.—Excursion to Boulder 86.—Coal mines at Erie 86.—Road from Erie to Boulder 87.— Reception at Boulder 88

CHAPTER VIII.

Scenery around Boulder 90.—Excursion up the Canyon 95.—Flora in same 96.—Grand scenery of 96.—Eagle Cliff 99.—Rocky Mountain sheep 100.—Castle Rock 101.—Water grade of Canyon 104.

CHAPTER IX.

Trip to Caribou 105.—Upper valley of the Boulder 105.—Beaver 106.—New Flora 107.—First snow field 108.—Mountain storm cloud 108.—Road up the mountain 108.—Cardinal 109.—First view of Snowy Range 109.—Caribou 110.—The first snow bank 111.—Prospect holes and mining shafts 111.—Evening ramble over the mountain 113.—Peak of the Snowy Range 113.—Accoustic effect of attenuated atmosphere 114.—Effect on breathing of animals 115.

CHAPTER X.

Morning ramble over the mountains 116.—Longcrested Jay 117.—Four striped ground squirrel 118.—Talk with a miner 118.—Caribou Lode 119.—Magnetic iron ore 120.—Orderly conduct of the miners 122.—Grand Island 122.—Metals in the district 122.—Woods on fire 123.—Another view of Mountain sheep 125.—Falls of North Boulder 126.—Singular conduct of a Rocky Mountain blue bird 127.—Return to Boulder 128.

CHAPTER XI.

Morning ramble 129.—Apostrophe to the Waters 130.—Photograph stones 130.—Explanation of them 135.—Visit to Marshall's coal mines on South Boulder 134.—Extent of coal 134.—Irrigation 135.—Advantages of 137.—Agricultural effects of 135.—Grasshoppers 136.—Excellence of flour 138.—Crystalized soda incrusting soil 138.—Premium awards for field productions 139.—Extent of Arable land in Platte Valley and affluents 140.—Desirable grazing region 140.—Arable and grazing land on the Mountains 141.

CHAPTER XII.

Colonial schemes in Colorado 143.—Difficulties suggested 144.—Drawbacks even in mining towns 145.—Greensborough colony 147.—Col. Wuesten's German Colony 148.—Mountain ranches product of 149.—Chicago Colorado Colony 149.—Climate of Colorado not determinable by empiric laws 150.—Sanitary condition of Colorado 152.—*Par excellence* the climate for invalids 150.—Directions and warnings to consumptives 154.

CHAPTER XIII.

Inevitable hardships and privations in forming new settlements 156.—Where immigration in Colorado goes 157.—The mountains not a barren waste 157.—Climate on lower Plains severer than at base of the mountains 159.—Proposition of irrigating canal from Platte canyon eastward over the Plains 160.—Advice to emigrants 161.

CHAPTER XIV.

Different orders of plants demand different kinds of food 163.—Difficulty of keeping a supply of plant food in the soil 164.—How fertility is spread 165.—Irrigation in the Orient, etc., 166.—System carried to America 167.—Products of vegetation 167.—Estimated amount of plant food carried on and deposited in the soil by irrigation 168.—The problem of perfect manure solved 169.

CHAPTER XV.

Middle Park 170.—Mecca for invalids 170.—Precious metals in 171.—Flexure of Snowy Range enclosing it 171.—Pertains to Pacific slope 172.—Elevation above tide 172.—Surface and vegetation of 173.—Contemplated railroads through 174.—Agricultural adaptations of 174.—Grand Lake 174.—Coal beds in 175.—Precious stones 175.—Sulphur springs 176.—Eroded stone monuments 176.—Passes over the Range leading into it 177.—Area of three northern parks 178.—Upper basin of the Arkansas 178.—San Luis Park 179. Lake Saguache, singular phenomenon in 179.—Singular facts about harvest 181.—Public land in San Luis Park 182.—Review of attractions and inducements to all classes of tourists 184.

CHAPTER XVI.

Difference between *views, vistas* and *sights* stated 187.—Difference between works of Nature and of Man 189.—Contrast between the Yosemite and Boulder Canyon 190.—Vistas and views in the mountains 192.—Top of Mount Lincoln 195.—Lakes 197.—The Divide 197.—Monument Creek 198.—Gardens of the Gods 199.

CHAPTER XVII.

History of Colorado 201.—Peoples Courts 202.—Party divisions when the Rebellion broke out 203.—The Colorado side of the Sand Creek affair 205.—Indian insolence punished 207.—The heroes of the Mountains 208.—Col. Pfeifer 209.—Ruins and their traditions 211.—Mountain Jim 214.—Indian history of 215.—Advent of the white man 216.—Contrast between civilization and barbarism 216.—Cause of Indian troubles 217.—Where the responsibility lies 219.

CHAPTER XVIII.

Mining in Colorado 221.—Cause of early failures 222.—Disastrous experiments 224.—Who responsible for them 225.—Products of mines 226.—Rusty gold 227.—Waste of stamp-mills 228.—Success of smelting works 229.—Investments in mining recommended and advise how to do it 230.—English capitalists, their proceedings and opinions about Colorado 231.—Why formerly so many failures 232.—Shameless swindles 235.

CHAPTER XIX.

Skylark 239.--Leaving for home, haze on Plains 240.—Denotes electric disturbances *Ib.*—Produces the phenomenon of mirage 241.—On board the cars 242.—Last look at the Mountains *Ib.*—Farewell to them 243 to 248.—Arrival and departure from Denver 249.

CHAPTER XX.

Rains at Kit Carson in Eastern Colorado 250.—Pond Creek experimental station *Ib.*—Buffalo trails on Plains 251.—The Prairie dog 252 to 256.—Snow fences 256.—Siroccos in Summer and "Nebraska zephyrs" in Winter on the Plains 258.—Herds of Buffalo 259.—Night storm of rain 261.—Arrival at home 262.

KANSAS PACIFIC R. R. CO.

Our road runs

FROM KANSAS CITY, MO.,

TO

DENVER, 638 MILES.

ALSO,

A Branch from Leavenworth to Lawrence, 33 Miles.
We have also, the Denver Pacific, from Denver to Cheyenne, 106 miles. Also the Boulder Valley Railroad, now completed to Erie; will be completed to Boulder City this summer. We are building a road from Junction City, Kansas, to Clay county, Kansas; and a road from Kit Carson to Fort Lyon, Colorado. We probably will build a road from Lawrence, Kansas, to Carboudale coal-fields, thirty-two miles, this summer.

Passengers leaving St. Louis at 8:30 a. m., will reach Kansas City in time to take the westward express leaving at 10:00 p. m.; arrive at Brookville at 9:45 a. m. and Denver next morning at 7:00. Time, 46 1-2 hours. Distance, 923 miles.

PULLMAN'S
PALACE SLEEPING CARS

Are Attached to Each Train.

Passengers leaving St. Louis in the evening express train, will arrive at Brookville at 9:00 p. m. next day, and have a good night's rest.

Rob't E. Carr, President.
    Adolphus Meier, V. President.

C. S. Greeley, Treasurer.
    Edmund S. Bowen, Gen'l Sup't.

OUR SPECIALTIES

ARE

AND

EPICURE BROILERS,

Either of Which are Perfectly Indispensable in every Well Regulated Household.

Unequaled in the Combined Merits of

Economy, Durability, Convenience, Cleanliness, and Excellence of Operation.

A single Trial is all we ask, being satisfied that they will not fail to give Perfect Satisfaction.

SOLD BY

Excelsior Manufacturing Co.

612 & 614 N. Main Street, St. Louis,

AND ALL

Live Stove Dealers.